In Praise of *The Hemingway Cookbook*

"**A** wonderful culinary biography of one of America's premiere writers. . . . Cooks, cookbook collectors, and of course, fans of Hemingway will find much to savor in this wonderful volume."

—JENNIFER A. WHEELER
Executive Director, The Ernest Hemingway Foundation of Oak Park

"**F**or someone who reads cookbooks like novels, what a delight to find both in one publication. What a pleasure to romp with Hemingway as he eats and drinks his way through life. Liberally sprinkled with appropriate quotations, citations, and biographical data along with detailed recipes and menus, this book will certainly find a place in the kitchen and on the bookshelf of gourmets, gourmands, and the literati."

—HOWARD B. CARRON, PH.D.
editor-in-chief, *Cigar Lovers Magazine*

"**P**apa had some pungent comments about wine then that still ring true today."

—HARVEY STEIMAN
editor at large, *Wine Spectator*

"**A**uthentic recipes from Hemingway's favorite places bring to life an aspect of his life and writings long overlooked. Food was obviously very dear to Hemingway's heart and an integral part of his expansive love of life. ¡Olés! for *The Hemingway Cookbook*."

—PENELOPE CASAS
author, *Tapas: The Little Dishes of Spain*

The Hemingway Cookbook

An early-morning writing session while on safari.

The
HEMINGWAY
COOKBOOK

Craig Boreth

CHICAGO
REVIEW
PRESS

Published by Chicago Review Press, Incorporated
814 North Franklin Street
Chicago, Illinois 60610

ISBN 1-55652-297-5
Printed in Singapore by CS Graphics.
5 4 3 2

Library of Congress Cataloging-in-Publication Data
Boreth, Craig
    The Hemingway cookbook / Craig Boreth.
        p. cm.
    Includes bibliographical references (p. 205).
    ISBN 1-55652-297-5 (alk. Paper)
    1. Cookery. 2. Hemingway, Ernest, 1899–1961. I. Title.
TX714.B642   1998
641.5—dc21   98-20246
                                                          CIP

Cover photos: (Inset) An early-morning writing session
while on safari in 1953–1954. Hemingway's rod, reel, and
freshly caught trout. Both photographs courtesy of
Earl Theisen/Look/ John F. Kennedy Library

Distributed by Independent Publishers Group
www.ipgbook.com

This book is for Corinne

Contents

Introduction

Dining with Hemingway

WILD GASTRONOMIC ADVENTURES

xi

1

The Early Years

A TASTE FOR LIFE

1

2

Italy

REMEMBRANCE AND WAR

15

3

France

AN IMMOVABLE FEAST

37

4

Spain

THE FIESTA CONCEPT OF LIFE

79

5

Key West and Cuba

SAILING THE STREAM

109

6

East Africa and Idaho

A HUNTER'S CULINARY SKETCHES

143

7

The Hemingway Wine Cellar

159

8

The Hemingway Bar

171

Epilogue

An After-Dinner Treat

THE FABLE OF THE GOOD LION

195

Notes   199

Bibliography   205

Acknowledgments   208

General Index   211

Recipe Index   214

"I have discovered that there is romance in food
when romance has disappeared from everywhere else.
And as long as my digestion holds out I will follow romance."

— ERNEST HEMINGWAY

DINING WITH HEMINGWAY

Wild Gastronomic Adventures

"Ernest had a talent for making people feel that any pretension toward an appetite of life must be backed up with a healthy appetite for food."

—Peter Griffin, *Less than a Treason*

Hemingway writing as a young boy.

Have you ever encountered a storyteller who could engage your imagination as if it were his or her own, someone who can describe a person or place and you feel that you hold in your imagination a nearly complete and genuine experience of that person or place? Then, if you are fortunate enough to encounter that person or visit that place, they are exactly as you expected them to be? For me, Ernest Hemingway is one of those storytellers. I find myself drawn in, participating wholly in the creation of the intricate, near-reality he creates. That is the primary reason why I enjoy reading his writing, and that is why I am privileged enough to have you read mine.

Ernest Hemingway was in many ways an explorer. He lived in several different countries and traveled far from home for months at a time. He also traveled deep inside his own imagination and the minds of his characters, uncovering dark vestiges of torn and hardened individuals. He had an insatiable appetite for new and novel geographies, experiences, and people, attending to each detail with the dexterity and acumen of a natural historian. It is no surprise, then, that so many have followed him in search of that same newness, that same disconcerting, energizing imbalance that must be overcome in a new place. When I follow Hemingway, I am continually amazed at his great talent for taking me away to the landscape that he paints on the page. When I visit the settings, it feels exactly as I imagined when reading his work. It is a wonderful experience, and it makes reading Hemingway that much more of a personal adventure.

Ernest Hemingway was also a tremendous eater and drinker. For better and worse, he indulged his appetites to the fullest. His books are filled with episodes about food and drink, sometimes spectacular, other times intriguing in their mundane presentation. Regardless, *The Hemingway Cookbook* is a product of my belief that the same gut-warming, mind-racing sensation enjoyed by the follower of Hemingway's journeys may be evoked by the preparation and enjoyment of his food and drinks.

The sounds of the words themselves—Aguacates, Purée de Marron, Chambéry Cassis, or Amontillado—linger beyond the turn of the pages. The textures, tastes, and smells remain on the palate long after the dust jacket earns its keep. This was the foundation of Hemingway's art: to not only provide for his readers a description of the emotion evoked but to communicate the source of that emotion, creating for the reader that very same sensation. He crafted a fiction that stalked us and struck more quickly and fiercely than reality ever could. And there, sustaining, defining, and redefining the characters that we sense so profoundly, are the details of their eating and drinking endeavors.

Hemingway uses native foods and drinks to convey his characters' insider status. Participating in the local cuisine with the knowledge of the native, Hemingway's characters feel at home, and so do we, the readers. Amid their epic struggles with death and love they find treasure and foundation in the cuisine of the lands in which they are adrift. Participation in the life of the fiction and, thus, in the life of the writer himself may explain why Ernest Hemingway has inspired every generation since his own to embark in pursuit of that elusive sense of what has been called "more-being": to attain a sort of world-citizenry from the Plaza de Toros to the Parisian café to the Gulf Stream.

In our own enduring quest to gain some membership in his fiction and his legend, the preparation and consumption of the food and drink included here in *The Hemingway Cookbook* evoke the solitude of fishing his trout streams, the drama of watching his bullfights, and the camaraderie of hunting his game. It is as individual an adventure as the fiction itself.

There is no easy way to arrange a book about a man as prolific and well traveled as Ernest Hemingway. This book is laid out roughly chronologically, focusing on the central country or region of each time period. Within each chapter, focus is placed on the novels and short stories that take place in that region or were written in that time period. I have tried to include some pertinent biographical information, particularly

if the anecdotes pertain directly to the recipes included. For the complete picture of Hemingway's life, read Carlos Baker's seminal work, *Ernest Hemingway: A Life Story*, or any volume of Michael Reynolds's brilliant series of Hemingway biographies.

I have tried to provide a taste of the food and drink that were most important in Hemingway's life and the life of his fiction. It would be virtually impossible to include every recipe. (For a fascinating analysis of the role of food and drink in Hemingway's fiction, as well as a complete index to the references to food and drink therein, read Samuel J. Rogal's *For Whom the Dinner Bell Tolls*, 1997.) Therefore, I have chosen recipes that accompany important moments in Hemingway's life and art.

I have tried to stay true to the original recipes of the time. Thus, many of you may find yourself buying lard for the first time in many years, or frying in a lot of butter, or mixing some serious drinks. If you know the old adage "whatever doesn't kill me makes me stronger," you may want to keep it in mind as you prepare some of these Hemingway feasts.

The sources for the recipes themselves are varied. Several, such as the Roast Suckling Pig and the *Paella de Langosta*, come from the original restaurants where Hemingway enjoyed them. Other recipes, primarily those from the Cuba and Idaho years, are based on written records or interviews with Hemingway's closest friends from those days, such as Forrest "Duke" Mac-Mullen, Tillie Arnold, Gregorio Fuentes, and his fourth wife, Mary. Of the remaining recipes, the very traditional ones are based on cookbooks from that time.

It is my hope that by preparing the recipes in this book you may revisit the first time Hemingway's, or any author's, prose truly touched you. One of the wonders of Hemingway's work is that it may be enjoyed on so many levels, from the starkly empirical to the analytically profound. Through preparing these dishes, a new dimension of enjoyment may be added, strengthening the personal ties that each reader once had with the fiction alone.

I have written a book that I believe will satisfy the full spectrum of Hemingway readers and will help everyone enjoy the world he created for us. Maybe you will read a book of his you never read before. Maybe you will see something new in your favorite short story that reminds you why it's your favorite. Regardless, I wish every reader the wonderful experience of cooking these meals and spending some more time in the thralls of your own imagination, sated and rapt, at the feet of a master storyteller.

THE EARLY YEARS

A Taste for Life

"Don't be afraid to taste all the other things in life that aren't here in Oak Park. This life is all right, but there's a whole big world out there full of people who really feel things. They live and love and die with all their feelings. Taste everything, Sis."

—Ernest to his sister Marcelline, 1919

HEMINGWAY COLLECTION, JOHN F. KENNEDY LIBRARY

(Top row, left to right) Ernest, Ed, Grace, (bottom row) Ursula, Sunny, and Marcelline.

Ernest Miller Hemingway was born July 21, 1899, and ate meat, vegetables, eggs, and fish shortly thereafter. His father, Dr. Clarence Edmonds Hemingway (known commonly as Ed), believed such foods were essential for nursing babies to grow up strong and healthy. His mother, Grace Hall Hemingway, lamented the decision. She noted in her daughter Marcelline's baby book her annoyance at receiving the babies for nursing with onions on their breath.[1]

The Hemingways lived in the affluent and proper Chicago suburb of Oak Park. Grace Hemingway, once an aspiring opera singer, remained ambitious in her endeavors as a music teacher, suffragist, and painter. Mothering six children did not lessen her distaste for housework, and she continued her pursuit of the fine arts over the culinary arts. In fact, she was such a stranger to the kitchen that when she finally mastered a recipe from her mother's cookbook, she decided to quit while she was ahead. When Marcelline suggested that she learn to make a layer cake, Grace replied, no doubt with chin up and eyes beaming, "I proved I could cook with my tea cake, and I'm not going to take a chance of spoiling my reputation by trying anything else."[2]

This recipe is based on Grandmother Hall's English tea cake recipe, which Grace contributed to the 1921 edition of the *Oak Park Third Congregational Church Cookbook*. The author would like to thank Jennifer Wheeler and the Ernest Hemingway Foundation of Oak Park for their generous assistance in obtaining this recipe.

Ernest Hemingway and his sister Marcelline, 1916.

3

Grace Hall Hemingway's English Tea Cakes

The original recipe for these tea cakes is rather vague in its instructions. Grace shared the recipe with Liz Dilworth, the mother of Ernest's best friend from upper Michigan, where the Hemingways had a summer cottage on Walloon Lake. The Dilworths lived in Horton Bay on Lake Charlevoix. Mrs. Dilworth, known as Aunty Beth to the Hemingway children, ran a small restaurant called Pinehurst Cottage, famous for its fried chicken dinners. Mrs. Dilworth worked out the exact proportions of the recipe and taught Grace how to prepare it. After secretly mastering the recipe at the Dilworths', Grace finally prepared the hot bread in the Hemingway kitchen and served it with great pride and joy. Ed could hardly contain his praise: "Delicious! Gracie, delicious!"[3]

12 SERVINGS (4 TO 6 9-INCH CAKES)

    1½ teaspoons active dry yeast

    ½ teaspoon salt

    1½ cups warm water (110° F)

    4 cups all-purpose flour

    1 tablespoon butter, melted

    2 teaspoons lard or shortening

    2 large eggs, beaten

    ½ cup plus 2 tablespoons sugar

    ¼ cup warm milk

    1 cup dried currants or raisins

    Plenty of extra melted butter for swathing

To set the sponge, whisk together the yeast, salt, and water in a mixing bowl for several minutes until the yeast is completely dissolved. Stir in 1½ cups of the flour and mix until smooth. Cover with a towel and let stand in a draft-free space for 2 hours.

When the sponge has risen, stir in the butter and lard, along with the remaining flour, beaten eggs, sugar, milk, and currants or raisins. Mix thoroughly to form a stiff batter. Cover and let stand up to 1 hour.

Preheat the oven to 350°F.

Divide the batter evenly into four buttered pie tins and let rise for at least 2 hours. Bake in the center of the oven for about 20 minutes, or until golden brown. Remove the cakes to a cooling rack, brush with a lot of melted butter, cut into wedges, and serve while still warm.

———————————

Grace's tea cake recipe was also published in *The Nineteenth Century Women's Club Historical Centennial Cookbook*, along with a recipe for "Ernest Hemingway's Cold Cucumber Soup." Ernest's connection with this sweet cucumber and leek broth is unclear, but here it is:

Ernest Hemingway's Cold Cucumber Soup

4 TO 6 SERVINGS

 3 cucumbers
 1 tablespoon butter
 1 tablespoon chopped fresh dill or mint
 1 leek, white part only, sliced, or ¼ cup
   chopped onion
 1 bay leaf
 1 tablespoon all-purpose flour
 2 cups fresh chicken stock or canned broth
 1 teaspoon salt, or to taste
 White pepper (optional)
 1 cup half & half
 Juice of ½ lemon
 1 tablespoon honey (optional)

Peel and slice two of the cucumbers. Peel, seed, and grate the remaining cucumber. Heat the butter in a large, heavy saucepan. Add the sliced cucumbers and cook over low heat for a few minutes. Add the dill or mint, leek, and bay leaf and cook over low heat until tender, about 20 minutes. Stir in the flour and cook for a few more minutes, stirring constantly. Add the stock and salt and simmer gently for 30 minutes. Remove the bay leaf and let the mixture cool slightly. Purée the mixture, half at a time, in a blender or food processor. Return to the pan and add the white pepper to taste. Add the half & half, lemon juice, and honey; then taste and adjust the seasoning. Stir in the grated cucumber. Refrigerate until ready to serve. Serve in a chilled bowl.

Ed Hemingway extended the same moral sense of discipline and responsibility that ruled all aspects of his life to food and eating. He was a passionate outdoorsman, hunting a vast array of game for the Hemingway table. This was particularly useful when the family would retreat from Oak Park each summer to their cottage on Walloon Lake in upper Michigan. Dr. Hemingway would often stay behind to work at his family practice, but when he was out in the country he was truly in his element. He quickly began to share his passion with his young son.

5

Ernest at age 5 with his first gun.

Ed Hemingway believed in hunting for food and eating everything that he killed. So, in Ernest's fourteenth summer, when Ernest and summertime chum Harold Sampson returned triumphant after hunting and killing a porcupine that had injured a neighbor's dog, Dr. Hemingway did not shower them with praise as expected. Instead, in his typical firm and unforgiving tone, Dr. Hemingway made them eat the animal, which turned out to be "about as tender and tasty as a piece of shoe leather."[4]

Ernest's older sister Marcelline, in her memoir

Ed Hemingway in the Great Smoky Mountains in North Carolina, 1891.

of those early years, *At the Hemingways*, shares one of her father's anecdotes that displayed his skills and experience as a chef and outdoorsman. It is a story that Ernest no doubt heard repeatedly and loved, for details of Ed's youthful adventure show up years later in his son's early writings. It was not the last time that Ernest would take the stories of others and make them his own.

In the summer between his graduation from Oberlin College and his medical training at Rush Medical College in Chicago, Ed was asked to participate in a geological expedition in the Smoky Mountains. The expedition lasted longer than expected, and the supplies began to run low. Determined to provide a good meal (he was, after all, asked on the trip because he could cook), Ed shot some partridge and a few squirrels, coaxed honey from a bee's nest, and whipped up a meal of fried game, biscuits, and blackberry pie. To his fellow campers' amazement, Ed explained how he rolled out the piecrust using a beer bottle as a rolling pin.[5]

His father awakened Ernest's love of the outdoors, of fishing and hunting, in those first summers on the lake. Ernest would eventually take that same, all-consuming passion for sport and adventure and apply it to the bullfights, deep-sea fishing, big game hunting, and virtually any endeavor upon which he embarked. As a young boy, though, the cottage door opened into deep woods, trout streams, campfires, and endless adventures. He saved the sights, sounds, and smells, as he would throughout his life. Eventually he would return through that same door, this time into his imagination, when his gift beckoned and he could not resist.

The summers in Michigan served Ernest in both his fiction and his journalism. In an early article for the *Toronto Star*, Ernest offered a how-to guide to cooking in the bush. Later, in one of his finest short stories, he follows Nick Adams on a fishing trip to the "Big Two-Hearted River." In both cases, he takes particular care to share the sensation of the foods.

Trout fishing in Sun Valley, Idaho, 1939.

Hemingway trout fishing at Horton Creek, July, 1904.

Camping Out

In January 1920, Ernest traveled from Oak Park to Toronto to act as companion and tutor to the son of wealthy parents he met in Michigan while speaking on his wartime adventures. While there, he began writing for the *Toronto Star*, whose editor found Ernest's straightforward prose and good humor perfect for the paper's new direction. Young Hemingway had his own byline and received a penny a word for his articles. Hemingway would eventually work as a European correspondent for the *Toronto Star* during his time in Paris.

In his article "Camping Out: When You Camp Out, Do It Right," Hemingway shows that, even as a very young man, he had a knack for writing with an air of gentle, humorous authority. When he lectures on exactly how to prepare a delicious meal in the bush, it seems only wise to listen carefully.

Fried Trout

Ernest loved trout fishing and he loved eating trout. He enthusiastically shared his pleasure with his earlier readers, as he would later do after visiting the Spanish Pyrenees (see Trucha a la Navarra, *page 84) and Switzerland (see* Trout au Bleu, *page 58). Interestingly, our first introduction to Hemingway's trout is very similar to its Spanish counterpart. So we may take this campfire version as an introduction to trout, a dish that will reach great heights of gastronomic pleasure as the years pass. For now, let us follow young Ernest as he sets up camp and begins to prepare the day's catch, and we will learn what to do and what not to do.*

4 SERVINGS

> 1 cup Crisco or vegetable shortening
> 4 whole trout, cleaned
> 1 cup cornmeal
> 8 slices bacon

Hemingway fishing in Michigan at Walloon Lake, summer 1916.

Hemingway instructs: "The proper way to cook is over coals. Have several cans of Crisco or Cotosuet or one of the vegetable shortenings along that are as good as lard and excellent for all kinds of shortening. Put the bacon in and when it is about half cooked lay the trout in the hot grease, dipping them in cornmeal first. Then put the bacon on top of the trout and it will baste them as it slowly cooks. . . .

"The trout are crisp outside and firm and pink inside and the bacon is well done—but not too done. If there is anything better than that combination the writer has yet to taste it in a lifetime devoted largely and studiously to eating."[6]

Heat the Crisco in a skillet over medium heat (or over coals, not open flame, if cooking by campfire). While heating the shortening, coat each trout in cornmeal and set aside. When the shortening is hot, cook the bacon halfway. Just before it browns, remove from the pan. Place the trout in the pan (this may require two batches, depending on your luck on the river). After 5 minutes, turn the trout and place 2 strips of bacon over each fish. Cook for another 10–15 minutes, depending on the size of the fish.

———————

While the trout are cooking to perfection, Hemingway suggests you placate the hungry mob with coffee and pancakes.

Pancakes

When camping, Hemingway carried with him a sack of prepared pancake flour so that he could simply add water, mix until most of the lumps are out, and cook on a hot, greased skillet. To this day, nothing takes the hard edge off a campsite hunger like a hot stack of pancakes. Ernest's favorite toppings were apple butter, syrup, or sugar and cinnamon.[7] While today you may simply bring along any instant pancake mix, the purist would want to prepare the following pancake mix before leaving home. You can find the powdered milk and eggs at any well-stocked outdoor store.

2 SERVINGS

1 cup all-purpose flour
¼ teaspoon salt
½ tablespoon sugar
½ tablespoon baking powder
2½ tablespoons powdered milk
3 tablespoons powdered eggs
¼ cup shortening

Before leaving home, mix all the dry ingredients together. Add the shortening and stir with a fork until thoroughly incorporated. Store the mix in an airtight container.

To make the pancakes, add slightly less than 1 cup of water per cup of pancake mix. Mix well, but don't worry about all of the lumps. Pour out mix to form round pancakes on a hot, greased griddle. When the edges are just browned and bubbles form, flip the pancakes and cook the other side until lightly browned. Any of Ernest's recommended toppings go wonderfully with the pancakes.

Stewed Apricots

The stew kettle was an essential implement around the Hemingway campfire. In it he would soak, overnight, dried apricots in plenty of water. By the next morning, the fruit would have returned to its "predried plumpness,"[8] and could be cooked until very tender and enjoyed as a sweet snack after the pancakes were gone. Ernest would also use the kettle to cook macaroni or to ". . . concoct a mulligan in. . . ."[9] Of course, the thoughtful camper will be boiling water in the stew kettle for washing dishes while it's not in use for cooking.

Hemingway hiking around Walloon Lake in Michigan, summer 1916.

Campfire Apple Pie

In this recipe, Ernest takes a page from his father's book of cooking tricks, suggesting that the reader roll out the piecrust using a bottle. It also shows an attention to detail and presentation, most likely attributed to Ed's deliberate teachings. Hemingway recommends using a reflective campfire baker. These days, such devices are hard to come by. If you have one, by all means dust it off and start baking. Otherwise I would recommend using a Dutch oven or a baking device such as the Outback Oven Ultralight, which converts your own cooking pot into a fine campfire baker.

For the filling

> 1½ cups dried apple slices
> ½ cup sugar

For the piecrust

> 2½ cups plus 2 tablespoons sifted
>   all-purpose flour
> 1 teaspoon salt
> ¾ cup shortening, preferably chilled,
>   plus a little more
> 4–5 tablespoons cold water, or more if
>   needed

Soak the apples in 3 cups cold water overnight.

Mix 2½ cups flour with salt. Blend in the ¾ cup lard with a fork until it reaches the consistency of coarse meal. Add just enough water to work into a "...good workmanlike dough..."[10]

Flour any clean, flat surface available. Divide the dough into two pieces, with one piece slightly larger than the other, and use a bottle to roll out the dough in circles large enough to fill a pie tin, preferably the kind with holes. Spread a little more lard on the dough, sprinkle with flour, then roll one piece around the bottle and unroll it into the bottom of the pie tin.

Drain the soaked apples, mix in the sugar and 2 tablespoons flour, and place in the pie tin. Drape the top dough over the pie, crimping the edges with your fingers. Then, "cut a couple of slits in the top dough sheet and prick it a few times with a fork in an artistic manner. Put it in the baker with a good slow fire for forty-five minutes and then take it out, and if your pals are Frenchmen they will kiss you."[11]

These recipes, direct from Ed's storytelling, are as intricate as any Hemingway would ever provide for his readers. While he wrote many spectacular descriptions of exquisite dishes and extravagant meals, Hemingway was not a particularly skilled cook. In fact, when Ernest was prevailed upon to instruct on the preparation of "The Hamburger" in Venice in 1954, he took haste in delegating that responsibility to friend and biographer A. E. Hotchner.[12] The food that Nick Adams prepared in "Big Two-Hearted River" is a much better representation of the foods Ernest himself would prepare when out in the wild on his own.

Hemingway trout fishing in 1913.

"Big Two-Hearted River"

In the late summer of 1919, Ernest and two friends took the train to Seney, on Michigan's upper Peninsula, to fish and camp by the Fox River. Seney was a ghost town, just as the fictional Nick Adams found it when Ernest brought him there. Hemingway wrote "Big Two-Hearted River" in Paris in 1924, telling the story of a young man on a fishing trip. He included in this story his acute focus on the most minute details, implanting "it in geography and, insofar as possible, . . . [knowing] what time it was on every page."[13] This newly developed characteristic in his emerging style is seen clearly when Nick settles by his campfire to eat:

> Nick put the frying pan on the grill over the flames. He was hungrier. The beans and spaghetti warmed. Nick stirred them and mixed them together. They began to bubble, making little bubbles that rose with difficulty to the surface. There was a good smell. Nick got out a bottle of tomato catchup and cut four slices of bread. The little bubbles were coming faster now. Nick sat down beside the fire and lifted the frying pan off. He poured about half the contents out into the tin plate. It spread slowly on the plate. Nick knew it was too hot. He poured on some tomato catchup.[14]

Pork and Beans and Spaghetti

Never before have pork and beans been afforded such heroic status as when Nick Adams settled in to eat by the shores of Hemingway's "Big Two-Hearted River." While this dish may seem simple and common, when eaten alone in the bush by a favorite trout stream after a long journey you may understand its ascension into the pantheon of haute cuisine littéraire.

2 SERVINGS

    1 can prepared pork and beans
    1 can prepared spaghetti
    Ketchup
    4 slices bread

Pour the can of pork and beans and the can of spaghetti into a saucepan. Warm over a medium fire until the bubbles come fast to the surface. Pour half out onto a plate (preferably tin). Add ketchup to taste. Allow to cool sufficiently before eating. Serve with bread for wiping up the sauce.

Canned Apricots

Nick Adams also brings apricots along on his camping adventure. Contrary to Hemingway's suggestion in "Camping Out," Nick enjoys canned apricots rather than stewed. One need only imagine the sweetness of the syrup from the can to understand his preference for this canned version. Either way, apricots provide a succulent dessert, simply prepared and profoundly enjoyed by the fire.

Coffee According to Hopkins

Hemingway closes Nick's meal and Part One of "Big Two-Hearted River" with a pot of coffee. Not just any coffee, but coffee according to the specific method of Nick's friend Hopkins, a "very serious coffee drinker."[15] Most likely Hopkins is loosely based on Charlie Hopkins, Hemingway's friend and editor at the Kansas City Star. *Hemingway made the fictional Hopkins an oil millionaire who had a particular penchant for coffee making. Nick argued with him at every point but eventually saw the light. The following recipe is "straight Hopkins all the way."[16]*

2 SERVINGS

> 2 cups cold water
> 3 heaping spoonfuls ground coffee
> Sugar

Pour the water into a coffeepot. Use ice-cold stream water, if available. Add the coffee. Bring the water to a boil, allowing it to overflow and run down the side of the pot just to assure yourself that it is, in fact, boiling. Remove the pot from the fire and sprinkle in a little cold water to settle the grounds. Pour coffee into apricot cans or coffee cups as per your preference. Do not let the coffee steep in the pot. Add sugar to taste.

These were the foods of Ernest Hemingway's youth, expressions of the characters of his mother and father, and symbols of the freedom and adventure of the Michigan woods. He would return again to Michigan, and its summer people would be on his mind for years to come as he lived and wrote. He would rarely return to Oak Park and would never write explicitly about his hometown. He lost his father to suicide in 1928, and grew continually more distant from his mother, who died in 1951.

Growing up in Oak Park and Michigan, his father had instilled in him a voracious appetite for new experiences. He had tasted adventure, and he longed for more and greater ones. He could never have imagined what awaited him in northern Italy and later in Paris and beyond. And yet in many ways he was always well prepared for what lay ahead.

ITALY

Remembrance and War

"'I like a retreat better than an advance,' Bonello said. 'On a retreat we drink barbera.'

'We drink it now. To-morrow maybe we drink rainwater,' Aymo said.

'To-morrow we'll be in Udine. We'll drink Champagne.'"

—*A Farewell to Arms*

Ernest in uniform.

Ernest graduated from Oak Park High School in 1917 and faced the prospect of work, college, or war in Europe. Through his uncle Tyler (Hemingway), who was in the lumber business in Kansas City, Ernest learned of a position with the *Kansas City Star* that would be available in the fall. After yet another joyous summer in Michigan, Ernest left for Kansas City. His work at the *Star* was as close to a formal education in the fundamentals of writing as he would ever have. "Use short sentences," the *Star*'s stylebook said. "Use short first paragraphs. Use vigorous English, not forgetting to strive for smoothness."[1] He acquired his first tools. The raw material from which he "whittled a style for his time"[2] lay in wait close by, though never close enough until it was upon him in a blanket of fire, earth, and metal.

In the spring of 1918, the war in Europe beckoned. Ernest could not imagine missing out on "the most exciting drama ever produced."[3] Although his poor eyesight kept him out of the armed services, he quickly volunteered when the American Red Cross began recruiting ambulance drivers.

On the morning of May 22, 1918, Hemingway left New York on the French liner *Chicago*, bound for Bordeaux. After chasing incoming German shells around Paris and taking a spectacular train ride through the Alps, he was assigned to ARC Section Four in Schio, 24 kilometers northwest of Milan.

After three weeks with Section Four, Ernest was impatient to get out and find the war. His opportunity came when the Austrians increased their assault on the Piave River Valley above Venice and volunteers were needed for emergency canteens. About two weeks later, as Ernest was delivering cigarettes and chocolate to soldiers in a riverside trench, the war found him. Everyone heard the dull, rhythmic flutter of the 420-caliber projectile. When it struck the ground, ". . . there was a flash, as when a blast-furnace door is swung open, and a roar that started white and went red . . . ."[4] Ernest was badly wounded in both legs by the trench mortar and by machine-gun fire that struck him hard as he attempted to carry a wounded Italian soldier to safety.

After the first of several operations to remove the shrapnel, a brief stay in a field hospital, and a grueling train ride to Milan, Ernest eventually found comfort in the American Red Cross hospital, where he found his first love. She was Agnes von Kurowsky, an American nurse seven years older than Ernest.

The true details of their love affair remain obscured beneath Ernest's youthful bragging and his eventual fiction. This woman, and this chapter of his life, became the basis of one of the great novels to emerge from the trenches of World War I—

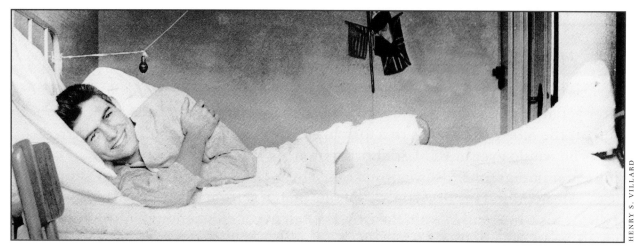

Recovering in the Red Cross Hospital, Milan, July 1918.

A Farewell to Arms. This novel, along with *Across the River and into the Trees*, whose main character could very well be Frederic Henry 30 years later, reflects Hemingway's lifelong, bittersweet love of northern Italy. Both of these books offer a rich and wonderful selection of Italian cuisine, providing for us, amidst the sorrow of lost battles, an indulgent sustenance.

A Farewell to Arms

It was almost 10 years after Ernest limped home from Europe before he had obtained the emotional distance and the skill to use his wartime experience for his fiction. He was bitter and hurt when Agnes, who remained in Europe, wrote that she had fallen in love with another. When the fiction finally came, he created Frederic Henry and Catherine Barkley and gave them evenings together and tense hours apart, much as he may have either experienced or hoped to experience with Agnes.

As Frederic was about to return to the front, he and Catherine took a room in a hotel across from the Milan train station and spent an evening together before they had to part. In this scene of passion, heightened by their imminent separation, Hemingway provides for Frederic and Catherine a meal befitting their love:

> "Monsieur and Madame wish dinner in their rooms?"
>
> "Yes. Will you have the menu brought up?" I said.
>
> "You wish something special for dinner. Some game or a soufflé?"
>
> The elevator passed three floors with a click

each time, then clicked and stopped.

"What have you as game?"

"I could get a pheasant, or a woodcock."

"A woodcock," I said. We walked down the corridor. The carpet was worn. There were many doors. The manager stopped and unlocked a door and opened it . . .

Catherine wore my tunic over her shoulders while we ate. We were very hungry and the meal was good and we drank a bottle of Capri and a bottle of St. Estephe. I drank most of it but Catherine drank some and it made her feel splendid. For dinner we had a woodcock with soufflé potatoes and purée de marron, a salad, and zabaglione for dessert.[5]

Hemingway with his first love Agnes von Kurowsky, in Milan, Italy, 1918.

THE MENU

Woodcock Flambé in Armagnac

Soufflé Potatoes

Purée de Marron

Salad

Zabaglione

Wines

Capri

St. Estephe

19

Woodcock Flambé in Armagnac

Hemingway shared his knowledge of wild fowl with Frederic Henry, who orders woodcock without hesitation. Frederic knows that woodcock is superior in delicacy to pheasant and is in season during the autumn frost. One can safely assume that Ernest also shared with Frederic his knowledge of hunting woodcock and the best way to prepare it as well:

> While the woodcock is an easy bird to hit, with a soft flight like an owl, and if you do miss him he will probably pitch down and give you another shot. But what a bird to eat flambé with Armagnac cooked in his own juice and butter, a little mustard added to make a sauce, with two strips of bacon and pommes soufflé. . . .[6]

While the game connoisseur would demand that woodcock be prepared without being drawn (with the intestines still in the cavity), it may be difficult to find woodcock these days that are not drawn. Frederic and Catherine no doubt enjoy their birds accompanied with a sauce flavored with the bird's intestines mixed with foie gras. The following recipe assumes that your birds have been drawn. If you are unable to find woodcock, you may substitute another dark-meat game bird, such as hazel grouse or snipe (2 snipes for each woodcock).

4 woodcocks
½ lemon, cut into 4 wedges
Salt
Freshly ground black pepper
8 slices bacon
4 tablespoons butter
1 teaspoon Dijon-style mustard
¼ cup Armagnac (or other fine brandy)

Preheat the oven to 400° F.

Rub the inside of each bird with a piece of lemon and season inside with a pinch of salt, and outside with a pinch of salt and pepper. Set aside.

Place the bacon in a large skillet and cook over medium heat. When the bacon is browned and plenty of fat is rendered, remove the bacon from the pan and set aside. Add the butter to the skillet and heat until it begins to foam. Truss the legs of the birds, place in the skillet, and brown on all sides, 5 to 8 minutes. Remove the skillet from the heat and transfer the birds to a roasting pan. Roast the birds for 10 to 15 minutes, basting frequently with the bacon fat. The birds are done when the juices run clear where the leg meets the body when the skin is cut.

Transfer the birds to a plate and remove the trussing. Place the skillet on the stove over medium heat. Stir the mustard into the leftover juices in the skillet. Place the birds and bacon back into the skillet and add the Armagnac. Heat briefly and ignite the brandy on the edge of the skillet. Use care doing so and keep your face

20

a safe distance from the skillet. When the flames die, transfer the birds and bacon to a warm serving platter. Pour the juices from the skillet over the birds and serve.

Soufflé Potatoes

The accidental invention of this dish dates back to the inaugural run of the first French railway in 1837 from Paris to Saint-Germain. The menu for the celebratory banquet included the requisite fillet of steak and fried potatoes. Setting a foreboding precedent, the official train carrying King Louis-Philippe and his queen was, of course, delayed. The cook therefore removed his frying potatoes from the oil and let them cool. When the train finally arrived, the chef courageously replaced the potatoes in the hot oil, not knowing what gastronomic aberration might result. What did result were these delicate and puffy chips, which have remained a dinnertime treat ever since.[7]

2 SERVINGS

> 2 cups vegetable oil, or enough to deep-fry
> 2 large potatoes
> Salt

Pour the oil into an 8- or 9-inch skillet or into a deep fryer and heat over medium-high heat. Peel the potatoes, then wash and pat dry. Cut the potatoes into slices, just less than ¼ inch thick. Wash and dry the slices. When the oil has warmed to approximately 300° F (150° C), place the potatoes in the oil. This will take a few batches. When the slices float to the surface, remove them and drain on paper towels or on a brown paper bag. Allow the slices to cool completely.

When the potatoes have cooled, reheat the oil to 350° F (180° C). Return the potatoes to the oil and fry until they are puffed up and lightly browned. Drain the potatoes, sprinkle with salt, and serve on a warm platter.

Purée de Marron (Chestnut Purée)

4 TO 6 SERVINGS

> 1 pound chestnuts, unshelled
> ¼ rib celery
> 1½–2 cups chicken stock
> 2 tablespoons butter
> ¼ cup heavy cream
> Freshly ground white pepper
> Pinch of salt, depending on saltiness of stock (optional)

To shell the chestnuts, cut a groove about ⅛ inch deep on the rounded side of the shells. Drop chestnuts into a pot of boiling water. Return water to boil and cook for about 5 minutes. Remove from heat. Take a few nuts at a time and remove the shells and the skins. If the nuts don't peel easily, return them to the pot and soak for a bit longer.

In a medium saucepan, combine the peeled chestnuts, celery, and chicken stock just to cover. More stock may be necessary if chestnuts are dry. Bring to a boil. Reduce heat, cover, and simmer until stock is absorbed and chestnuts are completely tender, 30 to 40 minutes. Put the mixture through a food mill, mash with a fork, or purée in a food processor. Transfer to a clean saucepan. Add the butter and stir until thoroughly mixed. Place the pan over medium heat and add the cream, pepper, and salt. Stirring constantly, bring the purée to a boil. Add more cream or milk to obtain desired consistency.

Zabaglione

4 SERVINGS

4 egg yolks
1 egg white
¼ cup sugar
¼ cup dry white wine
½ cup kümmel (or kirsch)

In the top part of a double boiler, combine the egg yolks, egg white, and sugar. Whisk until thickened and light yellow. In the bottom of the double boiler, bring a few inches of water to a boil, then reduce to a simmer. Place the top of the boiler over the water and continue whisking until foamy. Slowly add wine and liqueur. Whisk until the mixture is foamy and bubbling and begins to stick to the whisk. Remove from the heat. Serve immediately in dessert glasses.

Note: It is essential to continue whisking while the mixture is over the heat. If the mixture sticks to the pan or the yolks begin to coagulate, remove immediately from the heat and whisk vigorously. Zabaglione must be thick and frothy.

———————

Having brought Frederic and Catherine safely along the shores of Lake Maggiore to Switzerland—she is pregnant and he has escaped from the war—Hemingway was left alone to toil with the ending of his novel. During the novel's closing drama, Catherine struggles in labor all day long, as Frederic is sent away from the hospital three times to eat. These attempts at meals stand in stark contrast to the idyllic splendor of their feast together in Milan. Hemingway's taste for using food to illuminate the tenor of a scene, its fertile passion or its hollow fear, is exemplified by the final tragic passages of *A Farewell to Arms*.

Catherine goes into labor in the darkness of early morning. At the hospital, she sends Frederic away to have breakfast. As the light of day slowly emerges, he goes to a café to eat:

> I walked down the empty street to the café. There was a light in the window. I went in and stood at the zinc bar and an old man served me a glass of white wine and a brioche. The brioche was yesterday's. I dipped it in the wine and then drank a glass of coffee.[8]

Brioche

There is considerable variety to this traditional French pastry made from yeast dough augmented with eggs and butter. The most common forms are the Parisienne and the Nanterre. The Parisienne, or tête, *consists of a smaller ball of dough placed atop a larger one in a fluted mold. The Nanterre is loaf-shaped, made by placing large balls of dough in a loaf pan, creating a knobby effect. This recipe, adapted from Linda Dannenberg's book* Paris Boulangerie-Pâtisserie *makes two marvelous loaves of brioche or two large Parisiennes. The Parisiennes (even yesterday's) are fine for Frederic's breakfast, while the Nanterres will accommodate the red raspberry preserve that David and Catherine Bourne spread on their brioche in the opening pages of* The Garden of Eden.

- 2 tablespoons lukewarm water
- 2 tablespoons dry yeast
- 4 cups all-purpose flour
- ¾ cup milk
- 2 large eggs
- 1½ teaspoons vanilla sugar, or 1½ teaspoon sugar and ¾ teaspoon vanilla extract
- 1½ teaspoons salt
- ½ cup unsalted butter, softened
- ¼ cup plus 3 tablespoons sugar

For the glaze

- 1 large egg, well beaten
- 1½ tablespoons unsalted butter, melted

Pour the water into a small glass, sprinkle on the yeast, and set aside for about 10 minutes. At that time, place the flour in the bowl of a mixer fitted with a dough hook or on a flat work surface.

In a small saucepan, slowly heat the milk until lukewarm.

Form a well in the middle of the flour and pour in the yeast, milk, eggs, vanilla sugar, and salt. Mix the dough together on low speed, or with your fingers, until smooth.

In a separate bowl, combine the butter and sugar and stir until pale and smooth. If you have been working by hand, move the dough to a large buttered mixing bowl. Add the butter-sugar mixture,

23

very little at a time, pinching the dough together and stretching the dough up from the bottom of the bowl with each addition. When all of the butter and sugar is incorporated, the dough should be sticky and elastic. Form the dough into a ball. Cover the bowl with a damp towel and let dough rise for about 2 hours, or until doubled in size. At that time, punch the dough down, cover the bowl with plastic wrap, and refrigerate overnight.

The next day, remove the dough from the refrigerator and let stand for 1 hour. Turn the dough out onto a lightly floured work surface.

For Parisiennes, divide the dough in two. Cut one-third off each half of the dough. Quickly form the larger pieces into balls and drop into large, buttered brioche molds. Form the smaller pieces into pear-shaped balls. Make a small indentation in the center of the larger balls and place the smaller balls on top, pointed side down, pinching around the edges to seal the seam between the pieces. Cover and let rise another 2 hours, or until doubled in size. Preheat the oven to 350° F. Using wet scissors, make some small incisions in the base of the dough from the edges toward the crown. Lightly brush the dough with the beaten egg. Bake for 40 to 45 minutes, or until golden brown. Brush the brioche with the melted butter and let cool on a wire rack.

LUNCH

After breakfast, Frederic walks back to the hospital, stopping to root through a trash can to find something for a scavenging dog, but finds nothing but a gravelike pile of coffee grounds and dead flowers. At the hospital, Catherine has been moved to the delivery room and remains in labor into the early afternoon. At two o'clock, Frederick again leaves the hospital and returns to the same café for lunch:

> At two o'clock I went out and had lunch. There were a few men in the café sitting with coffee and glasses of kirsch or marc on the tables. I sat down at the table. "Can I eat?" I asked the waiter.
>
> "It is past time for lunch."
>
> "Isn't there anything for all hours?"
>
> "You can have *choucroute*."
>
> "Give me *choucroute* and beer."
>
> "A demi or a bock?"
>
> "A light demi."
>
> The waiter brought a dish of sauerkraut with a slice of ham over the top and a sausage buried in the hot wine-soaked cabbage. I ate it and drank the beer.[9]

Choucroute Garni
(Garnished Sauerkraut)

4 SERVINGS

4 cups fresh sauerkraut, or 1 2-pound can

8 slices lean smoked bacon

12 juniper berries

1 teaspoon caraway seeds

Dash of salt

1 teaspoon pepper

1 medium onion

1 whole clove

1 cup water

2 cups dry white wine, such as Riesling or other Alsatian wine

4 garlic sausages, or other high-quality sausage

2 slices cooked smoked ham

Preheat the oven to 325° F.

Strain and rinse the sauerkraut thoroughly with cold water. Place the bacon slices in a large heavy casserole. Cook over medium heat until a film of fat covers the bottom. Add half the sauerkraut. Slightly crush the juniper berries in a mortar and mix together with the caraway seeds, salt, and pepper, then add the mixture to the sauerkraut. Stick the onion with the clove and place it in the middle of the casserole. Add the remaining sauerkraut. Pour the water and wine over the sauerkraut. Cover the casserole and bake for 1½ hours.

Remove the casserole from the oven and, if the sauerkraut is too dry, add a little more water. Bury the sausages in the sauerkraut and place the slices of ham on top. Cover and bake for another 30 minutes.

Serve with large glasses of cold beer. Frederic orders a "demi," which is a half-liter glass.

DINNER

As the tragedy of Catherine's delivery unfolds, Frederic is sent to the café once again. This time it is brightly lit and crowded inside. Dinner, as with the two previous meals, consists of leftovers. This final meal at the café near the hospital, with the strange taste of eggs and beer, and the unfriendly clientele, sets the tone for Frederic's hurried return to Catherine. "Suddenly I knew I had to get back."[10] Hemingway has taken us through this ordeal, a day on the clock but the suffering of a lifetime, and engaged us through the otherwise benign act of eating. As Linda Underhill and Jeanne Nakjavani wrote in "Food for Fiction":

> As a result of this kind of specific detail, food and drink in Hemingway's fiction become, at moments of crisis in the story, a code to signify the mood, lending truth to the setting, and representing adventure.[11]

Across the River and into the Trees

Other than a few brief visits in the 1920s, Hemingway would not return to Italy until 1948. He had seen three more wars firsthand, and the initial romance of that first war seemed immeasurably distant. When he returned to the location of his wounding in 1922, newly married and living in Paris, he learned a hard lesson: "Chasing yesterdays is a bum show," he wrote in the *Toronto Daily Star*, "and if you want to prove it, go back to your old front."[12] And even with this knowledge and nearly 50 years old, he bent down to bury a 1,000-lire note in a small hole beside the very crater where he was first struck down.

Hemingway returned to Italy a celebrity, the single best-selling author in Italy since World War II. He would no longer be staying in hotels across from train stations without any luggage, but at the Gritti Palace Hotel in Venice and Locando Cipriani in Torcello, traveling with 14 pieces of luggage. He was the aging veteran of his war and his art, looking in mirrors and denying the truth. His book began as a story about duck hunting, but soon it too began chasing yesterdays.

Ernest arrived in Genoa in the fall of 1948, at the same port from which he had limped home, an injured and changed young man, in 1918. Hemingway spent the next few months exploring the northern Italian countryside, visiting his old front and enjoying his star status in "the magical city of Venice."[13] In December, on a hunting trip, Ernest met Adriana Ivancich, an 18-year-old Italian beauty descended from a long line of aristocratic Venetians. It was not long before Ernest was calling her "daughter." She was the same age as Hemingway when he was wounded by the riverbank in Fossalta.

Throughout this trip to Italy, Hemingway was looking back over 30 years. He saw his own experiences of the war mingle with those he created in *A Farewell to Arms*, and he saw Adriana, the figure of beauty and youth, enticingly close. As Carlos Baker wrote of this experience, the "past and present, the imagination and the reality, contended within him for mastery."[14] The only way he could wrest control again was to write. In the early spring of 1949, Hemingway began *Across the River and into the Trees*, the story of an old, embittered military man and his love for a very young, very beautiful Venetian countess.

Colonel Richard Cantwell, a composite of real-life military men, is primarily as Hemingway imagined himself had he become a professional warrior rather than a writer. Renata, the countess, is clearly based on Adriana. The details of their relationship, like Frederic and Catherine's, was a wishful fiction. The essence was true—the battle-weary veteran seeking to recapture his youth in the eyes and heart of a beautiful young woman. Ernest was well aware that the name *Renata*—which he had taken from role model Gabriele d'Annunzio's book *Notturno*[15]—translated as "reborn."

The Colonel's battles are elsewhere as he and Renata share Venice together. Whether hunting near Torcello in the Venetian Lagoon, dining at the Gritti Palace Hotel, or drinking martinis at

Harry's Bar, Hemingway's story is a "prose poem essentially devoid of action but rich in meditative discourse . . . on the courage and equanimity, toughness and resilience, the interconnectedness and distance of youth and old age."[16] As we saw when the war raged in *A Farewell to Arms*, the food and drink that Cantwell and Renata share reflect their indulgent passion. They feast, and Venice is alive.

HARRY'S BAR

> Then he was pulling open the door of Harry's bar and was inside and he had made it again, and was at home.[17]

Guiseppe Cipriani began his career at age 14 in a pastry shop in Verona. Like Hemingway, he enthusiastically went to war in 1918. Fortunately for Guiseppe, the armistice was signed and the fighting stopped on the eve of his departure for the front lines. Upon his return he began working as a waiter, eventually settling in Venice. He recognized in himself the essential traits of a restaurateur: a passion for food, a love of people, and a desire to bring the two together to create a truly enjoyable dining experience.

In 1927, Guiseppe became the barman at the Hotel Europa-Britannia because the owner recognized that he "had a way with the customers."[18] The following summer he met an American student named Harry Pickering, who came to Italy with his aunt to cure his alcoholism but ended up spending most of his time in the Europa bar. When Harry's money ran out, Guiseppe lent him 10,000 lire. Harry promptly left. He returned months later, carrying Guiseppe's money and another 40,000 lire with which they could open a bar together. On May 13, 1931, they opened Harry's Bar. For the complete story of this legendary Venice landmark, read Arrigo Cipriani's marvelous book, *Harry's Bar* (Arcade, 1996).

Hemingway discovered Guiseppe Cipriani's bar and restaurant in 1949 and quickly became its most famous regular customer. He and Cipriani became fast friends, and Guiseppe's son, Arrigo, who now runs Harry's, remembers that Hemingway was the first customer with whom his father drank.

As much as Ernest enjoyed the interior of Harry's (see The Montgomery, page 189), he loved the excellent duck hunting near the island of Torcello in the lagoon. Hemingway resided at the Cipriani's guesthouse on the island and took several wintertime hunting trips to the surrounding marshes and canals. In 1935, he had written an article for *Esquire* magazine that explained his passion for hunting these beautiful and spirited birds. The behavior and the calls of some seemed designed to aid the hunter, while he found that those that were harder to hear were better to eat:

> Why does the curlew have that voice, and who thought up the plover's call, which takes the place of noise of wings, to give us that catharsis wing shooting has given to men since they stopped flying hawks and took to fowling pieces? I think that they were made to shoot and some of us were made to shoot

them and if that is not so well, never say we did not tell you that we liked it.[19]

It is not surprising that Ernest took every opportunity to fight the early morning bitter cold to hunt again and again in the Venetian environs. One such trip provided the wonderful opening scene of *Across the River and into the Trees*:

> His head low, he swung the gun on a long slant, down, well and ahead of the second duck, then without looking at the result of his shot he raised the gun smoothly, up, up ahead and to the left . . . and as he pulled, saw it fold in flight and drop among the decoys in the broken ice.[20]

Arrigo Cipriani fondly remembers Papa's early morning duck hunting trips in Torcello with Emilio, his boatman. Cantwell reminisces about the ducks he once offered to the bellman at the Gritti Palace, who could not afford a meal of such expense. We, too, may feel that roast duck is, as the bellman put it, "outside of our way of life." And yet with the help of Signore Cipriani we may truly indulge ourselves in the spoils of Hemingway's love of hunting ducks in the icy waters outside of Venice.

> I never knew that anything could be so wonderful to eat. When your teeth close on the small slice of meat it is an almost unbelievable delight.[21]

Roast Duckling (*Anitra Arrosto*)

From *The Harry's Bar Cookbook*
6 TO 8 SERVINGS

For the Sauce

> 6 tablespoons olive oil
>
> Necks, wings, and giblets (except livers) from ducks
>
> Chicken bones or carcasses or extra duck carcass
>
> 2 ribs celery, cut into chunks
>
> 2 onions, coarsely chopped
>
> 2 carrots, cut into chunks
>
> 1 teaspoon chopped fresh thyme, or ¼ teaspoon dried
>
> 1 teaspoon chopped fresh rosemary, or ¼ teaspoon dried, crumbled
>
> 1 clove garlic, halved
>
> 1 cup Marsala
>
> ½ cup dry white wine
>
> 6 tablespoons flour
>
> 1 quart hot chicken stock, or more as needed
>
> Salt
>
> Freshly ground pepper

For the Ducks

> 2 3- or 4-pound ducks
>
> Salt
>
> Freshly ground pepper
>
> 6 flat-leaf parsley sprigs
>
> 6 fresh rosemary sprigs
>
> 4 fresh thyme sprigs
>
> 2 cloves garlic, halved
>
> 1 large onion, sliced
>
> ½ cup Marsala

Preheat the oven to 450° F.

To make the sauce, put 2 tablespoons of the olive oil and the duck necks, wings, and giblets and the bones and/or carcasses in a roasting pan and roast until they are well browned, about 30 minutes.

Meanwhile, heat the remaining oil in a soup pot over high heat. Add the celery, onions, carrots, herbs, and garlic and cook, stirring frequently, until they begin to brown, about 5 minutes. Pour the Marsala and white wine into the pot and boil hard, stirring constantly, until the wine has evaporated. Sprinkle on the flour, stir it in well, and cook over medium heat, stirring constantly, for 3 or 4 minutes. Add 3 cups of the stock to the pot and whisk it in until it forms a thickened sauce. Add the roasted bones to the pot.

Pour off the oil in the roasting pan and deglaze the roasting pan with the remaining cup of stock, scraping up all the brown bits from the bottom of the pan. Add this to the pot and bring it to a boil.

Stir the mixture as well as you can, reduce the heat, and simmer, uncovered, over low heat, for 1 hour. Season with salt and pepper to taste. Set aside.

To roast the ducks, place a shallow roasting pan with a rack in the oven to preheat at 450° F. (This will keep the ducks from sticking.) Season the cavities of the ducks with salt and pepper and fill with the parsley, rosemary, thyme, garlic, and onion. Place the ducks breast-side up in the preheated roasting pan and roast until golden brown, about 30 minutes. Prick the skin of the ducks well, especially the breast and thighs, reduce the heat to 350° F, and continue to roast for 1 to 1½ hours longer. Prick the ducks every 20 minutes to allow the fat to drain from beneath the skin. Start testing the ducks for doneness after 1 hour by piercing the flesh near the thigh bones with a sharp fork; when the juices run clear, with no sign of pink, the ducks are done.

While the ducks are roasting, finish the sauce. Strain it. If it is too thin, boil it, uncovered, to reduce it. Taste and carefully adjust the seasoning.

Remove the ducks and the rack from the roasting pan and spoon off as much fat as possible, leaving any juices in the pan. Set the roasting pan over the burner, pour in the Marsala, and cook over high heat until reduced by half, about 3 or 4 minutes, scraping up all the browned bits from the bottom of the pan. Add this to the sauce, stir to combine well, and heat through. Taste and adjust the seasoning. Carve the ducks and put them on a platter. Serve the sauce on the side.

From their large corner room on the third floor, Ernest and his fourth wife, Mary, commanded a magnificent view of the Grand Canal as it turned sharply to wrap itself around them. The luxurious Gritti Palace Hotel with its world-class restaurant served as a fitting domicile for the Hemingways (and Cantwell) as they sated themselves with Venetian charm. The Colonel and Renata dine repeatedly at the Gritti, enjoying dinner and breakfast served with wit and elegance. As they arrive, they are greeted by the Gran Maestro, a friend of the Colonel's from the war and a fellow member of *El Ordine Militar, Nobile y Espirituoso de los Caballeros de Brusadelli,* a fictitious organization named after a Milanese profiteer who, during a property dispute, publicly blamed his young wife for clouding his judgment through her "extraordinary sexual demands."[22] Nevertheless, the Colonel and Renata partake of a feast befitting their passionate reunion and their surroundings.

"I have saved your table. We have a very fine lobster if you would like him to commence with."

"Is he really fresh?"

"I saw him this morning when he came from the market in a basket. He was alive and a dark green and completely unfriendly."

"Would you like lobster, Daughter, to start your dinner?"

"I would love some lobster" the girl said. "Cold, and with mayonnaise. The mayonnaise rather stiff." She said this in Italian.[23]

Hemingway at Harry's Bar.

30

Dinner at the Gritti Palace Hotel, Venice

Lobster Salad

Scaloppine with Marsala

Cauliflower Braised with Butter

Artichoke Vinaigrette

Wines

Capri Bianco

Valpolicella

———

The Colonel and Renata do indeed commence with the lobster before moving on to the veal and vegetables. He's a big lobster and the Colonel likens him to George Patton. The Gran Maestro stems Renata's concern that he may be too tough: "He's truly not tough. He's only big. You know the type."[24]

Lobster Salad

2 SERVINGS

2 carrots, diced

1 parsnip, diced

1 leek, white part only, diced

1 rib celery, diced

1 onion stuck with 2 cloves

Bouquet garni (a few sprigs of parsley, thyme, rosemary, and a few bay leaves bundled and tied together or in a cheese-cloth bag)

1 clove garlic

2 cups dry white wine

Salt

Pepper

Pinch of cayenne pepper

2 small live lobsters (1¼ pound each), or 1 large lobster (about 2½ pounds)

Juice of ½ lemon

Hard-boiled egg and capers, for garnish

Wine

Capri Bianco, secco and really cold

To a large stockpot filled with 8 to 10 cups water, add the diced vegetables, onion, bouquet garni, garlic, wine, salt and pepper to taste, and cayenne. Bring to a boil. Lower heat and simmer, covered, for 30 minutes. Add the lobsters and simmer, covered, for about 20 minutes, or until the lobsters turn bright red.

31

Drain the lobsters and chill. Remove the tail and the tail meat. Crack the claws and remove the meat from the claws and the knuckles. Cut the lobster meat into uniform pieces. Arrange the meat on a bed of lettuce and season with salt and pepper to taste and a little fresh lemon juice. Cover with mayonnaise, garnish with quarters of hard-boiled egg and capers, and serve.

For the mayonnaise

MAKES ½ CUP

1 egg yolk
¼ teaspoon salt
1 teaspoon Dijon-style mustard
½ cup olive oil
1 teaspoon tarragon vinegar
Salt
Dash of freshly ground white pepper

Combine the egg yolk, salt, and mustard in a food processor. Pulse briefly to combine. With the food processor on, very slowly add the olive oil until the mixture is thickened and silky. Add the vinegar and salt and pepper to taste and process briefly to blend.

———————

The Colonel and Renata continue their meal with the attentive assistance of the Gran Maestro. The Countess orders a simple meal of steak with mashed potatoes and a plain salad. The Colonel orders the classic Scaloppine and accents it with braised cauliflower and an artichoke. He accompanies the food with the light, dry Valpolicella.

Scaloppine with Marsala

This recipe is adapted from Cuisine of Venice.

4 SERVINGS

2 pounds veal, thinly sliced
3–4 tablespoons all-purpose flour
3 tablespoons butter
3 tablespoons olive oil
½ cup dry Marsala
Salt
Pepper

Carefully trim any white skin from the veal. Place the slices of veal in a single layer between two pieces of wax paper. With a flat wooden mallet, pound the slices to approximately ⅓-inch thickness. Make several small incisions along the edges of each slice to prevent it from curling up while cooking. Dredge each slice lightly in flour. Shake to remove any excess.

Melt the butter in a large skillet over medium heat. Add the olive oil and heat almost until it begins to smoke. Add several slices of veal to the pan, being careful to leave plenty of room between the slices. Sauté for 3 minutes on each side, moving often to prevent sticking. Remove the veal to a warm serving plate while continuing to sauté in batches.

Deglaze the skillet with the wine, scraping up all the bits that have stuck. Season with salt and pepper to taste. Pour the Marsala over the scaloppine and serve.

Cauliflower Braised with Butter

2 SERVINGS

2 tablespoons butter

2 tablespoons olive oil

½ head cauliflower, cut into crowns

Salt

Pepper

1 cup chicken stock, or enough to cover

Combine the butter and olive oil in a large saucepan. Place over high heat until the butter is melted and frothy but not browned. Add the cauliflower and toss until well coated. Sauté the cauliflower for 2 minutes, or until just lightly browned. Add salt and pepper to taste. Pour in the stock. Lower the heat and simmer, covered, for 10 minutes, or until tender. Remove cauliflower with a slotted spoon and serve immediately.

Artichoke Vinaigrette

This was one of Hemingway's favorite vegetables,[25] and the Colonel enjoys this dish, once thought to be an aphrodisiac, "taking a leaf at a time, and dipping them, heavy side down, into the deep saucer of sauce vinaigrette."[26]

4 SERVINGS

Vinaigrette

¾ cup finest olive oil

¼ cup wine vinegar

Salt

Pepper

2 cloves garlic

Artichokes

4 artichokes

4 lemon slices

2 tablespoons lemon juice

Prepare the vinaigrette 2 hours before serving. Whisk together the olive oil, vinegar, and salt and pepper to taste. Add the garlic and steep for 2 hours.

Clean the artichokes by plunging them repeatedly, upside down, into cold water. Cut the stems off, leaving a flat bottom. To prevent discoloration, tie a slice of lemon to the bottom of the artichoke with kitchen string. Break off any tough bottom leaves. Cut off the top third of the artichoke and trim the top ¼ inch off the remaining leaves with scissors.

Bring a large pot of water, salted and with 2 tablespoons lemon juice added, to a boil. Add the artichokes and boil for about 30 minutes. The artichokes are done when an outside leaf pulls away easily. Remove the artichokes, drain upside down in a colander, untie and remove the lemon slices and rinse the artichokes thoroughly in cold water. When cooled, open them slightly, remove the very thin center leaves, and scoop out the choke with a spoon. Serve whole, one per person, with vinaigrette in a saucer for dipping the leaves.

The Market

Early one morning, before daylight, the Colonel embarks on an excursion that was one of Hemingway's favorites while in Venice. He would cross the Grand Canal at the Rialto bridge to the spectacular fish and vegetable market on the far side of the city by the Adriatic. Ernest loved the market, and shared its sensory feast, as well as his own taste for clams on the half shell, with the Colonel:

> He loved the market. A great part of it was close-packed and crowded into several side streets, and it was so concentrated that it was difficult not to jostle people, unintentionally, and each time you stopped to look, to buy, or to admire, you formed an îlot de résistance against the flow of the morning attack of the purchasers.
>
> In the market, spread on the slippery stone floor, or in their baskets, or their rope-handled

boxes, were the heavy, gray-green lobsters with their magenta overtones that presaged their death in boiling water. They have all been captured by treachery, the Colonel thought, and their claws are pegged.

He went past these, stopping to ask one seller where his clams came from. They came from a good place, without sewerage and the Colonel asked to have six opened. He drank the juice and cut the clam out, cutting close against the shell with the curved knife the man handed him.[27]

Clams on the Half-Shell

Shucking clams requires little more than a firm grip and a basic clam knife. Yet the rewards for this simple labor are exquisite. To prepare clams on the half-shell, first rinse the clams thoroughly under cold water and discard any clams that are broken or that will not close when squeezed shut a few times. Hold each clam with the hinge firmly wedged in the palm of your off hand. Holding the knife in your strong hand, wedge the knife into the seam of the narrower side of the clam. Pull the blade into the seam using the fingers of your off hand. Work the blade up and down slightly to separate the shells, keeping the clam level to hold the juice. The clam has two muscles on either side of the hinge, which must be severed. Place the tip of the blade against the inside of the upper shell, and sweep the knife first to one side to sever that mus-

cle, then to the other side. Sever the second muscle, then open the clam and discard the top shell. Run the knife under the clam to release it from the lower shell. Serve about 6 clams per person, and accompany them with lemon wedges.

The Colonel returns from the market "in the cold, hard Venice light of morning"[28] to meet Renata at Piazza San Marco to have breakfast at the Caffè Florian and to watch the crowds of people. Renata, though, decides that breakfast there is "worthless" and that she dislikes the square so crowded. She is very hungry, and they decide to return to the Gritti: "We'll give breakfast the full treatment," the Colonel said. "You'll wish you had never heard of breakfast."[29]

The Gran Maestro seats them in the empty dining room, gives the Colonel the situation report on bothersome compatriots and other potential intruders, and details for Renata her "breakfast to end breakfasts:"[30] "We can make our *fabricar rognons* grilled with champignons dug by people I know. Or, raised in damp cellars. There can be an omelet with truffles dug by pigs of distinction. There can be real Canadian bacon from maybe Canada, even."[31] Renata accompanies her meal with tea rather than coffee, and the Colonel orders a decanted flask of the Valpolicella to go with an order of the Canadian bacon.

Breakfast to End Breakfasts:
The Gritti Palace Hotel,
Venice

Rognons Grilled with Champignons

Omelet with Truffles

Canadian Bacon

———

Rognons Grilled with Champignons

2 SERVINGS

　　2 veal kidneys
　　Pinch of salt
　　Pepper
　　4–6 tablespoons melted butter
　　4 large mushroom caps

Preheat the broiler.

To prepare the kidneys, peel off the exterior membrane. Slice the kidneys in half, not quite severing them in two. Trim off any fat and skewer the kidneys on two metal skewers each to keep them flat when grilled. Season with a pinch of salt and pepper, brush liberally with melted butter, and place on a broiling pan.

Clean the mushroom caps with a damp towel. Brush with melted butter, season with salt and pepper to taste, and place on the broiling pan with the kidneys, cap-side up. Set the pan about 5 inches from the heat and broil the kidneys and mushrooms, basting with butter, for 6 to 8 minutes on each side. Remove the kidneys to a warm serving platter, slice the mushrooms, and place them around the kidneys. Drizzle on any remaining butter.

Omelet with Truffles

When buying truffles, choose carefully, as a purchasing error could cost you literally their weight in silver. The Italian white truffles used in this dish should be pale beige in color and very firm. Buy your truffles shortly before you plan to use them, as they will spoil quickly, which will be evident by their aroma—distinctly similar to a gas leak. Purchase a truffle slicer while you're at the store, for, if you acquire a taste for these pungent and costly fungi, this tool will be indispensable.

2 SERVINGS

    2 tablespoons butter
    1 truffle
    Pinch of salt

    Pepper
    4 large eggs
    1 tablespoon Madeira

Melt 1 tablespoon of butter in a skillet over medium heat. Slice the truffle and fry it in the butter for 10 minutes. Season with a pinch of salt and pepper to taste and allow to cool. Break the eggs into a bowl. Add salt and pepper to taste. Add the wine, and beat thoroughly. Add the truffles. Melt the remaining 1 tablespoon butter in a clean skillet. When the butter is sizzling but not yet brown, pour in the eggs. When the omelet begins to set underneath, prick the bottom a few times with a fork and lift to allow the uncooked egg to run through. When the eggs are only slightly runny and creamy on top, fold the omelet in half and slide onto a warm platter. Garnish with more slices of truffle, if desired.

Canadian Bacon

The Colonel enjoys an order of broiled bacon, which is thickly cut and broiled for about 1 minute on each side.

FRANCE
An Immovable Feast

"There is never any ending to Paris and the memory of each person who has lived in it differs from that of any other. We always returned to it no matter who we were or how it was changed or with what difficulties, or ease, it could be reached. Paris was always worth it, and you received return for whatever you brought to it."

—*A Moveable Feast*

Notre Dame, Île de la Cité, La Seine in 1920s Paris.

Hemingway returned from the war in January 1919. While he reveled in his role as hero and storyteller—wearing his uniform and cape and giving somewhat embellished talks around Oak Park and Michigan—he sorely missed Agnes and his adventurous life in Italy. In March, he received a letter from Agnes explaining that she could not continue their relationship and planned to marry another. Ernest was crushed, and yet he bragged to his friends that he had "set out to cauterize out her memory . . . with a course of booze and other women."[1] As usual, he was exaggerating and growing more and more impatient with provincial Oak Park and his mother's distaste for his "exuberant lifestyle and seeming lack of direction."[2] But that would change soon enough.

After his brief stint in Toronto with the *Toronto Star* weekly and one last summer at Horton Bay, Hemingway went to Chicago with Bill and Katy Smith and was introduced to an old friend of Katy's, Hadley Richardson. Their attraction was immediate, and they wrote to each other constantly after Hadley returned home to St. Louis. Like Agnes, she was tall and lovely and considerably older than Ernest. Their relationship continued to flourish, and they were married in Michigan in September 1921.

By Thanksgiving, the arrangements were made to sail for France. At the urging of Sherwood Anderson, a well-known writer whom Ernest met in Chicago, the Hemingways abandoned their initial plans to travel to Italy. Paris, Anderson insisted, was the place for serious young writers. He even volunteered to write introductory letters to the very elite of the expatriate literary community in Paris, including Ezra Pound, Gertrude Stein, and Sylvia Beach, owner of the Shakespeare and Company bookstore, soon to publish James Joyce's *Ulysses*. With income from Hadley's trust fund and the series of articles Ernest would write as part-time European correspondent for the *Toronto Star*, they could live quite well in Paris. Caught up in the romance of another European sojourn, Ernest was eager to begin the adventure. Many years later, he would share his memories of those early years, hungry and hard at work in Paris, in *A Moveable Feast*.

The Hemingways arrived in Paris on December 20, 1921. They quickly found a cheap apartment located above a noisy music hall and an herbalist. Ernest's work with the *Toronto Star* let him play at journalism in Paris and across Europe, from Genoa to Constantinople to Austria. He honed his acute powers of observation as he wrote on such diverse topics as peace conferences, tuna fishing, and Mussolini ("Europe's prized bluffer"). Wherever he found himself, he immersed himself in the people, culture, and cuisine of his host country.

Charles Scribner, Jr., called Hemingway "one of the most perceptive travelers in the history of literature."[3] He was also one of literary history's great eaters and drinkers, and when the haute cuisine of Paris, or the strong drink of Constantinople (see Deusico, page 182), or the hearty fare of Austria presented itself, he quickly became entrenched in the essence of the new and novel tastes.

Upon arrival in Paris, Hemingway was very shy and apprehensive about meeting Pound and Stein. It took only a week, though, before he encountered Sylvia Beach, "the postmistress and den mother of Left Bank Americans."[4] He never used the letter from Anderson, for his literary aspirations were introduction enough for Sylvia. Shakespeare and Company was also a rental library, and Ernest did not have enough money with him to join at first. Sylvia was impressed with Ernest, despite the address on his check-out card, and allowed him to take as many books as he liked and pay her whenever possible. He borrowed books by Turgenev, D. H. Lawrence, and Dostoyevsky. When he shared his wonderful discovery with Hadley, she insisted that they return immediately and pay the deposit for the books. The Hemingways were regular visitors to Shakespeare and Company over the next several years, borrowing books to read by lamplight at home or to take with them on skiing vacations and elsewhere.

That initial deposit cost them an evening out at a café, but they gladly made the sacrifice and ate at home that evening: "We'll come home and eat here and we'll have a lovely meal and drink Beaune from the co-operative you can see right out of the window there with the price of the Beaune on the window."[5] But, before they depart for the bookstore, they enjoy a fine lunch of radishes, foie de veau, mashed potatoes, endive salad, and an apple tart.

Hadley and Ernest in 1920s Paris.

*Lunch at Home on the
Rue du Cardinal Lemoine*

Radishes

Foie de Veau à l'Anglaise

Mashed Potatoes

Endive Salad

Apple Tart

Radishes

In the simple Parisian style, these radishes are served raw with butter and salt. It is assumed that the Hemingway's cook at the Rue Cardinal du Lemoine prepared all of the dishes for this menu in typical, classic Parisian styles.

2 SERVINGS

> 6 small pink radishes
> 1 baguette
> Butter
> Salt

Wash the radishes in cold water, trimming the root tip and cutting all the leaves to the same length. Pat dry thoroughly on a paper towel. Slice the bread and spread one side of each slice generously with butter. Place 1 radish on each slice, sprinkle with salt to taste, and serve.

Note: To serve the radishes without bread, simply place them in a small bowl, drizzle with melted butter, and season to taste.

41

Foie de Veau à l'Anglaise

2 SERVINGS

2 tablespoons butter

4 thin slices calf's liver, about ½ inch thick

4 thin slices bacon

2 tablespoons chopped fresh parsley

½ lemon

Heat the butter in a skillet over medium heat until frothy but not brown. Fry the liver slices quickly, about 3 to 4 minutes on each side. Remove the slices to a hot serving platter. Fry the bacon in the same pan to desired doneness. Garnish the liver with the bacon, sprinkle on the chopped parsley, squeeze on the lemon juice, and pour the cooking juices on top. Serve immediately.

Endive Salad

2 SERVINGS

2 endives

2 tablespoons minced fresh chives

½ cup artichoke vinaigrette dressing (see page 33) with ½ tablespoon Dijon-style mustard whisked in

Wash the endives thoroughly. Dry. Cut each endive in half lengthwise, then cut across into strips. Discard the bottom slice. Arrange each endive on a salad plate, sprinkle with the chives and dressing, and serve.

Mashed Potatoes

Parisian-style mashed potatoes have a much lighter consistency than those to which most Americans are accustomed. It is essential that you not spare the butter or the milk to reach the consistency of whipped cream in this dish. This recipe is adapted from the 1923 cookbook Colette's Best Recipes.

2 SERVINGS

3 medium potatoes

½ cup milk

3 tablespoons butter, plus have plenty more on hand

Salt and Pepper

Wash, peel, quarter, and boil the potatoes until tender, about 20 minutes. Drain thoroughly, then return to the boiling pot and heat over low heat until completely dry. Remove the potatoes from the pot, and press through a ricer back into the pot (you may also use a masher or a hand mixer to mash the potatoes, but I find a ricer works best).

In a small saucepan, heat the milk until very hot. While the milk is warming, add the butter and salt and pepper to taste to the potatoes and stir vigorously. When the milk is hot, place the potatoes over medium heat and add the milk. Whisk the potatoes until they are the consistency of whipped cream. You may need to add more milk or butter to reach this thickness. Simmer the potatoes very gently until they are very hot throughout. Serve immediately.

Apple Tart

1 10-INCH TART

For the Dough

> ½ cup butter
> 1½ cups all-purpose flour
> 2 tablespoons sugar
> ¼ cup ice water

For the Filling

> 4 baking apples, such as Granny Smith or
>   Stayman, peeled and cored
> 1½ tablespoons lemon juice
> 4 tablespoons sugar
> 2 tablespoons melted butter

To make the dough with a food processor, fit the processor with the metal blade. Cut the butter into small pieces and place in the bowl of the food processor. Add the flour and sugar. Blend together until dough just begins to adhere to the sides of the bowl. Add the ice water and continue blending until the dough starts to stick together. Turn the dough out onto a floured surface. Form the dough into a ball, wrap in plastic wrap, and refrigerate for at least 2 hours.

To make the dough by hand, cut the butter into small pieces. In a large mixing bowl, combine the flour and sugar. Cut the butter into the dry mix with a pastry blender or two knives until it has the texture of coarse crumbs. Add the ice water slowly and mix with a wooden spoon until completely incorporated. Turn the dough out onto a floured surface and knead gently, pushing part of the dough away from you with the heel of your hand, and folding it over onto itself. Repeat a few times. Form the dough into a ball, wrap in plastic wrap, and refrigerate for at least 2 hours.

When the dough has chilled, turn it out onto a floured surface. Roll the dough, lifting and turning a quarter-turn after each roll, to a circle of ¼-inch thickness. Transfer the dough to a buttered 10-inch tart pan by rolling the dough around the rolling pin and unrolling it onto the pan. Work the dough into the pan, gently lifting to cover the bottom and sides evenly. Fold over any excess and crimp decoratively. Refrigerate the tart shell for at least 30 minutes, or until ready for filling.

When the shell has chilled, preheat the oven to 350° F. Prick the bottom of the shell several times with a fork. Line the surface of the shell with aluminum foil and fill with dry beans to prevent shrinking or heaving. Bake the tart shell for 20 minutes.

To make the filling, cut the apples into thin slices and toss in a bowl with the lemon juice. Arrange the slices in the tart shell in two layers of overlapping, concentric circles, sprinkling half the sugar on each layer. Drizzle the finished tart with melted butter. Bake at 350° F for about 30 minutes, or until the crust is golden brown. Serve warm.

It was not until March 1922, that Ernest found the courage to call on Gertrude Stein at her studio at

Alice Toklas (left) and Gertrude Stein in the salon of their pavilion located in the courtyard of 27 rue de Fleurus.

44

27 Rue de Fleurus. He had no doubt borrowed her books from Shakespeare and Company and was eager to affirm Anderson's assessment of the importance of her experimental writings, but as a 22-year-old aspiring writer with roots in journalism and a taste for Kipling, he just didn't get it. When he and Hadley finally visited Gertrude and her partner, Alice Toklas, Ernest could not possibly understand the profound impact that this squat woman with the mobile face would have on his life and his ability to write:

> My wife and I had called on Miss Stein, and she and the friend who lived with her had been very cordial and friendly and we had loved the big studio with the great paintings. It was like one of the best rooms in the finest museum except there was a big fireplace and it was warm and comfortable and they gave you good things to eat and tea and natural distilled liqueurs made from purple plums, yellow plums or wild raspberries.[6]

Hemingway spent many afternoons sitting before Miss Stein in the studio, listening attentively to her instructions on the rhythm of words, the power of repetition, and sex and writers and life. She found him an extremely handsome young man, eager to learn. Their friendship grew into the relationship between master and disciple, and each benefited. Ernest, while working for Ford Madox Ford on the *Transatlantic Review*, insisted that Ford publish Stein's immense *The Making of Americans* serially in the magazine. As with most friends of those days, where Ernest was once the willing student, eventually the success of the disciple overshadowed that of the master. Ernest was often less than gracious, seeing clearly the faults and shortcomings of those whom he had once so deeply admired. Stein was no exception. He saw in her the cardinal vice of writers, one that he could never forgive: laziness. He saw her through new, seemingly clearer eyes, her genius turned to arrogance, and their friendship dissolved in venomous public critiques.

In the early days, though, when there was much to learn and a childlike eagerness to listen, Ernest drank in the warmth of Miss Stein's studio and partook of her philosophy as well as of her food and drink. The following recipes are adapted from *The Alice B. Toklas Cookbook*.

45

Visitandines

These small cakes were first prepared for Gertrude Stein and Alice Toklas by Léonie, an early femme de ménage in their home. She claimed that the name was derived from the religious order of the Visitation, the nuns of which first prepared them. Visitandines were invented to help the nuns use up their surplus egg whites.

ABOUT 36 CAKES

¼ cup butter

8 egg whites

⅔ cup sifted all-purpose flour

1 teaspoon vanilla extract

½ cup apricot jam

Preheat the oven to 400° F.

In a saucepan, heat the butter slowly until slightly browned. Remove from heat and allow to cool. Combine 6 of the egg whites in a bowl and stir very slowly with a wooden spoon until completely mixed. This step may take up to 15 minutes. Fold in the flour and mix until perfectly smooth. Add the vanilla and heated butter. Beat the 2 remaining egg whites to stiff peaks, then add to the batter.

Lightly butter small muffin tins. Fill halfway with batter and bake for 15 to 20 minutes, or until *visitandines* are pale gold in color. Remove from tins to a cooling rack. In a small saucepan, heat the apricot jam just to boiling. Strain through a fine sieve. Paint the cakes with apricot glaze.

Note: You may wish to frost the *visitandines* with kirsch icing, which is simply butter cream with a few tablespoons of kirsch added.

Black Currant Liqueur

ABOUT 2¾ QUARTS

½ pound raspberries

3 pounds black currants

1 cup black currant leaves

1 quart vodka

3 pounds sugar

3 cups water

Wash and drain the raspberries and black currants. Place the berries in a large ceramic or glass bowl and mash thoroughly. Cover the bowl with cheesecloth and set aside in a cool place for 24 hours.

After this time, add the black currant leaves and vodka to the bowl. Cover the bowl with a plate and set aside again for another 24 hours.

After the second day, pour the mash through a fine sieve into another bowl, forcing through all of the liquid with a pestle. In a large saucepan, combine the sugar and water and bring to a boil over low heat, stirring constantly. Boil for 5 minutes, stirring frequently. Remove the syrup from heat and allow to cool completely. Add the syrup to the berries, cover with a cloth, and allow to stand for several hours. Filter the liqueur through cheesecloth into bottles. It may be served immediately.

Hemingway lived in Paris, off and on, for eight years. He was educated at the feet of Stein and Pound and Fitzgerald, and he worked very hard to turn his writing into his art. He worked hardest in a small rented studio on the Rue Descartes, hunched over the Corona typewriter Hadley bought for him, sipping kirsch to keep warm by the fire and eating mandarins and chestnuts. He also discovered such Parisian cafés as the Café du Dôme, the Closerie des Lilas, and a "warm and clean and friendly"[7] café on the Place St. Michel. He would order a café au lait, a rum St. James, and a dozen of the very cheap oysters known as *portugaises* and wrote stories like "The Three Day Blow."

When there was no money, when he was unable to sell his stories and had given up journalism altogether and dared not gamble on the horses to support his wife and newborn son, he discovered strategies to hide his hunger or use it in his work:

> By any standards we were still very poor and I still made such small economies as saying that I had been asked out for lunch and then spending two hours walking in the Luxembourg gardens and coming back to describe the marvelous lunch to my wife. When you are twenty-five and are a natural heavyweight, missing a meal makes you very hungry. But it also sharpens all of your perceptions, and I found that many of the people I wrote about had very strong appetites and a great taste and desire for

food, and most of them were looking forward to having a drink.[8]

He often used the Luxembourg gardens to relieve his hunger, as "you saw and smelled nothing to eat all the way from the Place de l'Observatoire to the rue de Vaurigard."[9] In the Luxembourg museum, the paintings by Cézanne appeared sharper and clearer and more beautiful because he was "belly-empty, hollow-hungry."[10] One early afternoon late in 1924, Ernest decided to walk to Shakespeare and Company, carefully avoiding streets filled with aromatic restaurants and cafés. That day, Sylvia Beach had good news: a letter had arrived from *Der Querschnitt*, a German magazine, which had accepted two of his stories and paid him 600 francs. "Hunger is healthy and the pictures do look better when you are hungry," but "eating is wonderful too and do you know where you are going to eat right now? Lipp's is where you are going to eat and drink too."[11]

> There were few people in the brasserie and when I sat down on the bench against the wall with the mirror in back and a table in front and the waiter asked if I wanted beer I asked for a *distingué*, the big glass mug that held a liter, and for potato salad. The beer was very cold and wonderful to drink. The *pommes à l'huile* were firm and marinated and the olive oil delicious. I ground black pepper over the potatoes and moistened the bread in the olive oil. After the first heavy draft of beer I drank and ate very slowly. When the *pommes à l'huile* were gone I

ordered another serving and a *cervelas*. This was a sausage like a heavy, wide frankfurter split in two and covered with a special mustard sauce. I mopped up all the oil and all of the sauce with bread and drank the beer slowly until it began to lose its coldness and then I finished it and ordered a *demi* and watched it drawn.[12]

◁ **THE MENU** ▷

*Lunch at the
Brasserie Lipp*

Pommes de Terre à l'Huile

Cervelas with Mustard Sauce

Beer

———————

Pommes de Terre à l'Huile (Potatoes in Oil)

2 SERVINGS

1 pound potatoes
6 tablespoons very fine olive oil
2 cloves garlic, crushed
Salt
Pepper
2 tablespoons dry white wine
2 tablespoon red wine vinegar
1 tablespoon beef broth

Wash and peel the potatoes. Place in a saucepan with enough cold salted water to cover. Bring to a boil and cook until tender, about 20 minutes. Drain the potatoes and cut into slices as soon as they're cool enough to handle. Put the sliced potatoes into a medium bowl and toss gently with the olive oil, garlic, and salt and pepper to taste. In a small saucepan, heat the wine, vinegar, and broth until hot. Pour over the potatoes and toss gently. Be sure to include plenty of bread for mopping up the sauce.

Cervelas with Mustard Sauce

Cervelas are fat, short sausages made with pork and pork fat and seasoned with garlic or pepper. The name refers to brains, or cervelles, *with which these sausages were formerly made. If* cervelas *are unavailable, you may substitute any fine pork sausage with garlic.*

1 HUNGRY YOUNG WRITER OR 2 SERVINGS

2 *cervelas*, or other pork and garlic sausage
2 tablespoons butter

Bring a medium saucepan of water to a boil. Add the *cervelas*. Reduce heat and simmer for 5 minutes. Remove *cervelas* and rinse with cold water. Melt the butter in a skillet over medium heat. Cook the *cervelas* in the butter until lightly browned. Remove *cervelas*, cut in half lengthwise, and place on warm plate. Serve covered with mustard sauce.

Mustard Sauce

2 tablespoons butter
½ onion, finely chopped
½ cup dry white wine
1 tablespoon Dijon-style mustard
1 teaspoon vinegar
Juice of ½ lemon

Melt 1 tablespoon of the butter in a small pan over medium heat. Add the chopped onion and cook until translucent. Add the wine and cook until reduced by half. Stir in the mustard and vinegar. Add the lemon juice and the last tablespoon of butter. When the butter is melted, pour the sauce over the *cervelas* and serve immediately.

———————

As Hemingway used the Luxembourg gardens to relieve his hunger, he used the Seine for thinking things through. He browsed the bookstalls along the quais, or sat to edit manuscripts for Ford Madox Ford's *transatlantic review*, for which he worked as an unpaid assistant in the mid-1920s. He found that the thinking came easier along the river, "seeing people doing something that they understood,"[13] as the fishermen with the long, jointed cane poles understood their serious endeavors along the Seine:

> They always caught some fish, and often they made excellent catches of the dace-like fish that were called *goujon*. They were delicious fried whole and I could eat a plateful. They were plump and sweet-fleshed with a finer flavor than fresh sardines even, and were not at all oily, and we ate them bones and all. One of the best places to eat them was at an open-air restaurant built out over the river at Bas Meudon where we would go when we had money for a trip away from our quarter. It was called La Pêche Miraculeuse and had a splendid white wine that was a sort of Muscadet.[14]

49

Friture de Goujon (Fried Gudgeon)

2 TO 3 SERVINGS

Olive oil for frying

18 small gudgeon, or smelts

1 bottle beer

1 cup cornmeal

Salt

Lemon wedges

Heat the oil, deep enough for deep-frying, in a saucepan until just hot. Because these fish are too small to gut easily, simply wipe the fish with a cloth, then squeeze the underbelly to force the intestines and swim bladder out through the abdomen. Pour the beer into a small bowl. Dip each fish in beer, then dredge in cornmeal to coat. Shake off any excess.

Fry the fish in the barely hot oil until light yellow. Remove the fish and drain on brown paper or paper towels. Heat the oil until very hot (about 350° F). Return the fish to the very hot oil and fry until golden brown. Drain the fish again, sprinkle with salt to taste, and serve with lemon wedges.

50

Six Days at the Races

Spring was a magical season in Paris. "With so many trees in the city, you could see the spring coming each day until a night of warm wind would bring it suddenly in one morning."[15] The only truly sad time in Paris was the false spring, when cold rains would beat back the season "so that it would seem that it would never come and that you were losing a season out of your life."[16] And not just any season, but one that revived Ernest's appetites for the sports of the city. Hemingway enjoyed taking in the six-day bicycle races at the Velodrome d'Hiver, near the Eiffel Tower. In the early 1920s, Hemingway took friend, writer, and fellow adventurer John Dos Passos to the races. Dos Passos recalled Ernest's knowledge of the race and its riders but preferred to sit idly by eating and drinking:

> I did enjoy the six day bicycle races with him. The Six Jours at the Vélo d'Hiver was fun. French sporting events had for me a special comical air that I enjoyed. We would collect, at the stalls and barrows of one of the narrow market streets we both loved, a quantity of wine and cheeses and crunch rolls, a pot of paté and perhaps a cold chicken, and sit up in the gallery. Hem knew all the statistics and the names and lives of the riders. His enthusiasm was catching but he tended to make business of it while I just liked to eat and drink and enjoy the show.[17]

Lunch with John Dos Passos

Dos Passos was not alone in remembering those early days through gastronomic eyes. Hemingway simply would not allow his appetite for food and drink to impinge on his appetite for the intricacies of the sport. As we have seen (and will continue to see), Hemingway frequently enjoyed his food and drink as a postscript to sport and, of course, to writing. While Ernest wrote his biting satire of Sherwood Anderson, *The Torrents of Spring*, he remembered the food and drink he shared with Dos Passos while taking a break from work:

> I wrote the foregoing chapter in two hours directly on the typewriter, and then went out to lunch with John Dos Passos, whom I consider a very forceful writer, and an exceedingly pleasant fellow besides. This is what is known in the provinces as log-rolling. We lunched on *rollmops*, *sole meunière*, *civet de lièvre à la cocotte*, *marmelade de pommes*, and washed it all down, as he used to say (eh, reader?) with a bottle of Montrachet 1919 with the sole, and a bottle of Hospice de Beaune 1919 apiece with the jugged hare. Mr. Dos Passos, I believe, shared a bottle of Chambertin with me over the *marmelade de pommes*.[18]

Hemingway standing between Gerald Murphy and John Dos Passos in Schruns, 1926.

51

Rollmops

6 TO 8 SERVINGS

6 fresh herrings, or 12 fresh fillets
2 cups vinegar
6–8 small pickled gherkins
1 onion, coarsely chopped
1 bay leaf
1 sprig dill
6 juniper berries
6 white peppercorns
Salt

Marinate the fish in a mixture of 1 cup vinegar and 1 cup water for 24 hours.

Remove the fish and, if whole, fillet. Lay the fillets skin-side down. Place a piece of gherkin and a few pieces of chopped onion on each piece of fish. Wrap the herring around the vegetables and secure with a toothpick. Bring the remaining cup of vinegar to a boil and allow to cool completely. Place the rolls in a large glass jar. Add the herbs and berries. Dilute the vinegar with 2 cups of water. Add a generous pinch of salt. Pour the vinegar-and-water solution over the fish to cover completely. Cover the jar with a lid or cellophane. Let stand in a cool place for 3 to 4 days. The exact combination of herbs is "the secret of the cook." Some experimentation is necessary to find the combination to suit each individual taste.

Sole Meunière (Fillet of Sole Miller's Wife Style)

2 SERVINGS

½ cup all-purpose flour
2 large or 4 small sole fillets
Pepper
½ cup butter
Juice of ½ lemon
2 tablespoons chopped fresh parsley
Salt

Lightly flour all of the fillets on both sides. Season with pepper to taste. Heat ¼ cup of the butter over medium heat until very hot and foamy. Add the fillets, being careful not to overcrowd the pan (it may take two batches). Brown the fish on both sides, 5 to 6 minutes to a side. Remove the fillets to a heated serving plate. Garnish with lemon juice, parsley, and salt and pepper to taste. Pour out the frying liquid and wipe the frying pan clean. Melt the remaining ¼ cup of butter until very lightly browned. Pour the melted butter over the fish. Serve immediately.

Civet de Lièvre à la Cocotte (Jugged Hare)

1 hare, cleaned, gutted, and cut into pieces

4 cups red wine

8 onions, halved

1 carrot, coarsely chopped

1 sprig thyme

2 tablespoons butter

¼ pound salt pork, diced

2 tablespoons all-purpose flour

2 cups water

Bouquet garni (a few sprigs of parsley, thyme, rosemary, and bay leaf bundled and tied together)

4 cloves

1 bay leaf

½ pound mushrooms, halved

Salt

Freshly ground pepper

Marinate the hare overnight in 2 cups wine with 2 of the onions, the carrot, and the thyme. The following day, melt the butter in a casserole over medium heat. Add the salt pork and render until the pork is brown. Remove the pork and set aside. Remove the hare pieces from the marinade and pat dry. Brown the meat in the butter and pork fat. Stir in the flour, then add the 2 cups wine, water, bouquet garni, the remaining 6 onions, cloves, and bay leaf. Lower the heat and simmer, covered, for about 2 hours. Add the mushrooms and simmer for another 30 minutes. When the hare is cooked, place the pieces on a serving platter and keep warm. If you have the liver and blood of the hare, add the chopped liver to the blood and add to the cooking liquid. Bring the sauce to a boil, then strain through a fine sieve. Return the onions, mushrooms, and pieces of salt pork to the sauce. Season with salt and pepper to taste and pour over the hare.

Marmelade de Pommes (Apple Conserve)

6 apples, peeled, cored, and cut into quarters

1 cup sugar

2 tablespoons water

Place the apples, sugar, and water in a small saucepan. Cook over medium heat until the apples are soft. Purée the apples in a food processor or food mill. Return the purée to the saucepan and cook until bubbling. Allow to cool slightly and serve.

Beside the marathon bike races, there were boxing at the Cirque de Paris, tennis matches, and horse races. Ernest and Hadley occasionally took the cheap train to the steeplechase at Enghien or Auteuil, sat in the infield, ate a picnic lunch of sandwiches that Hadley made, and drank cheap wine from the cooperative in the Rue Mouffetard. As was the case with his writing, when there was a windfall of funds from a lucky day at the track, attitudes changed, fond memories returned, and thoughts turned to the haute cuisine of Paris. After one particularly fortunate outing, Ernest and Hadley stopped at Pruniers. Sitting at the bar, they dined on oysters and *Crabe Mexicaine*, enjoying their momentary affluence that lingered through the night until morning, when the all-too-familiar hunger returned and the writing resumed. Many years later, Papa would return to dine at Prunier with his fourth wife, Mary, and Marlene Dietrich. For now, though, Paris belongs to the young Hemingways, and hunger is elsewhere.

THE MENU

Dinner at Prunier

Oysters

Crabe Mexicaine

Wine

Sancerre

Oysters

Hemingway certainly enjoyed his oysters. In A Moveable Feast *he eats them on three separate occasions. When money was scarce, he went to "a good café on the Place St. Michel" for* portugaises, *the small, very cheap oysters with their faint metallic taste. But when there was money he knew exactly the place for the finest oysters in Paris: Pruniers. Alfred Prunier founded his restaurant in 1872 in the Rue Duphot. It quickly became, as Julian Street noted in* Where Paris Dines, *"the most fashionable place in Paris for oysters, fish and crustaceans."*[19] *Later, when Ernest Walsh was paying for lunch,*

Ernest once again took advantage of the opportunity to enjoy the superior quality marennes, *or cultivated oysters.* Marennes *are large and bright green in color. In the 1920s they were considered very expensive at about $1.50 a dozen.*

Preparing oysters on the half-shell at home is actually quite simple but takes some practice and understanding of this delicacy. Prepare about 6 oysters per person, although the portion is limited only by the oyster-passion of the eater.

When purchasing live oysters, make sure the shells are tightly closed. If one is open, squeeze the shell closed a few times until it tightens up. If the oyster will not close, discard it. Also, avoid oysters that feel either too light or too heavy. Purchase the oysters shortly before you plan to use them.

When home, store the oysters, covered with damp paper towels, with the larger sides down (allowing the oysters to sit in their juice). To open an oyster, hold it in your hand with the larger side down. Find a small gap in the hinge of the shell, and pry the shells apart with a pointed can opener. Run a small knife along the underside of the top shell, disconnecting the oyster. The oysters can be served on a bed of crushed ice. Be careful to retain as much of the oysters' juices in the shell as possible. Serve with wedges of lemon. Or you may serve the oysters with a sauce made by simmering together ½ cup white wine vinegar and 2 tablespoons minced shallots, allowing the sauce to cool and adding 1 teaspoon chopped fresh parsley.

Crabe Mexicaine

This recipe is adapted from Madame Prunier's Fish Cookery Book. *It is rather complicated, but once you have made the sauces and stocks (the remainder of which may be used again and again), the assembly of the final dish is rather simple.*

4 SERVINGS

For the Fumet

> 3 tablespoons butter
> 2 pounds raw fish trimmings and bones
> 1 onion, sliced
> 2 tablespoons chopped fresh parsley
> 12 peppercorns
> 4 cups white wine
> 5 cups water, plus a little more
> Pinch of salt

For the Fish Velouté

> ¼ pound butter
> 1 cup all-purpose flour

For the White Wine Sauce

> 2 egg yolks
> 2 tablespoons heavy cream
> 1 tablespoon butter

For the Tomato Sauce

- 4 tablespoons butter
- 2 onions, diced
- 2 carrots, diced
- 2 inner ribs celery, diced
- ½ bay leaf, crushed
- 2 sprigs fresh thyme
- 1½ tablespoons all-purpose flour
- 4 pounds tomatoes, seeded and juice squeezed out
- 2½ cups tomato purée
- Salt
- Pepper
- Pinch of sugar
- Bouquet garni (parsley, thyme, and bay leaf tied together)
- 3½ cups vegetable or chicken stock

The Rest

- 4 large mushrooms
- Olive oil, for brushing
- 5 tablespoons butter
- 2 tomatoes, peeled, seeded, and chopped
- 1 cup diced okra
- 1 sweet red pepper, diced
- 1 tablespoon chopped fresh parsley
- ½ pound crabmeat

To make the white wine sauce, you must first prepare a fish fumet (or concentrated stock) and a fish velouté (a white sauce made with fish stock). To make the fish fumet, melt the butter in a large skillet. Cut up and add the fish trimmings and bones. Add the onion, parsley, and peppercorns. Cover and stew for about 5 minutes. Then add the white wine and water. Add a pinch of salt and bring to a boil. Boil the fumet gently for 25 minutes. Strain through a fine sieve. Set aside.

Note: This recipe makes about 2 quarts, most of which will be used in preparing the *Crabe Mexicaine*.

Fish Velouté

First prepare a roux: melt the butter in a saucepan (do not use an aluminum pan) over low heat. Add the flour and stir with a wooden spoon until thoroughly mixed. Continue to cook the roux, stirring constantly, for 10 minutes, until the roux takes on a golden color. Transfer the roux to a stockpot. Whisk in 7 cups of the fish fumet (to avoid lumps, allow the fumet to cool thoroughly before adding to the warm roux). Bring the velouté to a boil and boil gently for 15 to 20 minutes. Pour the velouté into a mixing bowl and stir until well cooled.

White Wine Sauce

Now you're ready to make the white wine sauce. Begin by whisking together 1½ cups fish velouté with 4 tablespoons of fish fumet. Just before serving the dish, bring the stock to a simmer and remove from the heat. Add the egg yolks mixed with the cream. Stir until thickened. Stir in the butter.

56

Tomato Sauce

Make a *mirepoix* in a stockpot: melt the butter over medium heat. Add the onions, carrots, and inner celery, bay leaf, and thyme. Fry this slowly for about 5 minutes, without coloration. Add the flour and fry until slightly browned. Then add the tomatoes. Stir in the tomato purée, salt and pepper to taste, a generous pinch of sugar, the bouquet garni, and the vegetable stock. Cook the sauce, covered, over low heat for 30–45 minutes. Pass through a fine sieve and set aside. Reheat the sauce to a simmer just before serving. This recipe makes about 1½ quarts of sauce.

Crabe Mexicaine

Brush the mushrooms with olive oil on both sides and grill, either in a broiler or over coals, for about 15 minutes on each side. While the mushrooms are grilling, melt 4 tablespoons of the butter in a saucepan over low heat. When frothy, add the tomatoes, okra, and peppers and cook, covered, for 30 minutes. When the mushrooms are done, slice and arrange them decoratively on a warm serving platter, leaving an inch of space around the edge of the platter.

Melt the remaining tablespoon of butter in a skillet. Add the parsley and crabmeat and toss until hot. Arrange the crabmeat in the center of the mushrooms. Surround the crabmeat with the vegetable mixture. Do the final preparation of the white wine sauce, then cover the crabmeat and vegetables with the sauce. Reheat the tomato sauce to a simmer and pour a ribbon of tomato sauce around the edge of the platter.

Walking home from Pruniers, sated and very happy, the Hemingways strolled through *le Jardin des Tuileries*, a park he reserved for romance in his writing, and they admired the Arc du Carrousel and the Arc de Triomphe in the distant darkness. Far beyond, across an expanse of distance and time, through warm memories, they reminisced about days in Milan and Switzerland, again thinking of wonderful foods. Hadley recalls Biffi's in the Galleria Vittorio Emanuele in Milan, eating fruit cup with wine from a tall, glass pitcher (see Capri on page 163). Ernest recalls a pension in Chamby, owned by a German Swiss family named Gangwisch, who served a wonderful trout dish, boiled "in a liquor made of wine vinegar, bay leaves, and a dash of red pepper."[20] They "ate out on the porch with the mountainside dropping off below and [they] could look across the lake and see the Dent du Midi with the snow half down it and the trees at the mouth of the Rhône where it flowed into the lake."[21]

Trout au Bleu

By his mid-20s, Hemingway was a connoisseur of trout dishes. This method was one of his favorites, as " it preserves the true trout flavor better than almost any way of cooking."[22] Ideally, the trout should be alive immediately before cooking to produce the blue color in the skin and the freshest taste. You may, though, use very freshly killed fish from the market. Because of this necessity for very fresh or live fish, this dish is not very well known:

You have to go back in the country to get trout cooked that way. You come up from the stream to a chalet and ask them if they know how to cook blue trout. If they don't you walk on a way. If they do, you sit down on the porch with the goats and the children and wait. Your nose will tell you when the trout are boiling. Then after a little while you will hear a pop. That is the Sion being uncorked. Then the woman of the chalet will come to the door and say, "It is prepared, Monsieur." Then you can go away and I will do the rest myself.[23]

4 SERVINGS

1 pint vinegar
2 tablespoons salt
4 carrots, sliced
4 onions, quartered
Sprig of thyme
1 bay leaf
Sprig of parsley
Dash of crushed red pepper flakes
6 peppercorns
4 live or very fresh trout
2 tablespoons chopped fresh parsley
4 tablespoons melted butter

In a large pot, prepare a court-bouillon: to 5 quarts water add the vinegar, salt, carrots, onions, and herbs in a bunch (you may want to bundle herbs in cheesecloth). Bring to a boil, then decrease heat and simmer for 1 hour. After 50 minutes, add the red pepper flakes and peppercorns (if added earlier they will impart too much bitterness to the broth). When the court-bouillon is done, strain through a fine sieve and reserve the liquid.

Pour the liquid into a shallow pan and bring to a boil. For live trout, kill the fish with a sharp blow to the head (see *The Alice B. Toklas Cookbook* for an introduction to coping with the trauma of fish-murdering). With minimal handling, gut and clean the fish. Plunge the fish into the boiling broth and simmer for 6–7 minutes for small trout, 8–10 minutes for larger fish. Remove the fish, drain, garnish with fresh parsley, and serve immediately with the melted butter poured over the fish.

Hemingway after a successful day of trout fishing.

Fame Became of Him

The meal at Prunier shows that, even while relatively poor, Hemingway had an understanding of fine dining that would serve him well when he became "Papa" and abandoned the cafés of Montparnasse in favor of the Ritz or the Hôtel Crillon on the right bank of the Seine. When the poet Ernest Walsh invited Hemingway to lunch "at a restaurant that was the best and most expensive in the Boulevard St. Michel quarter," he once again took advantage of the oysters served at the finer establishments. Hemingway orders two dozen of the "expensive flat faintly coppery *marennes*, not the familiar, deep, inexpensive *portugaises* . . . picking them from their bed of crushed ice on the silver plate, watching their unbelievably delicate brown edges react and cringe as I squeezed lemon juice on them and separated the holding muscle from the shell and lifted them to chew them carefully."[24]

When the lunch is ordered, Hemingway chooses tournedos with sauce béarnaise, french-fried potatoes, and a bottle of Châteauneuf du Pape, an ambitious selection from a man who could hardly afford the appetizer. Nonetheless, it once again shows Hemingway's knowledge of gastronomy, both as a form of indulgence and as an expression of distaste toward his endowed host as he tempts young Hemingway with the promise of a literary award from the *Dial*, the most prestigious literary magazine in America at the time.

THE MENU

Lunch with Ernest Walsh

Marennes

Tournedos with Sauce Béarnaise

French-fried Potatoes

Wines

Pouilly-Fuissé with the marennes

Châteauneuf du Pape with the steak

Tournedos with Sauce Béarnaise

I figured the butter would be good for him.[25]

4 SERVINGS

For the Beef

> 2 tablespoons butter
> 4 slices fillet of beef, ¾ inch thick
> 4 slices white bread

For the Béarnaise Sauce

> 3 egg yolks
> 1 tablespoon heavy cream
> ½ teaspoon salt
> Dash of cayenne pepper
> 1 tablespoon tarragon vinegar
> 4 tablespoons butter, in small pieces
> 1 tablespoon chopped tarragon
> 1 teaspoon chopped chervil

Melt 1 tablespoon of the butter in a small skillet. Brown the beef slices well on both sides, with the meat still rare in the middle (this dish caters to Ernest's taste for rarely cooked meat; it should never be cooked well done). Cut the bread into large croutons the same size as the tournedos. In a clean pan, sauté the croutons in the remaining tablespoon of butter until they are golden brown. Place one tournedo on each crouton and serve with béarnaise sauce.

To make the sauce: Bring 2 inches of water to a simmer in the bottom of a double boiler. Combine the egg yolks, cream, salt, cayenne pepper, and vinegar in the top of the double boiler and whisk together. Place over the bottom half of the double boiler. Whisking constantly, add the butter, a little at a time. Whisk until the butter is melted and the sauce is thickened. Add the herbs. Pour the sauce over the tournedos.

French-fried Potatoes (*Pommes de Terre Frites*)

4 SERVINGS

> 4 medium potatoes
> 4 cups vegetable oil
> Salt and pepper

Wash, peel, and cut the potatoes into strips of ¼- to ½-inch thickness. Place the strips in a bowl of cold water until ready for frying. Pour the oil into a deep fryer. If you do not have a deep fryer, use a large saucepan and a wire basket to hold the potatoes. You may also simply place the potatoes in the oil and remove with a slotted spoon, but a wire basket makes the process much easier. Heat the oil to approximately 350° F. Dry the potatoes completely and gently lower them into the oil. Fry until just before the potatoes turn golden, about 10 minutes. Remove the potatoes and drain. Heat the oil to the smoking point, replace the potatoes, and fry until golden brown and crisp, 8–10 minutes. Season with salt and pepper to taste.

On the Road with F. Scott Fitzgerald

The first time I ever met Scott Fitzgerald a very strange thing happened.[26]

Legend has it that Hemingway first met Fitzgerald at the Dingo Bar in Paris in the spring of 1925. Fitzgerald, already famous, ordered champagne, lavished Ernest with praise for his Nick Adams stories from *in our time*, asked Ernest if he slept with his wife before marriage, and passed out. It was not the last time that Scott would praise Hemingway's work. Scott's lobbying eventually helped ensure Ernest's contract with Scribner's for the publications of *The Torrents of Spring* and *The Sun Also Rises* the following year. It was also not the last time Scott would pass out from drink in Hemingway's company.

Shortly after their initial meeting, Scott asked Ernest to accompany him down to Lyon to pick up the car that he and his wife, Zelda, had been forced to abandon due to bad weather. Hemingway, eager to see the beautiful springtime country, and having drunk again with Fitzgerald and seen none of the "... chemical changes in Scott that would turn him into a fool,"[27] agreed to go along.

After missing his train and abandoning Hemingway in Lyon for the night, Scott finally found Ernest the next morning, and they began their journey home. Ernest had already shrugged off the inconveniences of traveling with Scott so far and could only laugh in bemused astonishment to discover the reason why the Fitzgeralds were held up in Lyon in the first place. The car's top had been damaged in Marseilles, and Zelda, who detested car tops, had it cut away. So, Hemingway and Fitzgerald, with a picnic lunch from the hotel, departed for Paris in their Renault permanent convertible. They traveled about an hour before they were halted by rain, and continued the eating and drinking they began earlier that morning:

In that day we were halted by rain possibly ten times. They were passing showers and some of them were longer than others. If we had waterproof coats it would have been pleasant enough to drive in that spring rain. As it was we sought the shelter of trees or halted at cafés alongside the road. We had a marvelous lunch from the hotel at Lyon, an excellent truffled roast chicken, delicious bread, and white Mâcon wine and Scott was very happy when we drank the white Mâconnais at each of our stops.[28]

Truffle-Roasted Chicken (*Poularde Truffée*)

3 TO 4 SERVINGS

For this dish, we will simply follow the recipe for roasted chicken that appears on page 73 with one rather expensive exception. The day before roasting, gently loosen the skin on the breast and on each leg. Slide 3 thin slices of black truffle between each breast and the skin, and one slice between the leg meat and the skin. Refrigerate the bird for 24 hours to allow the chicken to take on the flavor of the truffles. Then proceed with the normal roasting recipe.

Later that afternoon, Scott's hypochondria kicked in and he developed a dread fear of dying of congestion of the lungs. They stopped for the night, tended to Scott's illness with aspirin and whiskey sours, and had another strange meal together.

After Ernest's and Scott's clothes dried, they retired to the hotel dining room and began their meal with snails and a carafe of Fleurie. Shortly after the snails were served, the telephone call to Zelda that Scott had placed earlier finally went through, and he left the table for an hour. Hemingway felt obliged to finish Scott's snails, "dipping up the butter, garlic, and parsley sauce with broken bits of bread . . ."[29]

Given the likelihood that Ernest and Scott sought refuge in Burgundy, these snails are served in the classic manner of the region, stuffed with butter, shallots, and garlic and served piping hot. One can hardly blame Ernest for finishing Scott's snails before they turned too cold.

Burgundy Snails
(*Escargots à la Bourguignonne*)

Ernest loved to eat snails for the rest of his life. Forrest MacMullen, a close friend from Ketchum, Idaho, recalled preparing "gourmet snails" with Ernest's last wife, Mary, when he couldn't join Ernest down country hunting. He fondly remembers when Ernest would return from the hunt and "inhale two or three racks of snails."

While you may want to prepare this dish using live snails, for practical purposes I prefer to start with the canned snails that come packaged with their shells. What you sacrifice in flavor you make up in availability. The elegance of this dish may easily be retained in its presentation.

2 TO 3 SERVINGS (OR 1, SHOULD THE OTHERS LEAVE THE TABLE FOR A WHILE)

> 1 can *escargots* (18 snails), with empty shells
>
> 6 tablespoons butter, softened
>
> 4 shallots, minced
>
> 3 cloves garlic, crushed
>
> 1½ tablespoons minced fresh parsley
>
> ½ teaspoon salt
>
> Black pepper

Preheat the oven to 425° F.

Wash the snail shells thoroughly. Drain the liquid from the snails.

Cream together the butter, shallots, garlic, parsley, and salt and pepper to taste with a fork or wooden spoon. Place a small dollop of this snail butter into each shell. Add a snail to each shell, then seal the opening of the shell with more butter.

Ideally the snails should be baked in metal snail dishes, which have small indentations to nest each snail, opened side up. Alternately, you may bake the snails on a baking pan so that the snails rest against each other and will not roll over. Or, you may fill a baking pan halfway with salt and rest the snails securely in the pan (although you do lose any butter runoff this way). The goal here is to retain as much of the snail butter as possible. Bake the snails for 4–5 minutes, or until very hot and bubbling. Serve immediately with plenty of bread for soaking up the snail butter.

Serving Note: In a fine restaurant, along with the snail dishes, *escargots* would be served with a snail-shaped clamp and small two-pronged forks. You may substitute any small tongs and seafood forks. Quite frankly, feel free to use whatever works.

Poularde de Bresse

We had eaten very good cold chicken at noon but this was still famous chicken country, so we had *poularde de Bresse* and a bottle of Montagny, a light, pleasant white wine of the neighborhood.[30]

Bresse is the ancient term for the region surrounding Lyon, and it remains famous for the outstanding quality of its chickens and capons. A poularde is a roasting hen or capon weighing between 3½ and 5 pounds. The two ingredients most commonly associated with poularde de Bresse are truffles and morels. We have already experienced the splendor of truffle-roasted chicken. For chicken with morels, we will sauté the chicken parts and top them with a sauce of these delicious mushrooms. This recipe is adapted from Suzane Rodriguez-Hunter's wonderful historical cookbook of Paris in the 1920s, Found Meals of the Lost Generation.

4 SERVINGS

- 1 5-pound *poularde*, or finest quality chicken, cut into pieces
- ½ cup flour, for dredging, plus 1 teaspoon
- 6 tablespoons butter
- 1½ teaspoons fresh lemon juice
- ½ teaspoon salt
- ¼ cup water
- 1 pound fresh morels, or 3 ounces dried
- 1 shallot, finely chopped
- 2 cloves garlic, finely chopped
- 3 tablespoons chicken stock
- ¼ cup tomato purée
- 1 tablespoon chopped parsley, plus extra for garnish
- Pepper

Note: If you are using fresh morels, carefully brush the furrowed caps of the mushrooms to remove any sand. If you have dried morels, brush them to remove sand, then reconstitute covered with hot water and a few tablespoons of brandy.

Rinse the chicken and pat dry with a paper towel. Dredge in flour, then place on a cooling rack to dry for 10 minutes.

In a large skillet, melt 4 tablespoons of the butter over medium heat until bubbling but not brown. Lower the heat and add the chicken (this may be done in two batches if necessary). Brown the chicken on all sides. Cover and allow the chicken to cook, turning occasionally, over low heat while you prepare the mushrooms.

In a small saucepan, melt the remaining 2 tablespoons of butter over medium heat. Add the lemon juice, salt, and water and bring to a simmer. Lower the heat and add the morels. Cook, stirring occasionally, until the liquid is almost gone.

When the chicken is nearly done, remove to a platter and keep warm. Return the skillet to medium heat. Add the shallots and garlic and sauté for one minute. Remove the pan from the heat. Stir in the remaining teaspoon of flour. Add the morels and any juice, the chicken stock, and tomato purée. Return the skillet to low heat and simmer for 5 minutes. Add the parsley and salt and pepper to taste. Return the chicken in the sauce and simmer for another 10 minutes, or until done. Place the chicken on a serving platter, pour the morels and sauce over, and garnish with a little chopped fresh parsley.

Scott hardly touched the chicken or the wine, for the day's drinking, the travel, and the "illness" had taken their toll:

> He passed out at the table with his head on his hands. It was natural and there was no theater about it and it even looked as though he were careful not to spill nor break things.[31]

A few days after their return, Scott brought Ernest a copy of his new book, *The Great Gatsby*. Hemingway was duly impressed and vowed to look after Scott more thoroughly than he had during their journey from Lyon.

Winter in Austria

> We went to Schruns in the Vorarlberg in Austria. After going through Switzerland you came to the Austrian frontier at Feldkirch. The train went through Liechtenstein and stopped at Bludenz where there was a small branch line that ran along a pebbly trout river through a valley of farms and forest to Schruns, which was a sunny market town with sawmills, stores, inns and a good, year-around hotel called the Taube where we lived.[32]

The Hemingways, with their infant son John (nicknamed Bumby), first arrived in Schruns just before Christmas 1924. At the suggestion of friend and painter Bertram Hartman, they rented two rooms at the Hotel Taube, a family-style inn run by Paul Nels. With their Paris apartment sublet and an exchange rate of 70,000 Austrian kronen to the dollar, they could afford to escape dreary wintertime Paris and spend the entire season skiing and sledding and enjoying the crisp and clear quality of life in the mountains. Early on, Ernest worked on his stories while Hadley knitted or practiced her piano and Bumby played with the local children in the Kinderhaus behind the hotel. Ernest was happily immersed in the local color, emulating the locals and letting his thick black beard grow in for the first time. He took great pleasure in hearing that the locals were calling him "the black, kirsch-drinking Christ," a testament to the presence that he and his appetites carved out in the mountain valley.

Hemingway consumed his newfound lifestyle voraciously, participating in illegal poker games with the chief of police and climbing the steep trail at the head of the valley to Madlener Haus or Wiesbadener-Hut, the Alpine Club stations from which they could ski back down across virgin slopes of freshly fallen powder. His hunger for the local food and drink matched his appetite for this new life.

In the warmth of the wood-planked bar of the Taube, Ernest enjoyed their selection of 36 kinds of beer, good and cheap wine, schnapps distilled from mountain gentian, and a locally made kirsch, which quickly became his favorite. Frau Nels ran the kitchen and prepared excellent, hearty meals:

> We were always hungry and every meal time was a great event. We drank light or dark beer and new wines and wines that were a year old sometimes. The white wines were the best. For other drinks there was kirsch made in the valley and Enzian *Schnapps* distilled from mountain gentian. Sometimes for dinner there would be jugged hare with a rich red wine sauce, and sometimes venison with chestnut sauce. We would drink red wine with these even though it was more expensive than white wine, and the very best cost twenty cents a liter. Ordinary red wine was much cheaper and we packed it up in kegs to the Madlener-Haus.[33]

The Hotel Taube remains much as Hemingway found it in the 1920s, with big rooms and large beds with good blankets. While Ernest may have enjoyed his venison served with a chestnut sauce, the local specialty is *Hirschfilet in Wacholder-rahmsauce*, venison fillet or cutlets in a juniper cream sauce. At the Taube, you may accompany your venison with the traditional red cabbage and potato croquettes. The author would like to thank Walter Nels, son of Paul Nels and the current proprietor of the Hotel Taube, for his assistance in developing these recipes for this book.

THE MENU

Dinner at the Hotel Taube

Venison in Juniper Cream Sauce

Red Cabbage

Potato Croquettes

Hotel Taube in Schruns, Austria.

Venison in Juniper Cream Sauce
(Hirschfilet in Wacholderrahmsauce)

4 SERVINGS

1 pound venison, pork, or beef bones, cut up

2 slices of bacon, or lard for frying

1 onion, coarsely chopped

1 carrot, chopped

1 rib celery, chopped

1 tablespoon all-purpose flour

1 tablespoon tomato paste

½ cup red wine

3½ cups beef broth

24 juniper berries, crushed

1 piece orange rind

1 piece lemon rind

1 teaspoon dried thyme

1 bay leaf

4 peppercorns

4 1½-inch slices of venison fillet, or venison cutlets

4 thin rashers of bacon or strips of fatty bacon

Salt

Pepper

Oil and butter for frying

½ cup heavy cream

Preheat the oven to 400° F.

In a large, heatproof casserole, roast the bones until brown, about 30 minutes. Remove the casserole from the oven and place over medium heat. Add the bacon and vegetables and sauté for a few minutes. Stir in the flour and tomato paste and cook, stirring frequently, for 5 minutes, until the mixture takes on a nice brown color. Add the wine, broth, half the crushed berries, lemon and orange rind, thyme, and bay leaf. Reduce heat to a simmer and cover. Cook for 1 hour, stirring frequently. After 45 minutes, add the peppercorns to the sauce and begin cooking the venison.

Wrap each cutlet in a rasher of bacon and secure with a skewer. Season with salt and pepper to taste. Heat oil and butter in a skillet over high heat. Sear the cutlets for 1 minute on each side. Place the cutlets on a warm serving platter and remove skewers. Deglaze the skillet with a little red wine, scraping up any bits stuck to the skillet. Reduce the heat to medium. When the sauce is finished, strain through a fine sieve and season with salt and pepper to taste. Pour the sauce into the skillet. Add the remaining crushed berries and cream. When hot, but not yet boiling, pour the sauce over the cutlets and serve.

Red Cabbage
(*Rotweinkraut*)

4 TO 6 SERVINGS

1 head red cabbage

½ cup red wine

Juice of ½ lemon

2 tablespoons butter

1 onion, finely chopped

2 tablespoons sugar

½ cup beef broth

1 teaspoon caraway seeds, crushed

1 apple, cored, peeled, and chopped

1 tablespoon all-purpose flour

Salt

Pepper

Begin preparation the night before. Clean the cabbage. Remove the stem and any imperfect leaves. Cut into fine strips. Marinate the cabbage overnight in the red wine and lemon juice.

The following day, melt the butter in a large casserole. When hot, add the onion and sauté briefly. Add the sugar and cook, stirring often, until caramelized. Add the cabbage, broth, and caraway. Lower the heat, cover, and cook for 45 minutes. After 30 minutes, add the chopped apple. Just before serving, stir together the flour with 2 tablespoons water in a cup and add to the cabbage to thicken. When thickened, season with salt and pepper to taste and serve.

Potato Croquettes
(*Kartoffelkroketten*)

18 TO 24 CROQUETTES

5–6 medium potatoes

1 egg yolk

2 tablespoons butter

1 tablespoon salt

½ teaspoon nutmeg

1½–2 cups all-purpose flour, or more as needed

2 large eggs, beaten with 1 tablespoon water

1 cup breadcrumbs

Vegetable oil, for deep-frying, to 1-inch depth

Boil the potatoes, unpeeled, in salted water for about 20 minutes, or until tender. Drain, peel, and purée in a food mill, or pass through a ricer. Add egg yolk and butter to potatoes and mix thoroughly. Add salt and nutmeg, using more or less to taste. Add flour to the potato mixture, a few tablespoons at a time, until you can form the potatoes into small, firm sausage-shaped or round croquettes. Dip each croquette into the egg-water mixture, then coat with breadcrumbs.

Heat the oil until hot (about 375° F). Add the croquettes, a few at a time, and fry until golden brown. Remove from the oil and drain on brown paper or paper towels.

The Hemingways returned to Schruns the following winter. Ernest worked as hard as he ever had to edit the manuscript about bullfighting and Paris that he had written in six weeks earlier that year. In August 1926, he sent the proofs of his first novel to Max Perkins at Scribner's. The dedication to his wife and son read: This book is for Hadley and for John Hadley Nicanor.

These were bittersweet words for Hemingway, for his marriage to Hadley was all but finished in the fall of 1926. Ernest had fallen in love with Pauline Pfeiffer, who came from Piggott, Arkansas to work for the Paris edition of *Vogue* and, as some would suggest, to find the right husband. In October, 1926, Scribner's published *The Sun Also Rises*, its author poised at the brink of a new marriage and yet another new life.

The Sun Also Rises

In the summer of 1925 Ernest began writing what started as a tribute to matador Cayetano Ordoñez and the bullfights of which he was quickly becoming an aficionado. As his writing flourished, the focus of the story expanded well beyond the bullring to include the equally compelling spectacle of Parisian café life and its destitute band of roving drunkards. "I'm writing a novel full of plot and drama," he told Kitty Cannell, who would appear as Frances Clyne in the novel. "He gestured ahead towards Harold [Loeb] and Bill [Smith]. 'I'm tearing those bastards apart,' he said. 'I'm putting everyone in it.'"[34]

He would, indeed, put everyone in it, capturing the decadent, barren soul of Montparnasse and expatriate Paris. *The Sun Also Rises* became one of the most famous (and infamous) *romans à clef* of all time. As intriguing as his readers found his fiction, the real people upon whom it was based were not quite as pleased. Jimmie Charters, well-known barman of the Dingo Bar, recalled in his memoirs the displeasure of the unwitting protagonists, who were described as "six characters in search of an author—with a gun!"[35]

The people are all gone now. What remains is Paris, Hemingway's Paris, complete with cafés, book stalls, dusk-tipped horse-chestnut trees, and smoke-filled bars. Hemingway also included a meal at the Rendezvous-des-Mariniers on the Ile St. Louis, a meal that Suzanne Rodriguez-Hunter, in her book *Found Meals of the Lost Generation*, claims "may well be the most famous

71

meal of the decade."[36] Jake Barnes and Bill Gorton —based in part on Hemingway and his childhood friend Bill Smith—dine at the Rendezvous, which had already lost its dingy charm as a hangout for the literary set and had been invaded by "too many compatriots."[37] In *Where Paris Dines*, Julian Street notes that Americans found this "shabby little eating place . . . invaluable for purposes of entertaining. 'To-night,' you would remark casually to your visitors, 'I'll take you to a queer little place, very French.'"[38]

> We ate dinner at Madame Lecomte's restaurant on the far side of the island. It was crowded with Americans and we had to stand up and wait for a place. Some one had put it in the American Women's Club list as a quaint restaurant on the Paris quais as yet untouched by Americans, so we had to wait forty-five minutes for a table. Bill had eaten at the restaurant in 1918, right after the armistice, and Madame Lecomte made a great fuss over seeing him.
>
> "Doesn't get us a table, though," Bill said. . . .
>
> We had a good meal, a roast chicken, new green beans, mashed potatoes, a salad, and some apple-pie and cheese. . . . After the coffee and a *fine* we got the bill, chalked up the same as ever on a slate, that was doubtless one of the "quaint" features, paid it, shook hands, and went out. . . .
>
> The river was dark and a bateau mouche went by, all bright with lights, going fast and quiet up and out of sight under the bridge. Down the river was Notre Dame squatting against the night sky. We crossed to the left bank of the Seine by the wooden foot-bridge from the Quai de Bethune, and stopped on the bridge and looked down the river at Notre Dame. Standing on the bridge the island looked dark, the houses were high against the sky, and the trees were shadows.
>
> "It's pretty grand," Bill said. "God, I love to get back."[39]

72

Dinner at Madame Lecomte's Au Rendezvous des Mariniers

Roast Chicken

New Green Beans

Mashed Potatoes

Salad

Apple Pie and Cheese

Coffee

Fine (Cognac)

Roast Chicken

Roasting chickens found in the United States tend to be much larger and fattier than those in France. For this recipe, a 3- to 4-pound fryer works perfectly.

2 SERVINGS, WITH LEFTOVERS

1 3- to 4-pound frying chicken
Salt
Freshly ground white pepper
4 tablespoons butter
1–2 tablespoons flour
¼–½ cup chicken stock

Preheat the oven to 400° F.

Season the cavity of the chicken with salt and white pepper to taste, and place 2 tablespoons butter inside. Truss the legs and wings of the chicken. Rub the breast of the chicken with 1 tablespoon butter, then salt and pepper to taste. Pour ½ cup water into a roasting pan. Place the bird on a rack, breast-side down, place the rack in the pan, and roast for 1–1¼ hours. Frequently baste the chicken with the pan juices, turning the bird breast-side up after 30 minutes. To test for doneness, pierce the skin at the thigh; if the juices run clear, it is done.

Remove the bird to a warm serving platter and let stand for 10 minutes before serving.

To make the gravy, pour off the pan juices and separate the fat, reserving both. Pour the fat back into the roasting pan and place on the stove over medium heat. Add the flour and stir to form a thick roux, scraping up any bits stuck to the pan. Pour the remaining pan juices into the roasting pan, adding enough chicken stock to make 1 cup, and cook for 4 to 5 minutes, stirring constantly, until thickened and smooth. Season with salt and white pepper to taste. Blend in the remaining tablespoon butter and serve with the chicken.

New Green Beans

Haricots verts, *which are much slimmer than common string beans, may be difficult to find in the United States. If you are unable to find them, substitute the smallest string beans you can find.*

4 SERVINGS

> 1 pound *haricots verts* or fresh green beans
> 4 tablespoons butter
> ½ teaspoon fresh lemon juice

Trim and wash the beans. Bring a medium pot of salted water to a boil. Add the beans and cook for 5–10 minutes. Beans should be crisp yet tender (or, of course, to your own personal taste). Drain the beans and rinse under cold water to halt cooking. In a saucepan, melt the butter; add the beans and lemon juice. Stir to coat the beans with butter. Serve immediately.

Mashed Potatoes

For Parisian-style mashed potatoes, use the recipe on page 42.

Apple Pie and Cheese

Unless Madame Lecomte's kitchen as well as her dining room had been corrupted by "too many compatriots," it is not likely that Jake and Bill had all-American apple pie and cheese, an unheard-of combination in France. Most likely they enjoyed a cheese course followed by a classic French apple tart.[40] *For the tart recipe, follow the one on page 43.*

Fine

Une fine *(pronounced* feen), *short for Grand Fine Champagne, is the common way to order Cognac in France. A* fine *is a blend of Cognac brandies from the Grand Champagne and Petite Champagne districts.*

The Garden of Eden

Later in life, Hemingway returned to France in his fiction, this time to the Riviera. In 1946, he began work on what he felt was a major novel. He worked on *The Garden of Eden* over the next 15 years, amassing a manuscript of 48 chapters and 200,000 words. The book was not published until 25 years after his death, severely diminished in size yet retaining its essential elements of love, obsession, loss, and hunger. This book alone, once called "the eggiest novel ever written,"[41] may very well wrest from Paris the title of gastronomic capital of Hemingway's France and relocate it on the Mediterranean coast.

Hemingway uses food in general, and eggs specifically, as symbols of the volatile relationship between the honeymooning David and Catherine Bourne and the dark and beautiful Marita, with whom they have both fallen in love. They eat eggs soft-boiled, egg whites cold and cut up, fried eggs, and omelets. There is even a Humpty Dumpty reference in David's African story-within-the-story. Between all of the eggs, and the other foods and drinks, we cannot ignore the central emphasis on appetites and hunger that rule *The Garden of Eden*. While it may often result in "wacky" humor[42] *The Garden of Eden* sets an abundant culinary table that is irresistible:

> They were always hungry but they ate very well. They were hungry for breakfast which they ate at the cafe, ordering brioche and café au lait and eggs, and the type of preserve that they chose and the manner in which the eggs were to be cooked was an excitement. . . . On this morning there was brioche and red raspberry preserves and the eggs were boiled and there was a pat of butter that melted as they stirred them and salted them lightly and ground pepper over them in the cups [Hemingway believed that pepper cleansed the morning stomach].[43]

> They were big eggs and fresh and the girl's were not cooked quite as long as the young man's. He remembered that easily and he was happy with his which he diced up with the spoon and ate with only the flow of the butter to moisten them and the fresh early morning texture and the bite of the coarsely ground pepper grains and the hot coffee and the chickory-fragrant bowl of café au lait.[44]

Breakfast in the Garden

Soft-Boiled Eggs

Brioche and Red Raspberry Preserves

Café au Lait

———————

76

Brioche

2 4-INCH BY 8-INCH LOAVES

To create brioche loaves, or Nanterres, simply follow the brioche recipe on page 23. After the dough has been refrigerated overnight, let it stand at room temperature for 1 hour. Divide the dough into four pieces. Quickly form four balls slightly less than 4 inches across. Place two of the balls in each of two buttered loaf pans (4 inches by 8 inches), one ball on each end of the pans. Cover the loaf pans and let stand until the dough has risen to the edge of the pans, about 2 hours. At that time, lightly brush the top of each loaf with the beaten egg. Bake in a 350° F oven for 40 to 45 minutes, or until loaves are golden brown. Turn onto cooling racks, brush with melted butter, and let stand for 1 hour. Slice brioche and serve with red raspberry preserves.

Café au Lait

To create the perfect café au lait to accompany the brioche, use a dark-roasted coffee blended with French chicory (the roasted and ground root of endive). Blends available in the United States include Café du Monde and Community New Orleans.

———————

In addition to the innumerable eggs in *The Garden of Eden*, Hemingway also introduces several dishes of mackerel as "crucial signs and thematic signals."[45] In the original manuscript for the book, after David valiantly fights and catches a sea bass too large to cook at the hotel, he and Catherine lunch on mackerel fresh from the fleet's morning catch. Afterwards they make love, reinforcing the role of the *maquerel*, the pimp or panderer who administers to their sexual exploits. In the novel that survives, though, they have fresh sea bass for lunch, forestalling the more lurid symbolism in favor of a celebration of David's skills as a fisherman:

> "I'm excited about the fish," she said. "Don't we have wonderful simple fun?"

> They were hungry for lunch and the bottle of white wine was cold and they drank it as

they ate the celery *rémoulade* and the small radishes and the home pickled mushrooms from the big glass jar. The bass was grilled and the grill marks showed on the silver skin and the butter melted on the hot plate. There was sliced lemon to press on the bass and fresh bread from the bakery and wine cooled their tongues of the heat of the fried potatoes. It was a good light, dry cheerful unknown white wine and the restaurant was proud of it.[46]

THE MENU

Lunch in the Garden

Sea Bass Grilled with Butter and Herbs

French-fried Potatoes

Celery Rémoulade

Small Radishes

Home-Pickled Mushrooms

Sea Bass Grilled with Butter and Herbs

We'll get a small one for us to eat. They're really wonderful. A small one ought to be grilled with butter and with herbs. They're like striped bass at home.[47]

2 TO 3 SERVINGS

    1 onion, chopped
    1 rib celery, chopped
    1 bay leaf
    ½ teaspoon fennel seeds
    1 sprig thyme
    2 cups dry white wine
    1 2- to 3-pound sea bass or striped bass, cleaned
    2 sprigs fennel
    4 tablespoons melted butter
    1 tablespoon chopped fresh parsley, for garnish
    1 lemon, sliced, for garnish

In a flat baking dish large enough to hold the fish, combine the onion, celery, bay leaf, fennel seeds, thyme, and wine. Make 2 diagonal incisions on both sides of the bass. Add the fish to the marinade, baste with the liquid and marinate, covered with plastic wrap, for 2 hours.

Heat a charcoal grill until hot, and add the sprigs of fennel to the coals. Remove the fish from the

77

marinade, pat dry with a paper towel, and brush liberally with melted butter. Grill the fish for 8 to 10 minutes on each side, brushing occasionally with more butter. Check the fish to see that the flesh is white to the bone beneath the cuts you have made. Remove the fish to a warm serving plate, pour the remaining butter over the fish, and garnish with parsley and lemon slices.

Celery Rémoulade

4 SERVINGS

2 cups peeled and coarsely grated celery root

1 hard-boiled egg

1 egg yolk

1 teaspoon Dijon-style mustard

2 tablespoons tarragon vinegar

½ teaspoon salt

Freshly ground black pepper

½ cup olive oil

1 teaspoon chopped fresh parsley

1 teaspoon finely chopped chives for garnish

Blanch the grated celery root in boiling water for 2 minutes. Drain and rinse with cold water. Allow to dry thoroughly.

In a small mixing bowl, mash the egg and egg yolk together with a fork. Stir in the mustard, vinegar, salt, and pepper. Vigorously whisk in the olive oil, a little at a time, until the sauce reaches the consistency of mayonnaise. Combine the celery root and the dressing, chill, and serve garnished with chopped fresh parsley and chives.

Small Radishes *(see page 41)*

Home-Pickled Mushrooms

4 SERVINGS

1 pound fresh button mushrooms

½ cup wine vinegar

½ cup extra-virgin olive oil

2 teaspoons chopped chives

1 teaspoon dried tarragon

1 clove garlic, finely minced

½ teaspoon salt

1 teaspoon sugar

1 tablespoon fresh lemon juice

¼ teaspoon freshly ground black pepper

Wipe the mushrooms clean with a towel and cut off the ends of the stems. Whisk all the other ingredients together in a mixing bowl. Put the mushrooms into a jar and cover with the marinade. Allow the mushrooms to marinate in the refrigerator at least overnight.

SPAIN

The Fiesta Concept of Life

"It was spring in Paris and everything looked just a little too beautiful. Mike and I decided to go to Spain. Strater drew us a fine map of Spain on the back of a menu of the Strix restaurant. On the same menu he wrote the name of a restaurant in Madrid where the specialty is young suckling pig roasted, the name of a pension on the Via San Jerónimó where the bull fighters live, and sketched a plan showing where the Grecos are hung in the Prado."

—*By-Line Ernest Hemingway*

The amateurs in the Pamplona Bullring.
Hemingway is the taunter in the white pants.

At the urging of Gertrude Stein and Ezra Pound, Hemingway made his first real excursion to Spain in the summer of 1923 (he had traveled through Spain en route to Paris in 1921). His destination was Pamplona on the nape of the Pyrenees, home to the Fiesta de San Fermín and some of the greatest bullfights in all of Spain. Ernest was immediately captivated by the country, the people, and the spectacle of the bulls. He would later write: "If the people of Spain have one common trait it is pride and if they have another it is common sense and if they have a third it is impracticality."[1] It was an alluring combination, one that would draw Hemingway back to Spain again and again for the rest of his life.

He used those early Spanish summers for *The Sun Also Rises*, paying homage to its earthly dominion, celebrating its trout streams and its all-consuming celebrations. In the early 1930s he wrote *Death in the Afternoon*, his treatise on the bullfights and writing and eating and living. In the mid-30s, war swept the country. He watched as the country he loved best was torn apart by civil war. While he watched as a journalist, he was seeing as an artist. Soon after his return he began *For Whom the Bell Tolls*. Much later, very close to the end of his life, he chased his final yesterday, following two of Spain's greatest matadors in *The Dangerous Summer*.

Spain inspired some of Hemingway's finest work. The writing is full of the rich colors of the country, the lowing of cows, the feel of solid earth underfoot, and the aromas of saffron and olive oil.

(Author's note: I would like to acknowledge a debt of gratitude to Penelope Casas, the author of such extraordinary books on Spanish cuisine as *Tapas: The Little Dishes of Spain* and *¡Delicioso!*

Upon returning from my first trip to Spain, I first learned to re-create the staples of Spanish cuisine from the pages of her books. Her influence may be seen and tasted in the following pages.)

The Sun Also Rises

July 1925: Duff Twysden, Harold Loeb, Bill Smith, and Hadley and Ernest Hemingway are in Pamplona for the Fiesta de San Fermín. The party seethes and rocks amidst the personal bitterness between Hemingway and Loeb, and by week's end a rift of legendary dimensions has split the group. The Hemingways travel south to Madrid, he scribbling in blue composition books a tale of destitution and decadence and the "Lost Generation." *The Sun Also Rises*, Hemingway's account of his travails in Paris and Spain, was published by Charles Scribner's Sons in 1926.

His was a physical world, violent and sensual, draped in the teasingly acrid aroma of drink and death. As accomplices to the drama, we continue our quest to this day for the world and the men and the life he revealed to us. This world thrives in the restaurants and bars of Spain. Spanish cuisine echoes the Hemingway prose, simple and coarse, subtly concealing great passion and bravado. It reflects the essence of this country, burning hottest in the stone-and-tile country inns and tapas bars of Hemingway's Spain. Following the author and his characters through Spain is culi-nary high drama, replete with conflict and climax, creating real-life memories to mirror and comple-ment those once etched in our imaginations by brilliant fiction.

By Hemingway's hand, Jake Barnes and Bill Gorton began their Spanish sojourn fishing and hiking around the mountain hamlet of Burguete, 40 kilo-meters above Pamplona. The Hostal Burguete,

CRAIG BORETH

Hostal Burguete where Hemingway and friends stayed in the early 1920s. This establishment played host to Jake and friends in *The Sun Also Rises*.

located on the north end of the town's only road, remains dark and drafty. Haunted by the ghosts of Hemingway and Jake, the rooms of the Hostal are as both men described them: "There were two beds, a washstand, a clothes-chest, and a big, framed steel-engraving of Nuestra Señora de Roncesvalles."[2] Peek in on the sitting room on the second floor above the Hostal's quaint dining room, where Jake, Bill and Harris, the fly-tying Brit, played three-handed bridge. True to the spirit of this reclusive region and Hemingway's genius, each step marks a path deeper into your own imagination and the lives, both real and fabled, that played upon this place. The mountains surrounding Burguete harbor the gray and majestic Monastery at Roncesvalles, refuge for pilgrims to Santiago de Compostela. Above the Monastery is the Pass at Ibañeta, where Charlemagne's nephew Roland met his demise in the climactic battle scenes of *The Song of Roland*.

The Hostal Burguete offers a classic mountain repast. The regional culinary specialty, *Trucha a la Navarra* is sweet and subdued. A small, fresh trout is cooked beneath a generous cut of bacon, which has basted the fish to indulgence. The sweet, pink flesh is to be picked from the bone and savored slowly. Dinner is followed by a bowl of wild strawberries. The cool brisk and mountain aroma of Burguete veils the meal with a pastoral stillness. A snifter of brandy and a smoke before bed staves off the blustery evening, and the spirit that drew Hemingway to this land is laid bare before us. Nuestra Señora de Roncesvalles bows her assent.

THE MENU

A Pyrenees Country Repast

Sopa de Navarra a la Burguete

Trucha a la Navarra

Wild Strawberries

Hot Rum Punch a la Burguete

83

Sopa de Navarra a la Burguete (Hot Vegetable Soup)

This recipe is adapted from the Hostal Burguete, which still serves this soup as a prelude to its tender trout.

4 SERVINGS

> 5 cloves garlic, crushed
> 1 onion, chopped
> 2 leeks, white parts only, sliced
> 2 tablespoons olive oil
> 1 1-pound piece cured ham
> 1 cup dried white beans
> Salt
> Pepper
> 1 cup thinly sliced cabbage
> 1 cup green beans, snapped in half
> 1 cup frozen peas

In a stockpot, sauté the garlic, onion, and leeks in the olive oil over medium heat until soft. Add 8 cups water and the ham, white beans, and salt and pepper to taste. Reduce the heat and simmer, covered, for about 2 hours, or until the beans are tender. Add the cabbage and green beans. Cover and simmer for another 20 minutes. Add the peas and cook for another 5 minutes. Remove the ham and serve.

Trucha a la Navarra (Trout Cooked with Cured Ham)

Trout fishing was a lifelong passion for Hemingway. This dish bestows upon the trout a posthumous honor truly worthy of such a beautiful fish. As you may recall, Hemingway offered a recipe for a similar dish in his Toronto Star *dispatch "Camping Out",* *(see page 9).*

There are innumerable recipes for Trucha a la Navarra. *This is a slightly more domesticated version than Hemingway's own.*

4 SERVINGS

> 4 small trout, cleaned and gutted
> Several sprigs mint
> ¾ cup dry white wine
> 8 thin slices serrano, prosciutto, or cured ham
> 4 generous slices bacon, thickly cut
> Flour for dusting
> 4 tablespoons olive oil
> Salt
> Pepper
> Lemon wedges

Stuff the trout with half the mint, pour wine over, and refrigerate, covered, for 2 hours. Remove the mint and discard. Roll 1 mint leaf inside each slice of the cured ham and stuff 2 rolls inside each fish. Heat the oil in a skillet until hot. Cook the bacon 1 minute on each side, until slightly browned. Remove the bacon from the pan and reserve, leaving the grease. Roll the fish in flour to lightly coat. Increase the heat and fry the fish in the bacon grease and oil for 10 minutes for each inch of thickness, turning once. After turning, place 1 slice bacon on each fish. Serve the fish whole with the bacon on top. Garnish with mint leaves. Season with salt and pepper to taste and serve with lemon wedges.

Wild Strawberries

Wild strawberries, the likes of which you will find in a Pyrenees inn, are exceedingly rare in the United States. If you are unable to find the very small, sweet wild strawberries, substitute the smallest, ripest strawberries available. Wash the strawberries in cold water. They need not be hulled. Allow to dry on paper towels. Fill a bowl with strawberries and serve plain.

Hot Rum Punch a la Burguete

For this soul-warming recipe, visit The Hemingway Bar *(page 190).*

Hemingway brings Jake and Bill from the mountain's earthly domain down into Pamplona for the Fiesta de San Fermín. They are consumed by swirling and dancing and drums pounding. The Fiesta burns for nine days, from noon on July 6th to midnight on the 14th. From dawn to dawn, there are exuberant celebrations of life and exhilarating confrontations with death. Each morning begins cold and raw, and each is shattered with the Running of the Bulls (*El Encierro*) from the corrals at Santo Domingo to the Plaza de Toros. Thousands of men (and a few women) prove their bravery before the horns of 2,000-pound brawlers. Each day is filled with parades and song, each afternoon with bullfights and drink and dance. The purity and splendor of Hemingway's time may seem a little worn, but the venerable spirit of San Fermín thrives to this day. ¡Viva San Fermín!

A Pamplona Fiesta

Bocadillo de Tortilla de Patata

Escabeche de Atún

Bacalao de Pamplona

––––––––––––

Amid the insanity of the Fiesta, dining is hardly a deliberate process. For most revelers, sustenance is found within the makeshift food shops and pedestrian bars of the town. Spain's hearty version of fast food, and a staple product of the Fiesta, is the *bocadillo de tortilla de patata*, or potato omelet sandwich, the national dish of Spain. Hardly glamorous, the *tortilla* is a taste of basic, traditional cuisine. As with Spain itself, the *tortilla* charms with its simplicity and subtle blend of elemental tastes. One must not miss the *tortilla*, as it above all else tastes of Spain.

Bocadillo de Tortilla de Patata (Potato Omelet Sandwich)

Few places haunt you when you are away as Pamplona during the San Fermín. With senses blurred all week, you depart only to find a sight, sound, or smell that evokes the madness of the Fiesta. It is a delicious torture, and you may indulge yourself in it each time you re-create the Tortilla de Patata. *The blend of oil and onions in a starchy omelet brings back the sleep-soaked damp and chilled mornings and wild, endless nights of* la fiesta más intensa.

4 SERVINGS

> 2 cups oil (mixture of olive and vegetable)
> 2 medium potatoes, peeled and sliced very thin
> 2 medium onions, finely chopped
> 4 large eggs
> 2 tablespoons water
> Salt
> 4 sub rolls

Heat 2 cups oil in a large saucepan over medium heat. Add the potatoes and onions in layers. Try to separate the potato slices as much as possible when adding them to the oil. Cook over low or medium heat. The oil should only reach a slow boil. In a separate bowl, whisk the eggs lightly, adding the water and salt to taste. Don't overbeat the eggs, as an overbeaten albumen results in a less-than-perfect texture.

Ernest with "the king of all fish, the ruler of the Valhalla of fishermen."

When the potatoes are tender, drain the mixture into a colander, placing a heatproof bowl under the colander to save the oil for later use (it has a wonderful potato/onion flavor). Add the vegetables to the eggs, pressing down gently until completely covered. Let stand for 10 minutes.

In a large skillet with high sides, heat enough oil to coat the bottom and sides of the pan (be sure ahead of time that you have a large plate that can cover the pan). Pour off the excess oil if necessary. When the oil begins to smoke, add the egg mixture quickly, lifting the sides to allow liquid to flow beneath. Lower the heat, rotating pan to be sure the *tortilla* is not sticking. Remember: Spanish cuisine is a cuisine of patience.

When the underside is browned, cover the pan with the large plate and invert to flip the omelet out. Wipe out the pan and add more oil. Bring to high heat again. Slide the *tortilla* back into the pan and cook the second side until brown. The *tortilla* is done when you tap the center and it is of similar consistence to your forearm. Of course, if you have manly Hemingway forearms, choose a slightly fleshier spot. Remove the *tortilla* from the pan, allow to cool, then serve in slices on sub rolls.

Escabeche de Atún (Marinated Tuna with Onions)

For Hemingway, tuna was "the king of all fish, the ruler of the Valhalla of fishermen."[3] *It is only fitting that tuna should make a special appearance at the Fiesta:*

> In the back room Brett and Bill were sitting on barrels surrounded by the dancers. Everybody had his arms on everybody else's shoulders, and they were all singing. Mike was sitting at a table with several men in their shirt sleeves, eating from a bowl of tuna fish, chopped onions and vinegar. They were all drinking wine and mopping up the oil and vinegar with pieces of bread.[4]

The smells and sounds evoked by this passage are absolutely inebriating. While Mike probably enjoyed a dish made with canned flaked tuna fish, the following recipe uses fresh tuna. It is still a very simple dish and will enliven any gathering with the festive culinary music of San Fermín.

4 TO 6 SERVINGS

2 pounds fresh tuna steak cut into small chunks

1 large onion, coarsely chopped

4 cloves garlic, finely chopped

2 bay leaves, whole

Salt

Freshly ground pepper

1 cup olive oil

1 cup vinegar

Preheat the oven to 300° F.

Place the tuna chunks in a heatproof casserole and cover with the onion, garlic, and bay leaves. Season the casserole with salt and pepper to taste, then pour the oil over the fish and let stand for 20 minutes. Add just enough vinegar to cover the fish. Cook, covered, for 20 minutes.

Serve at room temperature with plenty of bread for mopping. If you have time, prepare this dish and let it sit overnight. This allows the flavors to mingle and produces a more profound flavor.

Hemingway rarely traveled anywhere without making some bar or restaurant his own. In Venice there was Harry's Bar; in Paris there was the Closerie des Lilas; in Key West it was Sloppy Joe's; and in Havana it was El Floridita. In Pamplona, it was Casa Marceliano. Matías Anoz, owner of Marceliano's, befriended Ernest when he first visited Pamplona as an eager young journalist with dreams of writing about the Fiesta. He gave Ernest room and board and didn't mind when the bill went unpaid for a while. He also prepared *Bacalao de Pamplona*, which Ernest declared on several occasions to be his favorite dish. Casa Marceliano closed down in the early 1990s. What remains is a legacy of

friendship, of proud old men speaking longingly of the days of their youth, and a dish of cod, shrimp, vegetables, spices and herbs that bring that nostalgia to life.

Bacalao de Pamplona (Salt Cod)

The following recipe is based on the one that appears in José Maria Iribarren's book Hemingway y Los Sanfermines.

6 SERVINGS

89

1 pound salt cod

2 tablespoons olive oil

2 cloves garlic, crushed

2 tomatoes, peeled

1 large onion, finely chopped

1 green bell pepper, chopped

2 bay leaves

½ teaspoon sugar

¼ teaspoon cumin seeds

½ tablespoon minced fresh oregano, or ¼ teaspoon dried

½ tablespoon minced fresh marjoram, or ¼ teaspoon dried

Pinch of black pepper

¼ cup dry white wine

¾ pound crabmeat

1 cup peeled shrimp

½ cup sliced mushrooms

Begin preparation 1 day in advance. In a large bowl, cover the salt cod with cold water and let stand for 20 minutes. Drain the water. Cut the fish into 2-inch pieces, place in a medium saucepan, and cover again with cold water. Let the fish soak overnight, skin side down.

The next day, bring the water to a boil, then simmer over low heat for 45 minutes. Taste a small piece of the fish. If it is still too salty, rinse the fish thoroughly in hot water. Otherwise, drain the fish and set aside.

Heat the olive oil in a large pot. Add the garlic, tomatoes, onion, green pepper, bay leaves, sugar, cumin seeds, oregano, marjoram, pepper to taste, and wine. Cook slowly, covered, for 30 minutes. Add the cod and continue to cook, covered, for another 20 minutes. Add the crabmeat, shrimp, and mushrooms and cook, covered, for 10 minutes.

The cuisine of the Fiesta revolves around the wine, and in Navarra in July it flows freely. In the streets there is no delicacy of bouquet or concern for vintage. Volume, though, is very highly regarded. Shops throughout the town sell cheap wine and champagne in bottles and cartons. Regardless of price, the wines of this celebration must eventually embrace the leather tint of the bota (or wineskin). The white-on-white uniform of the Fiesta (accented rakishly with red sash and scarf) would not be complete without a Las Tres ZZZ wineskin hung wryly from the shoulder. The bota that Jake bought for four pesetas now costs 3,000 but remains essential. For a quick lesson, we'll follow Jake and Bill's ride atop a bus from Pamplona to Burguete:

Bill raised the wine-skin and let the stream of wine spurt out and into his mouth, his head tipped back. When he stopped drinking and tipped the leather bottle down a few drops ran down his chin.

"No! No!" several Basques said. "Not like that." One snatched the bottle away from the owner, who was himself about to give a demonstration. He was a young fellow and he held the wine-bottle at full arms' length and raised it high up, squeezing the leather bag with his hand so the stream of wine hissed into his mouth. He held the bag out there, the wine making a flat, hard trajectory into his mouth, and he kept on swallowing smoothly and regularly.

"Hey!" the owner of the bottle shouted. "Whose wine is that?"

The drinker waggled his little finger at him and smiled at us with his eyes. Then he bit the stream off sharp, made a quick lift with the wine-bag and lowered it down to the owner. He winked at us. The owner shook the wine-skin sadly.[5]

The Market was nearby, and I wanted to buy a few little appetizers that Ernesto was especially fond of: radishes, celery, capers, scallions, pickled peppers, green cloves of garlic, cod, fresh tuna, Spanish olives, and whatever else I could find, because Ernesto, the victor of so many battles, who still had enough energy to refuse to grow old, deserved every favorite tidbit of his that I could possibly offer him.[6]

Meanwhile the Fiesta burns about you. Its circus burlesque charges forth through stately processions and rituals, closing with a mournful candlelit ceremony at midnight on the fourteenth of July. The following morning Jake leaves to seek refuge from the Fiesta. San Sebastián is a tranquil space, its name alone evokes golden beaches, summer breezes, and the lazy dining style of the uniquely Spanish tapas bars.

San Sebastián is a Spanish resort, so replete with local flavor that the word *resort*, conjuring images of mirrored and brash hotels with cookie-cutter thoroughfares twining amidst manicured greens, simply doesn't fit. San Sebastián is home, sharing all day that certain early-morning quality that Jake found so intoxicating. It is a postcard of a caricature of a dreamy seaside town. Life is swell and the food divine in San Sebastián.

Few cities can boast the number of world-class restaurants found in tiny San Sebastián. And few Spanish cities can compete with the variety and character of the tapas offered in the dark personable bars above the gingerbread port in the Old Quarter. To indulge in the *tapeo*, or bar-hopping in search of elaborate appetizers, is uniquely Spanish, and in San Sebastián it is uniquely delightful.

HEMINGWAY COLLECTION, JOHN F. KENNEDY LIBRARY

With Pauline in San Sebastián, 1927.

The signs of great tapas bars are crowds of people at the bar and heaps of napkins on the floor. The crowds form before dinner, around eight or nine, and the trash accumulates soon thereafter. A stroll along Portu Kale is a walking tour of culinary bliss. Seafood is the specialty. Peering out beyond the flower garden of boats in the tiny port across to the Isla de Santa Clara, cradled in the arms of the town on the Bay of Biscay, one understands San Sebastián's bond to the sea. Enter a bar (my favorite is Portaletas in Portu Kale), order a glass of beer or wine, and partake of the tapas. Keep a running tab in your head, and pay the bartender when you're done. There is fish, shrimp, octopus and eel, serrano ham and chorizo. The variety is wonderfully daunting. The bartenders keep up a frantic pace matched only by the patrons, and the food and drink dance to the clamorous chatter of clinking glass and the spirited discourse of tipsy diners. This is dinner as it should be, a celebration of life, a spontaneous ritual replete with drama and comedy. When you return home, recapture the tapas lifestyle by creating your own.

THE MENU

A Tapas Menu

Pulpo a la Vinagreta

Patatas Alioli

Pimientos

Canapé of Fried Fish

Pulpo a la Vinagreta (Octopus Vinaigrette)

Hemingway loved octopus. In Cuba, he would catch them from his boat, the Pilar, *and dine on octopus in wine sauce and fricasse of octopus.[7] It is possible that Ernest experienced octopus for the first time in San Sebastián. At Bar Portaletas in the Old Quarter, you will find a perfect introduction to this delicacy. They serve tender pieces of octopus on a slice of bread with a dab of mayonnaise. You may also find it in countless tapas bars tossed in a vinaigrette. My all-time favorite is found at the Bar Gallego in Madrid, located just below the Plaza Mayor on the Plaza de Puerta Cerrada (very near to Casa Botín, which we will visit shortly).*

    1 small octopus, about 1 pound
    10 cups water
    1 bay leaf
    ½ cup olive oil
    Salt
    1–2 corks
    1 medium green bell pepper, diced
    1 medium onion, finely chopped
    ¼ cup pimientos (see page 94)
    4 tablespoons wine vinegar

Cooking an octopus is quite an adventure in itself. Begin by balling up the octopus in your hands and slamming it into the sink a dozen times to tenderize. Place the water, bay leaf, ¼ cup olive oil, a pinch of salt, and the corks in a stockpot and bring to a boil. Quickly dip the octopus into the boiling liquid three times to further tenderize it, then cook it in the liquid, covered, for about 1 hour. Taste a small piece after an hour and, if not yet tender, continue until it is. When done, remove the octopus and cut the tentacles into bite-size pieces with scissors.

Combine the octopus pieces with all other ingredients and the remaining ¼ cup olive oil. Allow the vinaigrette to sit for at least an hour. Serve at room temperature.

Note on buying octopus: If you are lucky enough to live near an excellent fish market, you may be able to purchase fresh octopus. Otherwise, try a local Portuguese market and buy frozen. And, although you didn't hear it from me, and I'll deny it if confronted, the canned octopus in olive oil that you can get in your local supermarket is an adequate substitute in this dish. Substitute 2 or 3 cans for the fresh octopus.

Patatas Alioli (Potatoes in Garlic Mayonnaise)

8 TO 10 SERVINGS

    1 pound potatoes
    ¾ cup mayonnaise (recipe follows)
    3 cloves garlic, mashed to a paste or very
        finely chopped
    1 tablespoon minced fresh parsley
    Salt

Peel the potatoes and cut them into ½-inch chunks. Boil in water to cover until tender yet firm, about 15 minutes. Rinse in cold water and allow to cool to room temperature.

Combine the mayonnaise, garlic, and parsley. Fold in the potatoes. Season with salt to taste. Or prepare ahead and refrigerate, then return to room temperature before serving.

Alioli
(Mayonnaise)

1¼ CUP (ENOUGH FOR *PATATAS ALIOLI* RECIPE)

   1 large egg plus 1 egg yolk
   ¼ teaspoon Dijon-style mustard
   Dash of salt
   2 tablespoons fresh lemon juice
   Mixture of ½ cup olive oil and ½ cup
      vegetable or canola oil

Place in the bowl of a food processor the whole egg, egg yolk, mustard, salt, and lemon juice. Blend for a few seconds. With the motor running, pour in the oil very gradually and continue beating until thickened and silky.

Pimientos

Pimientos, or roasted red peppers, are a simple, magnificent, and elemental part of any tapas feast. Set them out alone on a plate or use as a colorful and aromatic garnish to paella, tortillas, or other tapas.

4 TO 6 SERVINGS

   2 red bell peppers

Preheat the oven to 400° F.

Place the peppers on an ungreased baking pan and bake for 15 to 20 minutes. Turn the peppers and bake for another 15 minutes, or until the skins are black. Remove the peppers and place them in a closed brown paper bag until cool. When cool, remove the peppers from the bag. The blackened skins will virtually fall off the syrupy, tart flesh. Core and seed the peppers. Cut into thin strips and serve liberally throughout the meal.

Canapé of Fried Fish

Just up the street from Portaletas is another San Sebastián institution: Bar Alkalar. Indulge in their fried fish tapa: a generous chunk of fried hake, served on slices of baguette lightly fried in oil and swathed with alioli.

6 TO 8 SERVINGS

   1 pound hake or other firm, white fish
   Salt
   ¾ cup all-purpose flour
   ¾ cup cornmeal
   Oil for frying
   2 large eggs, slightly beaten

Cut the fish into 1½-inch square pieces. Lightly salt the fish. Combine the flour and cornmeal in a bowl. Roll the fish pieces in the flour and cornmeal mixture to cover. Pour the oil into a skillet to about ½ inch. Heat the oil. Coat fish in egg wash, then fry until brown, turning once. Drain the fish on paper towels. Serve on fried bread slices with mayonnaise.

This simple canapé can be garnished with pimientos, or even cured ham, but the Bar Alkalar serves them plain, and there are no complaints.

Madrid Beckons

An early morning swim, breakfast of a *bocadilla de tortilla* and a cup of the sweet viscous lava that passes as hot chocolate in Spain, and the road to Madrid unfolds to the south. As Brett once beckoned for Jake to rescue her in Madrid, so does the city itself now call us to indulge in its intemperate demeanor. A long bus ride along a flat ribbon of road through burnt bronze plains, and it is as if all that is Spain passes before you. The land's blaring fanfare announces your slow descent into Madrid: the living, breathing distilled essence of the Spanish heart.

In dynamic culinary swaths and broad cultural strokes, Madrid paints the whole of Spanish life on a sprawling urban canvas. With boundless charge day melts into evening, and evening fights the good fight only to be replaced, with regretful obligation, by morning. There is so much, and only in Madrid is there enough time to enjoy. The Spanish treasure their great city, and they make time. As Ernest wrote, "Nobody goes to bed in Madrid until they have killed the night."[8]

July in Madrid is hot. An early morning stroll to the Plaza Mayor and the bountiful and cool Market of San Miguel, and the heat arrives. A bustling café offers a respite of coffee and *churros*, a sweet and rich fried dough. The coffee, as you may have noticed, bears no pretense whatsoever of delicacy. As you will no doubt appreciate when you awake tomorrow afternoon, Spanish coffee is potent, for it assumes that you have had a rough night.

The day is reserved for the Prado museum and the grandeur of Goya, Velásquez, and El Greco. Housed in an only slightly grandiose building, the art speaks for itself, making the Prado one of the most accessible and personable big museums in the world. A stroll amidst the statues of Retiro Park, and thoughts once again turn to food.

In *The Garden of Eden*, David and Catherine Bourne visit Madrid and the Prado, afterwards dining at a restaurant in an old, stone-walled building. They sip glasses of manzanilla and eat jamón serrano, spicy sausage, anchovies, and garlic olives. Afterward they enjoy peppery gazpacho and drink Valdepeñas wine from a large pitcher.

Garlic Olives

1 cup small, green olives
3 cloves garlic, crushed
Virgin olive oil or brine, to cover

Combine the olives and garlic in a bowl or glass jar. Add enough olive oil or brine to cover. Marinate for several hours before using. Olives will keep for up to 1 month at room temperature or 3 months in the refrigerator.

These olives may also be used in a Super Montgomery (see page 189).

Gazpacho

It came in a large bowl with ice floating with the slices of crisp cucumber, tomato, garlic bread, green and red peppers, and the coarsely peppered liquid that tasted lightly of oil and vinegar.[9]

This bright-flavored, chilled soup was originally prepared in Spain for the farm workers as they left to work in the fields. It becomes a hearty meal in itself when served with wine and firm, crusty bread. You will often find gazpacho prepared as a thin blend of vegetables in a tomato base. In fact, it is served this way in the Hostal Burguete today, and it is exquisite. I for one cannot imagine a barrel-chested young Ernest Hemingway sitting down and sipping that broth. Like the farm workers themselves gazpacho must be rugged.

6 SERVINGS

2 cloves garlic, peeled and finely chopped, and 3 cloves garlic, peeled only

½ green bell pepper, coarsely chopped

½ red bell pepper, coarsely chopped

½ yellow onion, coarsely chopped

5 very ripe tomatoes, coarsely chopped

1 medium cucumber, peeled and chopped, and 1 medium cucumber, peeled and thinly sliced

¼ cup olive oil

2 tablespoons red wine vinegar

½ teaspoon cumin

1 tablespoon Tabasco sauce

1 cup ice water

2 cups tomato juice

Salt

Pepper

Garlic bread croutons (see below)

Combine all of the ingredients, except the whole garlic cloves and the croutons. Taste repeatedly and adjust seasoning to your own taste. I often add another ½ cucumber, finely chopped, and a splash more Tabasco.

Chill well, pour into bowls, and garnish with croutons.

For the croutons, slice French bread thin, lightly fry on both sides in olive oil, then rub both sides of the bread with the whole cloves of garlic. You can either cube the bread or leave it whole, and place a few pieces in each bowl.

For Jake and Brett in *The Sun Also Rises*, dining in Madrid means only Casa Botín, the oldest continuous restaurant in the world. The Antigua Casa Sobrino de Botín, opened in 1725, was forever a Hemingway favorite, so much so that the next restaurant up the street has written on its awning (in English), "Ernest Hemingway never ate here." Casa Botín may be full of tourists, but its long history before Don Ernesto secured a culinary tradition of country fare that remains unmatched. The wine flows hearty and deep beside a giant brick oven offering suckling pig and roast lamb. In Casa Botín you truly feast. Hemingway, infamous for hosting marathon lunches and dinners throughout Spain, wouldn't have it any other way. We may leave Casa Botín just before midnight, yet the evening in Madrid is just beginning.

CRAIG BORETH

Casa Botín, Madrid, Spain.

Dinner at Casa Botín

Cochinillo Asado

Wine

Rioja Alta

————

98

Cochinillo Asado (Roast Suckling Pig)

We lunched up-stairs at Botín's. It's one of the best restaurants in the world. We had roast young suckling pig and drank rioja alta. Brett did not eat much. She never ate much. I ate a very big meal and drank three bottles of rioja alta.[10]

This recipe is adapted from Casa Botín in Madrid, the oldest restaurant in the world. I would like to thank Antonio Gonzalez II, and everyone at Botín, for their hospitality and charm.

6 SERVINGS

  1 8- to 10-pound suckling pig
  ½ pound lard
  Salt
  Pepper
  2–3 sprigs fresh parsley
  1 sprig fresh thyme
  2 bay leaves
  2 cloves garlic
  1 small onion
  1 cup dry white wine
  2½ cups water

Preheat the oven to 450° F.

Have your butcher butterfly the pig, or do it yourself by opening the underside, leaving the backbone and the head intact. Rub the skin with the lard and season with salt and pepper. Place the pig in a large clay casserole, skin-side down. Chop the herbs, garlic, and onion and spread evenly across the body of the pig. Pour the wine and water into the casserole. Place the casserole in the oven and cook for 45 minutes. Drain off the extra liquid and melted fat and roast for another 45 minutes. Turn the pig over, skin-side up, and roast for another 30 to 45 minutes, or until golden and crunchy. Pour off the juice and serve it in a gravy boat. Pig may be accompanied with a salad or surrounded with roasted potatoes.

Alternative: To truly re-create the wood-fired stoves of Botín's, use an outdoor grill and add pine or ash wood chips to the coals.

Madrid is a city, indeed Spain a country, of endless adventure. Each turn in the road finds succulent diversions for all of the senses. In Madrid your head swims with memories and dreamy landscapes of food and wine. The clay-brown plains and stormy dark seas. The mountains and churches, of equal antiquity. In the early hours in Madrid, the world celebrates this land. The gift of Spain shall not go unappreciated. It is in good hands.

For Whom the Bell Tolls

In July 1936, the civil war began in Spain, pitting the right-wing Nationalist forces led by Francisco Franco against the Republicans, also known as Loyalists. Initially Hemingway remained neutral. Eventually, through the urging of many people, including journalist and would-be third wife Martha Gellhorn, Ernest came to see the Loyalists as the lesser of two evils. Much more clearly he saw the conflict in Spain as a prelude to war across Europe, and in February 1937, he left for his first of four tours as war correspondent for the *North American Newspaper Alliance* (NANA).

Sensing that a larger war was imminent, Hemingway did not wait 10 years to write his novel of this war, as he had with *A Farewell to Arms*. He began *For Whom the Bell Tolls* in March 1939, six months before Germany invaded Poland. It was published in October 1940 and was a huge success, becoming the biggest best-seller since *Gone with the Wind*.

The novel takes place northwest of Madrid, high in the Sierra de Guadarrama mountains, late in May 1937. Robert Jordan, a young Spanish professor from Montana, has joined a band of Loyalist guerrillas well behind the fascist lines. Through telling the story of Jordan's mission— the destruction of a steel bridge coordinated with a surprise Loyalist attack—Hemingway expressed his distaste for both sides and the deep sorrow he felt at seeing his beloved Spain torn apart. He showed us the nightmares of the characters' present lives and shared their fond daydreams of a past that grew more and more distant each day of the war.

With the guerrillas in the mountains, we dine on rabbit stew and coarse red wine. Robert Jordan sits with the band of *guerrilleros* for their first meal, drinking wine and eating together. He meets María, a beautiful young girl who suffered terribly at the hands of the fascists. She brings the rabbit stew, prepared by Pilar, the woman of Pablo, described as "Something barbarous . . . Something very barbarous. If you think Pablo is ugly you should see his woman. But brave. A hundred times braver than Pablo. But something barbarous."[11]

Pilar's Rabbit Stew

They were all eating out of the platter, not speaking, as is the Spanish custom. It was rabbit cooked with onions and green peppers and there were chick peas in the red wine sauce. It was well cooked, the rabbit meat flaked off the bones, and the sauce was delicious. Robert Jordan drank another cup of wine while he ate. The girl watched him all through the meal.[12]

4 SERVINGS

1 3- to 4-pound rabbit
2 cups red wine
4 onions, coarsely chopped
4 green bell peppers, coarsely chopped
1 cup chickpeas

1 bay leaf
2 tablespoons paprika
2 teaspoons salt
3 tablespoons all-purpose flour

Cut the rabbit into pieces. Place in a stew kettle with the wine, onions, peppers, chickpeas, bay leaf, paprika, and salt. Add enough cold water to cover and cook covered over low heat for 2 hours. Combine the flour with 4 tablespoons cold water and mix until smooth. Add to the stew and stir until slightly thickened. Serve with plenty of crusty bread.

A Valencia Escape

For now, newly arrived in the hills and hungry, Robert Jordan savors the simple stew. When the war turns bad in the north, and the food remains the same meal after meal, Jordan, too, may lift his spirits with Pilar's reminiscence of high-spirited Valencia, and the food and drink that only memory and tragedy can hold so well.

We ate in pavilions on the sand. Pastries made of cooked and shredded fish and red and green peppers and small nuts like grains of rice. Pastries delicate and flaky and the fish of a richness that was incredible. Prawns fresh from the sea sprinkled with lime juice. They were pink and sweet and there were four bites to a prawn. Of those we ate many. Then we ate *paella* with fresh sea food, clams in their shells, mussels, crayfish, and small eels.

Then we ate even smaller eels alone cooked in oil and as tiny as bean sprouts and curled in all directions and so tender they disappeared in the mouth without chewing. All the time drinking a white wine, cold, light and good at thirty centimos the bottle.[13]

For the paella, we will defer to the forthcoming section on The Dangerous Summer *(page 104), in which Hemingway enjoys* Paella de Langosta *at La Pepica on the Levante Beach in Valencia. For now, though, there remains the delicious* Empanadilla de Pescado *and the baby eels cooked in oil and garlic.*

101

COURTESY OF LA PEPICA, VALENCIA

Hemingway at La Pepica, Valencia, Spain, 1959. On the far right is Juanita Balaguer.

Pastry of Fish, Peppers, and Pine Nuts (*Empanadilla de Pescado*)

6 SERVINGS

For the Dough

1 cup water
¼ teaspoon salt
3 tablespoons butter
3 tablespoons vegetable oil
2½ cups all-purpose, unbleached flour
1 large egg

For the Filling

2 tablespoons olive oil
1 onion, chopped
1 green bell pepper, chopped
1 pound fillet of haddock, cod, or sole, cut into thin strips
1 tomato, peeled and chopped
2 cloves garlic, minced
1 tablespoon chopped fresh parsley
½ teaspoon paprika
1 teaspoon salt
Freshly ground black pepper
¼ cup chopped olives
1 hard-boiled egg, chopped
¼ cup pine nuts
Oil for frying

To make the dough, in a medium saucepan, heat the water, salt, butter, and oil over medium heat until butter is melted. Remove from heat. Add the flour to the saucepan and stir, incorporating flour completely. Add the egg and beat with a wooden spoon until the dough is smooth. Turn the dough out onto a floured board and knead lightly. Add more flour, if necessary, and continue kneading until the dough is no longer sticky. Form dough into a ball, cover with a towel, and let stand for 30 minutes. Roll out dough until very thin and cut out 3- to 4-inch circles.

To make the filling, heat the olive oil in a skillet. Add the chopped onion and green pepper and sauté until soft, about 10 minutes. Add the fish, tomato, garlic, parsley, paprika, salt, and pepper to taste. Reduce heat and cook, stirring frequently, for about 10 minutes. Remove from the heat, allow to cool, and mix in the olives, chopped egg, and pine nuts.

To assemble the *empanadillas*, place a heaping tablespoon of the fish mixture in the center of each round of dough. Bring up the sides of the sides of the dough and pinch closed around the semicircle. Lay the *empanadilla* flat and press the seam with the tines of a fork to seal. Pour oil into a skillet to a depth of at least 1 inch, or into a deep fryer. Heat the oil until hot. Fry the *empanadillas*, turning once, until golden brown on both sides. Drain on brown paper or paper towels.

Sharing a table in Pamplona, Spain, 1926. (Left to right) Gerald and Sara Murphy, Pauline Pfeiffer, and Ernest and Hadley Hemingway.

Fried Baby Eels

4 SERVINGS

3 cups (about ¾ pound) baby eels
½ cup olive oil
3 cloves garlic, sliced
Salt

Rinse the eels and pat dry on paper towels. Heat the olive oil in a large skillet over high heat. Add the garlic, fry until lightly browned, and remove. Add the eels and toss gently until golden. Drain the eels on paper towels or brown paper, dust with salt to taste, and serve.

The Dangerous Summer

Twenty years later, Hemingway wrote the final chapter of his Spanish adventures, covering one of the greatest bullfighting duels in the country's history. *Mano a manos* are unusual. *Mano a manos* between two of Spain's greatest matadors are rare indeed. Seldom is there one truly great matador in Spain, let alone two fighting at the same time. In the summer of 1959, there were Luis Miguel Dominguín and Antonio Ordoñez, both great matadors, both friends of Ernest Hemingway, and brothers-in-law besides. When they fought together, the only two men on each afternoon's card, fighting three bulls each instead of the usual two, it was a summer of great rivalry and danger. When one man did something in the ring that was truly brave and artistic and without fear, the other must match it if he was to win the competition. It was a supreme display of Spanish pride, and death was never closer at hand.

Hemingway turned 60 that summer. He went back to Spain to cover the *mano a manos* for *Life* magazine and to update *Death in the Afternoon*. *Life*, which had found great success serializing *The Old Man and the Sea* in 1952, commissioned Hemingway to write a 10,000-word article. The first draft ran 120,000 words and eventually became *The Dangerous Summer*, a complete chronicle of the rivalry between the two matadors. Of equal importance is its value as a window into the life and mind of the aging master. In Pamplona, the fiesta is in some ways changed, in others exactly the same:

In Pamplona we had our old secret places like Marceliano's where we went in the morning to eat and drink and sing after the encierro; Marceliano's where the wood of the tables and the stairs is as clean and scrubbed as the teak decks of a yacht except that the tables are honorably wine-spilled. The wine was as good as when you were twenty-one, and the food as marvelous as always. There were the same songs and good new ones that cracked and suddenly pounded onto the drums and the pipes. The faces that were young once were as old as mine but everyone remembered how we were. . . . Nobody was defeated.[14]

Matador's Feast

There was great food during that summer, including picnics back at the Irati River above Pamplona, lunches of cold, smoked trout, eggplant, pimientos, and Navarra black grapes before returning to Pamplona for the afternoon bullfights. But the meal that takes center stage during this epic drama is dinner at Pepica's, on the beach in Valencia:

> Dinner at Pepica's was wonderful. It was a big, clean, open-air place and everything was cooked in plain sight. You could pick out what you wanted to have grilled or broiled and the seafood and the Valencian rice dishes were the best on the beach. Everyone felt good after the fight and we were all hungry . . .
>
> We drank sangria, red wine with fresh orange and lemon juice in it, served in big pitchers and ate local sausages to start with, fresh tuna, fresh prawns, and crisp fried octopus tentacles that tasted like lobster. . . . It was a very moderate meal by Valencian standards and the woman who owned the place was worried that we would go away hungry.[15]

Sangría

Most sangría recipes you encounter these days have brandy, Cointreau, or other liquor. This classic, simple recipe is just wine, citrus, and sparkling water.

2 TO 4 SERVINGS

> 1 bottle full-bodied, dry red wine
> Juice of 1 lemon
> 1 orange, sliced
> ¾ cup sparkling water, or to taste

In a large pitcher, combine the wine, lemon juice, orange slices, and sparkling water. Add ice. Stir and serve.

Fried Octopus

4 APPETIZER SERVINGS

Meat from 1 small octopus
3 large eggs, slightly beaten
3 tablespoons milk
Salt and Pepper
Oil for frying

Prepare the octopus as for *Pulpo a la Vinagreta* (see page 92), to the point when the tentacles have been cut into pieces.

Combine the eggs, milk, and salt and pepper to taste in a bowl. Add the octopus pieces and stir to coat. Heat the oil in a skillet over high heat. When hot, add the octopus, a few pieces at a time. Fry until lightly browned, turning a few times. Remove the octopus, drain on brown paper or paper towels, and serve immediately.

Paella de Langosta

Hemingway remembered a great many foods at La Pepica that summer. Juanita Balaguer, who still runs La Pepica today in her nineties, remembers Ernest's fondness for this one dish in particular. I would like to thank Luis and José, as well as Juanita herself, for their generous assistance in developing a written record of this dish. Of course, without the real hardwood charcoal, the paella pans cured over generations, and a certain magic that exists only in the Valencian kitchen, we may only hope to create a respectable facsimile of the genuine article. For the true effect, one must dine, as Hemingway repeatedly did, at La Pepica. It is truly, as Penelope Casas claims, "the paella mecca of the world."[16]

4 SERVINGS

2 small lobsters, about 1¼ pound each
3 cups clam juice
1 cup water
1 bay leaf
1 cup dry white wine
Large pinch of saffron threads
½ cup olive oil
6 cloves garlic, minced
1 tablespoon chopped fresh parsley
1 red bell pepper, coarsely chopped
2 tomatoes, peeled and seeded
1 tablespoon Spanish paprika
2 cups arborio or other short-grain rice
Salt
Lemon wedges, for garnish

To prepare the lobster stock, you must first kill the lobsters. This may be done one of two ways: either insert a knife in the first joint behind the head, which instantly kills them, or place them in boiling water for about 5 minutes. If you choose the latter method, add the lobster pieces to the paella pan just before adding the rice, rather than at the very beginning.

Remove the tail and claws from the lobsters, setting the bodies aside. Crack the claws and knuckles and cut the tail (with the shell still on) into 3 or 4 pieces with kitchen scissors. Place the lobster pieces in a bowl, cover with plastic wrap, and refrigerate.

In a medium stockpot, combine the lobster bodies, clam juice, water, and bay leaf. Bring stock to a boil, reduce the heat, and simmer for 20 minutes. Strain the stock. There should be about 3½ cups of stock. If there is more, return the stock to the pot and continue to simmer until reduced to 3½ cups. Stir in the wine and saffron.

In a food processor, combine ¼ cup of the olive oil,

CRAIG BORETH

Today at age ninety, Juanita Balaguer pictured with Luis and José, still runs the restaurant.

2 cloves of garlic, and the parsley. Pulse together quickly and set aside. This mixture is known as *picado*.

Preheat the oven to 400° F.

Place a 14-inch paella pan or large cast-iron skillet over high heat. Add remaining ¼ cup oil and the lobster pieces and sauté for a minute or two. Add red pepper and sauté for 1–2 minutes. Add the tomato and remaining 4 cloves of garlic and sauté 1 minute more. Stir in the paprika and *picado*. Then add the rice and stir to coat completely. Stir in the lobster stock and cook, simmering vigorously, for about 15 minutes, or until most of the fluid has been absorbed. Taste the broth and add salt to taste. Place the paella in the oven and cook for 10 to 15 minutes, or until the rice is slightly browned on top. Remove pan, cover, and let stand for 5 to 10 minutes. Garnish with lemon wedges and serve.

5

KEY WEST AND CUBA

Sailing the Stream

"What do you have to eat?" the boy asked.

"A pot of yellow rice with fish. Do you want some?"

"No. I will eat at home. Do you want me to make the fire?"

"No. I will make it later on. Or I may eat the rice cold."

"May I take the cast net?"

"Of course."

There was no cast net and the boy remembered when they had sold it. But they went through this fiction every day. There was no pot of yellow rice and fish and the boy knew this too.

"Eighty-five is a lucky number," the old man said.

—The Old Man and the Sea

Ernest and Joe Russell raise a toast.

ANITA

V. 10748

The *Anita* was the model for Harry Morgan's boat in *To Have and Have Not.*

Key West

Hemingway first discovered Key West, Florida, more by accident than design, in 1928. He and his second wife, Pauline Pfeiffer, had stopped there briefly en route from Paris to Piggott, Arkansas, and Kansas City where she would give birth to Ernest's second son, Patrick. Pauline's wealthy Uncle Gus had arranged for a man from Ford to meet the Hemingways upon their arrival and present them with a new Ford Roadster. There was no man from Ford and no car, and the Hemingways spent most of April and May 1928 in Key West. Ernest was in high spirits. His work on *A Farewell to Arms* was going well, and he was discovering saltwater fishing in the afternoons and the saloons of Key West at night (Prohibition never quite caught on in Key West). His fondness for the charming yet dilapidated little island grew along with the manuscript, and when it came time for Ernest and Pauline to return to Paris they chose instead to spend the winter of 1928 in the warmth and sun of Key West.[1]

Fitzgerald had a theory that Ernest would need a new woman for each new novel. Apparently there would be new homes as well. Ernest lived in Key West, in the house at 907 Whitehead Street that Uncle Gus bought, until he left for Cuba and another wife in April 1939. In the years between, he became (and remained long after his death), Key West's most famous resident. The Hemingway House, filled with cats, would become its most famous landmark, and Sloppy Joe's, his favorite old watering hole, would thrive forever on the legacy of his patronage.

Hemingway arrived in Key West working on *A Farewell to Arms*, and some say he left while starting *For Whom the Bell Tolls*. The Key West years were the most productive in his career, also including *Death in the Afternoon*, *The Green Hills of Africa*, and the short stories "The Short Happy Life of Francis Macomber" and "The Snows of Kilimanjaro."

Cuba

When you do something which people do not consider a serious occupation and yet you know, truly, that it is as important and has always been as important as all the things that are in fashion, and when, on the sea, you are alone with it and know that this Gulf Stream you are living with, knowing, learning about, and loving, has moved, as it moves, since before man, and that it has gone by the shoreline of that long, beautiful, unhappy island since before Columbus sighted it and that the things you find out about it, and those that have always lived in it are permanent and of value because that stream will flow, as it has flowed, after the Indians, after the Spaniards, after the British, after the Americans and after all the Cubans and all the systems of governments, the richness, the poverty, the martyrdom, the sacrifice and the venality and the cruelty are all gone.[2]

Upon settling in Key West, Ernest immediately took full advantage of Cuba's proximity, fishing in the Gulf Stream and taking writing retreats to the Ambos Mundos Hotel in Havana. In April 1939, when his marriage to Pauline was all but over and his marriage to journalist Martha Gellhorn only awaited the divorce papers, he moved to Cuba to live with Martha. His fame and need for privacy had outgrown his hotel room, and Martha soon rented an old estate called the Finca Vigía in the hills of San Francisco de Paula outside Havana, for $100 a month. For Christmas 1940, Hemingway purchased the estate, whose name means "Lookout Farm," an appropriate title given the clear view of San Francisco de Paula and Havana it commands from its hillside perch.

It was there that the celebrity and legend of Ernest Hemingway grew to its full stature. He wrote little fiction in the first years in Cuba, spending his time on correspondence and fishing. He had purchased the *Pilar*, a 38-foot Playmate cabin cruiser, in 1934 while living in Key West. The *Pilar* had the range to take him on 100-mile cruises to fish for giant marlin in the warm Cuban waters. Now that he lived in Cuba, with the *Pilar* moored in Cojimar or Havana Harbor, the lure of the big fish was as strong as that of the bullfights or the wild game. It became one of his greatest passions, and his happy years fishing the Gulf Stream aboard the *Pilar* and its rented predecessor, the *Anita* out of Key West, inspired such works as *To Have and Have Not*, *Islands in the Stream*, and *The Old Man and the Sea*.

Hemingway brought to both Key West and Cuba his appetites for food and drink. Aboard the *Pilar* he was treated to native dishes by his mate and cook, Gregorio Fuentes, whom Hemingway would pit against the chef of the Ritz in Paris in their own culinary *mano a manos*.

Closer to home, the Finca Vigía's kitchen was eventually ruled by Mary, another journalist who Ernest met while in Europe during World War II. In 1946 Mary became Hemingway's fourth wife. She was the only one of his wives to take a genuine interest in cooking, and she enjoyed the experimentation and challenge of overseeing the meals prepared for her husband and the endless stream of visitors to the resort that their home had become. The diversity of notables who visited was only surpassed by the variety of cuisine. Mary recalled one dish and one visitor in particular: "I baked a wahoo roast, basting it in Brut champagne, lime juice and chicken broth, for Jean-Paul Sartre when he was here, and he liked it."[3]

Our culinary tour of Key West and Cuba begins with the first of Ernest's novels to feature a Cuban setting: *To Have and Have Not*. Throughout our tropical sojourn, we will experience the splendor of Cuban cuisine, the dangerous watering holes of Prohibition-era Key West, and the characters and anecdotes that surrounded a man whose appetite for food, drink, and life only seemed to grow (often despite doctor's orders) as the years went by.

TO HAVE AND HAVE NOT

Considered by Socialists to be Hemingway's "coming out" novel, *To Have and Have Not* is more likely a product of his gut reaction to the social and financial polarization of Depression-era Key West. It is a story of one man's desperate struggle to simply survive, and no amount of political interpretation can mask the stark humanity of Harry Morgan's failure to do so. The story opens violently in a café in Havana, La Perla de San Francisco, and in the aftermath the food mingles with the fear:

> I went in the Perla and sat down at a table. They had a new pane of glass in the window that had been shot up and the showcase was all fixed up. There were a lot of gallegos drinking at the bar, and some eating. One table was playing dominoes already. I had black bean soup and a beef stew with boiled potatoes for fifteen cents. A bottle of Hatuey beer brought it up to a quarter. When I spoke to the waiter about the shooting he wouldn't say anything. They were all plenty scared.[4]

THE MENU

*La Perla de
San Francisco Café Menu*

Black Bean Soup

Beef Stew with Boiled Potatoes

Hatuey Beer

113

Black Bean Soup

I would like to thank Teresa Merenges-Berry for her assistance with this and several other traditional Cuban recipes in this chapter. She embodies the spirit and character of Cuba and its flavorful and spirited cuisine. Feel free to adjust all of the seasonings to taste. Teresa claims, happily and with a certain degree of pride, that her preparation of this dish has never tasted the same twice. This recipe will create a thick soup that is wonderful by itself or served over rice.

6 SERVINGS

1 pound dry black beans

3 large green bell peppers

1 bay leaf

3 tablespoons olive oil

1½ cups chopped onion

3 cloves garlic, chopped

1 tablespoon cumin

1 tablespoon chopped fresh or ½ teaspoon crushed dried oregano

4–5 small cilantro leaves

Salt

1 tablespoon vinegar

Hot sauce

Rinse the beans, removing any stones. Place the beans in a large bowl and cover with cold water to about 2 inches above the beans. Let soak overnight.

Rinse the beans and place them in a large stockpot. Cover the beans once again with cold water to 2 inches above the top. Add one whole green pepper and the bay leaf to the pot. Bring the pot to a boil. Reduce heat, cover, and simmer for about 1 hour, or until the beans are tender. Discard the pepper and the bay leaf.

Wash, seed, and cube the 2 remaining peppers. Heat the olive oil in a large skillet over medium heat. When the oil is hot, add the peppers and cook for 1 minute. Add the onion and cook for 1 minute. Add the garlic and cook for 1 minute more. Stir the vegetables into the beans. Add the cumin, oregano, cilantro, and salt to taste. Cook, uncovered, for about 30 minutes, or until thickened to taste. Add the vinegar and hot sauce and adjust seasonings to taste.

Beef Stew with Boiled Potatoes

This recipe for beef stew and potatoes is based on Gregorio Fuentes's version. It is among the handful of treasured secrets that he shared with Mary Hemingway over the years of their acquaintance.[5] As was characteristic of Fuentes's cooking style, it is simply prepared, with just a touch of magic. Mary recalls that Gregorio usually served this dish with white rice. While he never seemed to measure the rice, water, or timing, it always seemed perfectly prepared. She fondly remembers lounging on the afterdeck aboard the Pilar, *when suddenly Gregorio would leap down to the galley and remove the pot from the fire. His secret was the*

Mealtime aboard the *Pilar*.

smell. When the rice began to "smell faintly, barely noticeably, of mothballs," then it was cooked to perfection. I would suggest following the directions on the package, as not all of us are blessed with Gregorio's gastronomic inspiration.

4 SERVINGS

¼ cup lard

2 onions, chopped

3 cloves garlic, minced

1¼ cups tomato purée

¾ cup chopped tomatoes

1 can, or 2 whole, pimientos, finely chopped

1 cup sherry

1 tablespoon crushed dried oregano

1 bay leaf

1 pound stew beef, cut into bite-size pieces

3 medium potatoes, cut into small chunks

First prepare the sauce, with plenty of garlic (feel free to add more if desired): heat the lard in a kettle over medium heat. When hot, add the onions and garlic and sauté until the onions are translucent. Add the tomato purée, chopped tomatoes, pimientos, sherry, oregano, and bay leaf. Simmer for 15 minutes, adjusting the seasoning to taste. Add the beef. Simmer the stew over low heat for 1 hour. Add the potatoes and continue cooking for an additional 20 minutes, or until potatoes are just tender. Serve over rice.

116

HATUEY BEER

Hemingway's palate for wine and stronger drinks overshadowed his taste for beer. That is not to say he didn't enjoy and write about beer frequently throughout his life. His favorite during the Cuban years was Hatuey, brewed in Cotorro, a town near his home in San Francisco de Paula, by the good people at the Bacardí Company. Aboard the *Pilar* there was always a generous supply of Hatuey (or another beer called Tropical) in the ice box that ran across the stern of the boat. Hemingway mentioned the brew in both *To Have and Have Not* and *The Old Man and the Sea*, when the owner of the Terraza sends along two returnable bottles of Hatuey along with the plates of food. The owners of Hatuey and Bacardí did not allow Hemingway's endorsement to go unrecognized, although it's likely he wished they had.

On August 13, 1956, the owners of the brewery organized a tribute to Hemingway, in honor of his presence in Cuba and his receiving the Nobel Prize in 1954. Hemingway was celebrated for his friendship with local fishermen, his larger-than-life character and talent, and, of course, his assistance in promoting the cosponsors, Hatuey and Bacardí, in his novels.

Sloppy Joe's: The Fiction and the Facts

"It's a strange place," said Professor MacWalsey. "Fascinating, really. They call it the Gibraltar of America and it's three hundred and seventy-five miles south of Cairo, Egypt. But this place is the only part of it I've had time to see yet. It's a fine place though."[6]

It is not clear exactly when Ernest first entered the little, cavelike bar on Green Street, although we could safely assume it was very shortly after checking into the La Concha Hotel in early April 1928. One thing we do know is that in many ways he never left. The bar has changed names a few times, but its legacy of intrigue, utility, romance, superstition, and literature has remained. When Hemingway first ordered a Scotch at the Silver Slipper, he hitched his youthful legend to a bar that could hold its own as far as legends were concerned. When Joe Russell, who owned the bar in the 1930s, cashed a Scribner's royalty check for Ernest, the legends of man and bar would henceforth be immutably intertwined.

In 1851, the Key West icehouse was built from disassembled pirate ships confiscated off South America. Shortly thereafter, well before its inventory would be used to chill whiskey, it was used to chill dead bodies. By the mid-1850s, the building was converted to the city morgue. Ten years later, a tremendous hurricane struck Key West, causing severe flooding and burying many of the morgue's inhabitants under several feet of mud.

Hemingway with friends and a bottle of Hatuey beer.

There they remain to this day, under what is now the pool room. Not to worry, though—their spirits have been mollified. Several members of the large Bahamian population of Key West warded off any wayward spirits with bottles of holy water, the empty remains of which may still be found there today.

This nondescript little building also served as the first telegraph station of Key West and was home to the city's hanging tree, both of which prompted its inclusion in the National Historic Registry. In the late 1870s, it first became a bar, the Silver Slipper. And there Hemingway found it on a hot spring afternoon, having just arrived from Paris.

After Joe Russell bought the bar in 1933, it became the successful young writer's favorite watering hole, Sloppy Joe's. There Hemingway

117

Ernest in the *Pilar* trailed by Mary in the *Tin Kid*, sailing past Morro Castle in 1947, Cuba.

found a setting for the barroom brawls of *To Have and Have Not* and met his eventual third wife, Martha Gellhorn, in December 1936.

Sloppy Joe's moved to Duvall Street in 1937, where it remains the epicenter in name, if not in place, of Hemingway's presence in Key West. Where the original Sloppy Joe's stood is now a bar called Capt. Tony's Saloon, the oldest bar in Key West. In the 1960s Tennessee Williams lived upstairs, Truman Capote dropped by for a while, and Jimmy Buffett found a place to sing. To this day Hemingway's legacy has been preserved at Capt. Tony's. While Sloppy Joe's may thrive on his name and face and the Papa Dobles they serve, Capt. Tony's will always play host to Hemingway's spirit in Key West.

119

Captain Tony's Saloon was the original Sloppy Joe's from 1933 to 1937.

Islands in the Stream

As he had done in Key West with Sloppy Joe's, Hemingway began to mingle his legend with local institutions in and around Havana as well. He would later claim that his attraction to bars and restaurants like El Floridita and La Terraza in Cojímar was not solely the food or drink. Even though he would often go through a dozen Daiquirís in one sitting, it was more the characters that inhabited these places that he truly enjoyed. Many of them appear in *To Have and Have Not* as well as in the posthumously published *Islands in the Stream*, which was originally part of his Sea trilogy. This story, begun in the early 1950s, is about Thomas Hudson, a good painter who will not get better. Hudson bears a striking resemblance to his creator, not solely for his hunting for German submarines, as Hemingway did aboard the *Pilar*. In addition they share the pleasure of La Terraza, a bar in Cojímar "built out on the rocks overlooking the harbor."[7] It was here that Hemingway may have founded his Royal Order of Shrimp Eaters and where he bestows upon Thomas Hudson the semifictional cat, Boise, with the presumptuous eating habits:

> The proprietor of the bar had asked him, "Do you want some shrimps?" and brought a big plate piled with fresh cooked prawns and put it on the bar while he sliced a yellow lime and spread the slices on a saucer. The prawns were huge and pink and their antennae hung down over the edge of the bar for more than a foot and he had picked one up and spread the long whiskers to their full width and remarked that they were longer than those of a Japanese admiral.

> Thomas Hudson broke the head off the Japanese admiral prawn and then split open the belly of the shell with his thumbs and shucked the prawn out and it was so fresh and silky feeling under his teeth, and had such a flavor, cooked in sea water with fresh lime juice and whole black peppercorns, that he thought he had never eaten a better one; not even in Málaga nor in Tarragona nor in Valencia. It was then that the kitten came over to him, scampering down the bar, to rub against his hand and beg a prawn.[8]

120

Prawns in Sea Water

4 SERVINGS

  8 cups sea water (fresh water with sea salt will suffice)

  4 tablespoons fresh lime juice

  6 whole black peppercorns

  2 pounds prawns (with the heads still attached) or jumbo shrimp

  2 limes, quartered

Combine the water (and salt, if necessary), lime juice, and peppercorns in a saucepan and bring to a boil. Add the prawns or shrimp and boil for 5 minutes, or until the prawns turn bright pink. Drain the prawns and plunge immediately into a bowl of ice water. Drain again and serve, piled on a plate with lime quarters.

ROYAL ORDER OF SHRIMP EATERS

Hemingway had a penchant for turning the mundane into the regal and renowned (if not infamous). We encountered a fictional example of this with Colonel Cantwell's *El Ordine Militar, Nobile y Espirituoso de los Caballeros de Brusadelli* (see page 30). In real life, Hemingway once formed a legal partnership with friend, biographer, and traveling companion, A. E. Hotchner, known as Hemhotch, Ltd. The partnership was originally formed as a racing syndicate to cover their bets on the steeplechase at Auteuil. Eventually, they had greeting cards made (as was the European custom at the time) announcing the partnership's diversification beyond the races and into such endeavors as duck hunting, the bullfights and other masculine pursuits.[9]

In Havana, Hemingway introduced Hotchner to yet another quasi-formal order he had founded. As the two sat before a heaping plate of unpeeled shrimp, Hemingway informed Hotchner that should he wish to join The Royal Order of Shrimp Eaters, there is but one membership requirement: that he eat the shrimp complete with the heads and tails. Hemingway happily crunched one of the large shrimp. Hotchner followed, with markedly less enthusiasm.[10]

If you so choose, you may take this opportunity to induct yourself into this prestigious order. I won't recommend repeating the initiation often enough for it to grow on you, though. That's for inductees to decide on their own.

In the novel, the proprietor of La Terraza gives Thomas Hudson the prawn-begging Angora Tiger cat as a Christmas gift. It was Gregorio Fuentes who gave Hemingway the real-life cat, named Boise, who maintained the same high gastronomic standards as her owners. Mary Hemingway thought Boise "one of the world's most sophisticated cats in his food preferences,"[11] who, even after eating melons and sauerkraut and chili and pie, "still jumps like a feather in the breeze."[12] Soon after Thomas Hudson takes Boise home from La Terraza, he learns of the cat's rather precocious eating habits:

Then when the alligator pear trees, the big, dark green *aguacates* with their fruit only a little darker and shinier than the foliage, had come into bearing this time when he had been ashore in September for overhaul, preparing to go down to Haiti, he had offered Boise a spoonful out of the shell, the hollow where the seed had been, filled with oil and vinegar dressing, and the cat had eaten it and then afterwards at each meal, he had eaten half an *aguacate*.[13]

122

Boise's Avocado

Note: A ripe avocado should be firm but forgiving. Be careful to buy neither too hard nor too soft a fruit. To seed the avocado, cut along the fruit laterally, down to the round central pit, then twist the two halves apart. To remove the pit, strike the pit with a large, sharp knife, firmly enough that the blade will stick. Twist the knife and remove the pit.

3 HUMANS AND 1 CAT

> 2 avocados
>
> Lime juice
>
> 6 tablespoons olive oil
>
> 2 tablespoons white vinegar (or a combination of white and wine vinegars)
>
> Pinch of salt

Cut the avocados in half, remove the pits and sprinkle with lime juice to prevent browning. Whisk together the olive oil, vinegar, and salt. Fill the hollow of each half with dressing.

Islands in the Stream is a mosaic of Hemingway's reminiscences, including his memories of his three sons, his third wife, his early days in Michigan, his life in Paris, and his later adventures in the 1930s and 1940s. Sitting on his hillside Cuban perch, Ernest had endless opportunities to remember—looking back through time and across the ocean—to his former lives. From Paris to Marseilles to Hong Kong, these memories are invariably infused with the tastes and smells of the foods therein. Hemingway would not begin to write his full memoirs of Paris until 1957, when he began *A Moveable Feast*. In *Islands in the Stream*, we get a taste of things to come:

> "Papa, tell us some more about when you and Tommy and Tommy's mother were poor. How poor did you ever get?"

> "They were pretty poor," Roger said. "I can remember when your father used to make up all young Tom's bottles in the morning and go to the market to buy the best and the cheapest vegetables. I'd meet him coming back from the market when I would be going out for breakfast."

> "I was the finest judge of poireaux in the sixth arrondissement." Thomas Hudson told the boys.

> "What's poireaux?"

> "Leeks."

> "It looks like long, green, quite big onions," young Tom said. "Only it's not bright shiny like onions. It's dull shiny. The leaves are green and the ends are white. You boil it and eat it cold with olive oil and vinegar mixed with salt and pepper. You eat the whole thing, top and all. It's delicious. I believe I've eaten as much of it as maybe anyone in the world."[14]

Young Tom Hudson's Leeks

It is fitting that Tom Hudson had become such a connoisseur of leeks and that young Tom had enjoyed them so regularly during the lean years in Paris. Poireaux is known in France as les asperges de pauvre *("the asparagus of the poor").*

1 SERVING

> 1 leek, as small as possible
> 3 tablespoons olive oil
> 1 tablespoon vinegar
> Salt
> Pepper

Cut only the very top green and bottom root off the leek. Carefully clean out any sand from between the layers. Bring water to a boil in a pan large enough to hold the whole leek. Plunge the leek into the boiling water and cook for 10–15 minutes, or until the white part is tender. Drain the leek, pat dry, and refrigerate until chilled. Whisk together the olive oil, vinegar, and salt and pepper to taste. Serve sliced in half lengthwise and drizzled with the vinaigrette.

Back in Cuba a strong northwester churns the sea, blowing severe and cold and forcing Thomas Hudson ashore. He is content to let the Germans rule the sea for a few days and enjoys the company of his cats and his memories. He longs to make love to a princess, wanton and feline, and remembers his one royal affair, with a "plain girl with thickish ankles and not very good legs."[15] They were sailing from Mombasa, returning from safari, aboard a super luxury liner, and the denial of their passion became more dangerous than their possible discovery by the Prince. Hudson and the Baron, who was also on board ("Isn't it nice to have a wicked Baron just as in olden times?"),[16] get off the ship in Marseilles. Hemingway himself shared those cold afternoons in Marseilles in November 1933. He waited to depart for East Africa aboard the *SS General Metzinger*, hardly a luxury liner, like the Gripsholm upon which he would eventually return and on which Thomas Hudson's affair must have occurred. He held onto the memories of the city, of its sidewalk restaurants in the Vieux Port, and when he brought Thomas Hudson's memories there in *Islands in the Stream*, he knew exactly how to welcome him:

> It was blowing colder than ever outside. It reminded him of the cold day there on the steep street in Marseilles that ran down to the port, sitting at the café table with their coat collars up eating the moules out of the thin black shells you lifted from the hot, peppery milk broth with the hot melted butter floating in it, drinking the wine from Tavel that tasted the way Provence looked . . .
>
> "Do you want some more moules?"
>
> "No. I want something solid."
>
> "Shouldn't we have bouillabaisse, too?"
>
> "Two soups?"
>
> "I'm hungry. And we won't be here again for a long time."
>
> "I should think you might be hungry. Good. We'll have a bouillabaisse and then a good Châteaubriand very rare. I'll build you up, you bastard."[17]

*Lunch in Marseilles
with the Baron*

Moules in Peppery Milk Broth

Bouillabaisse de Marseilles

Châteaubriand

Wine

Tavel

Moules (Mussels) in Peppery Milk Broth

2 TO 3 SERVINGS

1 pound mussels

Several tablespoons cornmeal

1½ cups dry white wine

Bouquet garni (a few sprigs of parsley, thyme, rosemary, and a few bay leaves bundled and tied together)

3 cloves garlic, crushed

¼ cup olive oil

½ onion, coarsely chopped

1 tablespoon all-purpose flour

¼ cup milk

Plenty of coarsely ground fresh black pepper

Salt

Pinch of cayenne pepper

Juice of ¼ lemon

2 tablespoons heavy cream

1 tablespoon butter

Scrub the mussels, removing any mussels with broken shells or that don't close up tight when placed under running cold water. Debeard the mussels (pull or cut off the fibrous growth attached to the shell). Place the mussels in a large bowl and cover with cold water. Sprinkle on the cornmeal, which will help the mussels to expel their sand and fatten up a little. Let the mussels soak for about 15 minutes then drain.

125

In a large skillet over high heat, combine the wine, herbs, and garlic. Add the mussels and cook, tightly covered, until the shells open, 5–7 minutes. Remove the mussels, disregarding any that have not opened. Remove the empty half of each shell and arrange the mussels in a shallow serving dish. Cover with foil to keep warm.

Strain the mussel cooking liquid through a fine mesh sieve or cheesecloth and set aside. In a large saucepan over medium heat, add the olive oil and onion and sauté until the onion is soft. Stir in the flour and cook a few minutes more. Remove the pan from the heat. Beat in the cooking liquid and the milk. Return to the heat and bring to a boil. Add the pepper, salt, and cayenne to taste, and lemon juice. Reduce heat and simmer for 10 minutes. Stir in the cream and butter and pour the sauce over the mussels. Serve immediately.

Bouillabaisse de Marseilles

As Thomas Hudson and the Baron acknowledge, true bouillabaisse is, in fact, a soup rather than a stew. Marseilles is the home of bouillabaisse, and this recipe attempts to follow the strict traditional guidelines of the genuine article. The key element is the variety of fish that flavor the broth. As this dish was originally prepared on the beach by local fishermen, it included those fish least suited for sale in the marketplace, such as the scorpion fish or rockfish.[18] Even if this and other local fish are unavailable, a respectable facsimile is achieved through use of four or five different types of local fish.

6 TO 8 SERVINGS

> 4 cloves garlic, crushed
>
> 2 onions, chopped
>
> ¾ cup olive oil
>
> 3 tomatoes, skinned and finely chopped
>
> 1 tablespoon chopped fresh parsley
>
> Pinch of dried fennel
>
> 1 bay leaf
>
> 1 sprig thyme
>
> Freshly ground black pepper
>
> Small pinch of saffron threads
>
> 4–5 pounds of fish (such as whiting, bass, red snapper, haddock, cod, or any other firm-fleshed fish), cut into medium-size pieces

1 cup dry white wine

Several cups of boiling water

1 pound mussels (see preparation tips in preceding recipe)

1 pound large shrimp or prawns, sliced in half lengthwise

Parsley for garnish

Several thick slices of bread

In a soup kettle or large heatproof casserole, sauté the garlic and onion in the olive oil until lightly browned. Add the tomatoes, parsley, fennel, bay leaf, thyme, pepper to taste, and saffron. Allow to simmer for a few minutes, then add the fish, white wine, and boiling water to cover. Cover and cook over high heat for 7–8 minutes. Add the mussels, shrimp, and more water to cover. Continue to cook, covered, for another 8 minutes, or until the mussels are open. Remove the fish and shellfish and place in a serving bowl, garnished with chopped parsley. Arrange thick slices of bread in a soup tureen. Strain the bouillabaisse and pour over the bread. Serve the soup and the fish at the same time.

Châteaubriand

Châteaubriand is simply a thickly cut tournedo of between ¾ and 1½ pounds, cut from the thickest part of the fillet. For two people, ¾ pound will suffice. As with tournedos, it is important that they not be overdone but merely seared on the outside and underdone inside.

¾ pound beef fillet

2 tablespoons butter, melted

Salt

Coarsely ground pepper

Preheat the broiler.

Slightly flatten the meat with a cleaver. Brush the meat with butter and lightly season with salt and pepper to taste. Broil the Châteaubriand for about 1 minute on each side, basting with additional butter. Lower the oven temperature to 450° F. Transfer the meat to a rack in a baking dish and roast for 12 to 15 minutes. For very rare, the meat should reach an internal temperature of 115°–120° F. Place the meat on a heated platter and let stand 5 minutes before serving. Serve with béarnaise sauce (see page 61).

Hemingway takes time to share a traditional meal in Hong Kong. March 1941, while covering the war in China.

Thomas Hudson also remembers his time in China, describing Hong Kong for Honest Lil, a prostitute at El Floridita. Hemingway had followed Martha Gellhorn to China in January 1941. They were both covering the China-Japan War, and witnessed the destruction and the squalor of the front in Canton. Hemingway foresaw the eventuality of war between Japan and the United States as well as Communist domination of China after the war. He would not use his experience as the subject of a novel or story, but he would share with Thomas Hudson his image of Hong Kong. As he had done with Richard Cantwell in Venice, Hemingway takes this opportunity to share his pleasure in experiencing the color and flavor of a Hong Kong market:

I would wake in the mornings and even if it were raining I would walk to the fish market. Their fish are almost the same as ours and the basic food fish is the red grouper. But they had very fat and shining pompano and huge prawns, the biggest I have ever seen. The fish market was wonderful in the early morning when the fish were brought in shining and fresh caught and there were quite a few fish I did not know, but not many and there were also wild ducks for sale that had been trapped. You could see pin-tails, teal, widgeon, both males and females in winter plumage . . . as delicate and complicated as our wood ducks. I would look at them and their unbelievable plumage and their beautiful eyes and see the shining, fat, new-caught fish and the beautiful vegetables all manured in the truck gardens by human excrement, they called it "night-soil" there, and the vegetables were as beautiful as snakes. I went to the market every morning and every morning it was a delight.[19]

The Old Man and the Sea

The Old Man and the Sea is an idyll of the sea as sea, as un-Byronic and un-Melvillian as Homer himself, and communicated in a prose as calm and compelling as Homer's verse. No real artist symbolizes or allegorizes—and Hemingway is a real artist—but every real work of art exhales symbols and allegories. So does this short but not small masterpiece.
—Bernard Berenson, art historian

He held the story in his mind for fifteen years before making it his own. In the mid-1930s he heard the tale of an old Cuban fisherman, fishing alone in a skiff in the Gulf Stream, who hooked into a great fish. The giant marlin pulled the old man far out to sea. He fought the fish for two days and nights, and was finally able to raise the fish and harpoon him. When the sharks came, the old man fought them alone and lost. When the fishermen found the old man, crying and exhausted in his skiff, the sharks were still circling.[20]

Hemingway began writing *The Old Man and the Sea* in 1951. It was completed in eight weeks, and he would not rewrite a word. He appeared to have reached the pinnacle of the art for which he strove most of his life. *The Old Man and the Sea* was a tribute to the "simple strength of character, deeper than [the] will."[21] Hemingway won the Pulitzer Prize for the book in 1952, and it was cited specifically when he won the Nobel Prize for Literature in 1954.

The story begins as the old man returns yet again from the Gulf Stream with an empty skiff. The boy, who now fishes with a lucky boat, helps the old man carry home his tattered sail and gear. They speak of baseball and inexperience and wisdom. The boy leaves the shack for sardines. He returns with supper—black beans and rice, fried bananas, stew, and two bottles of Hatuey beer—in a metal container from the Terrace, compliments of Martín, the owner. The old man is proud, accepting the gift, assured that he will return the favor with the belly meat from a great fish.

"What have you got?" he asked.

"Supper," said the boy. "We're going to have supper."

"I'm not very hungry."

"Come on and eat. You can't fish and not eat."

"I have," the old man said getting up and taking the newspaper and folding it. Then he started to fold the blanket.

"Keep the blanket around you," the boy said.

"You'll not fish without eating while I'm alive."

"Then live a long time and take care of yourself," the old man said. "What are we eating?"[22]

Fried Bananas

Hemingway calls this dish fried bananas in The Old Man and the Sea, *but Santiago and Manolin no doubt enjoy fried plantains* (platanos)*, a larger, flatter version of the common banana with more starch and less sugar. The cooking method depends on the ripeness of the fruit, with the less ripe, very green plantains requiring an additional cooking stage.*

4 SERVINGS

 2–4 plantains, either very green or almost completely black
 Oil for frying

To peel the plantains, cut the tips of both ends, make slits in the skin lengthwise, and unwrap the peel of the plantain under running water.

For green plantains: Cut the plantain into 1-inch slices. Deep-fry over low heat until tender. Drain on brown paper. When cool enough to touch, flatten each slice with the palm of your hand. Reheat the oil over high heat until very hot. Dip each plantain slice in a bowl of iced, salted water. Pat dry, then fry quickly until browned. Drain on brown paper and serve.

For black plantains: Slice the plantains thinner, about ¼ to ½ inch thick, and cut diagonally to produce longer chips. Deep-fry in hot oil until dark brown. Drain on brown paper and serve.

Note: Learn from Nick Adams's example in "Big Two-Hearted River": wait awhile for the plantains to cool before eating them, otherwise a burned tongue may put you off these delicious treats for years.

Aboard the *Pilar*

More than the local characters in the bars and restaurants, stronger than the windswept memories of Paris and Africa and the East, more than the early morning processionals from fishing villages along the coast, it was the sea itself that mingled Hemingway's soul with that of Cuba. Sailing out into the Gulf Stream, fishing for giant marlin, Hemingway engaged his passion head on. As we saw with the bullfights, and will soon see with the safari, when Hemingway was truly living, his appetite grew accordingly.

Aboard the *Pilar*, Ernest's beloved fishing boat, food took on epic proportions. Even something as simple as a peanut butter and onion sandwich, his lunchtime favorite, can be elevated to heroic status while at sea:

> "Well, go down to the galley and see if that bottle of tea is cold and bring it up. Antonio's butchering the fish. So make a sandwich will you, please?"

> "Sure. What kind of sandwich?"

> "Peanut butter and onion if there's plenty of onion."

> "Peanut butter and onion it is, sir."

> He handed a sandwich, wrapped in a paper towel segment, to Thomas Hudson and said, "One of the highest points in the sandwich-maker's art. We call it the Mount Everest Special. For Commanders only."[23]

Mount Everest Special

A. E. Hotchner, in his biography, Papa Hemingway, *notes that this sandwich, along with a glass of red wine, was Hemingway's favorite.*[24]

1 SERVING

    2 slices white bread
    Peanut butter
    2 thick slices onion

Spread 1 slice bread thickly with peanut butter. Place onion slices on top. Cover with second slice of bread.

In 1928, aboard Sloppy Joe Russell's fishing boat, the *Anita* out of Key West, Hemingway sought shelter from a squall in the Dry Tortugas islands. There he encountered a run-down sailboat, the *Joaquin Cisto*, and its amiable skipper, Gregorio Fuentes. Fuentes helped the young and inexperienced Hemingway contact Key West and served him wine and raw onions, a favorite combination. Hemingway and Fuentes became great friends, and Gregorio would help Ernest out of many tight spots similar to the Dry Tortugas, eventually working aboard Hemingway's own boat. In the mid-1930s they parted company, only to reunite in Cuba in the early 1940s when Fuentes accepted the job as mate, deckhand, and cook of the *Pilar*.

Gregorio was not only an excellent cook but also took charge of the "Ethylic Department," a duty of great importance aboard the *Pilar*. Fuentes was a meticulous and thoughtful bartender, complementing Ernest's desire to be a gracious and generous host. Hemingway kept the ship's bar well stocked, aiming to satisfy the thirsts of all those aboard. Ernest had a habit of not drinking from a bottle opened the previous day and so would open a new bottle every day. Fuentes kept the drinks refreshed, believing that a cold drink should be held no more than half an hour and then be discarded and replaced. After the drinks were served and it was time to eat, Fuentes truly made his name and reputation. Fuentes took great pride in pleasing those for whom he cooked. His dishes display the simple techniques and subtle tricks of a master and should be enjoyed in the spirit of camaraderie and adventure that flourished aboard Hemingway's boat. Gregorio could turn the galley of the *Pilar* into a kitchen worthy of the Ritz in Paris. In fact, when Charlie Ritz visited Cuba in 1954, Ernest bet him that Gregorio was a better chef than anyone in the Ritz's employ. It was a challenge that Gregorio embraced with pride. Fuentes set out to astound the Frenchman with three dishes, the likes of which he had never tasted.

Spaghetti

Gregorio's recipe for spaghetti sauce is more delicious than even Charlie Ritz had ever tasted. The following recipe is based upon the instructions he gave to Norberto Fuentes, author of Hemingway in Cuba.

4 SERVINGS, WITH SAUCE LEFT OVER

For the Special Broth

> Plenty of olive oil
>
> 3 pounds beef and pork bones
>
> 3 medium onions, halved
>
> 1 cup manzanilla sherry
>
> 6 sprigs fresh thyme, or 1 teaspoon dried
>
> 6–8 sprigs oregano, or 1 teaspoon dried
>
> 1 bay leaf
>
> 2 cloves garlic

For the sauce

> Olive oil
>
> 1 3- to 4-pound chicken, cut into pieces
>
> ½ cup country-style ham, cubed
>
> ½ cup chorizo, cubed
>
> Generous pinch of paprika
>
> Salt
>
> Pepper
>
> 1 pound spaghetti
>
> Pinch of sugar

Preheat the oven to 400° F.

Coat the bottom of a roasting pan with olive oil. Add the bones and onions and roast, stirring occasionally, until the bones are browned, about 45 minutes. Place the bones and onions in a large stockpot. Deglaze the empty roasting pan by adding the sherry and scraping up any bits that may stick. Pour the contents of the roasting pan into the stockpot with the bones and onions. Add enough water to cover plus 1 inch, bring to a boil, then reduce heat and simmer. You may skim the stock, if you like, or just let it be. After about 1 hour, bundle the thyme, oregano, bay leaf, and garlic together in a piece of cheesecloth and tie tight with string. Add the herbs to the stockpot. Simmer stock, covered, for at least 4 to 5 hours.

Heat a little olive oil in a large skillet. Add the chicken parts and cook over medium heat until browned. Add enough stock to cover and bring to a boil. (Reserve any remaining stock for future use.) Lower the heat and simmer until done, almost 20 minutes. Remove the chicken and strain the cooking liquid, reserving both the liquid and the crumblike bits that remain in the sieve. When the chicken is cool enough to handle, remove as much meat as possible from the bones. Add a pinch of salt plus the bits in the sieve to the meat and grind in a meat grinder. Grind the ham and chorizo as well. Combine the ground meats in a skillet, add 1 cup of the stock from the cooked chicken, paprika, and salt and pepper to taste. Simmer over low heat until thickened. Transfer the sauce to a bowl.

Break the spaghetti in half and add to a large pot of boiling water. Cook to desired tenderness. Strain the spaghetti and transfer to serving plate. Add a pinch of sugar and serve with the sauce.

Swordfish á la *Pilar*

"How did you make this?" asked Señor Ritz.

"Easy," I answered. "With just a little bit of salt."[25]

In reality, Gregorio's swordfish recipe involves more than just a bit of salt, but not much more.

2 TO 4 SERVINGS, DEPENDING ON APPETITES AND SIZE OF STEAKS

2 very fresh swordfish steaks
Juice of 4 limes
4 cloves garlic, crushed
½ pound butter
1 lemon
Salt

Be sure that your fish is as fresh as possible. Place the steaks in a large bowl. Stir together the lime juice and garlic and pour over the fish. Let stand at least 20 minutes, turning steaks occasionally. Melt the butter in a large skillet over low heat. Fry the swordfish for 8–10 minutes. Squeeze the juice from ½ lemon over each steak. Turn and fry on the other side for an additional 8–10 minutes. Cooking time will be slightly longer for thicker steaks. Season with salt to taste.

Dorado Fillet in Damn Good Sauce

Dorado is another name for mahimahi or dolphin fish.

4 SERVINGS

2 pounds dorado fillets, about ½ inch thick
Juice of 2 limes
Salt
Freshly ground pepper
Olive oil for frying
1 clove garlic, crushed
2 green bell peppers, diced
½ pound asparagus, very finely chopped
1½ cups Gregorio's Special Broth (see page 133), or fish broth
½ cup chopped fresh parsley
¼ cup raisins
¼ cup capers
1½ cups dry white wine

Marinate the fillets in the lime juice and salt and pepper to taste for at least 1 hour. In a large skillet, heat the olive oil. Sauté the garlic, peppers, and asparagus for a few minutes. Add the broth, parsley, raisins, and capers and simmer, covered, for 10 minutes. Add the fillets and dry white wine and continue to simmer, covered, for 5–8 minutes, or until the fillets are cooked through.

In addition to these three dishes, Hemingway enjoyed Gregorio's preparation of octopus in wine sauce, lobster enchilada, crab cooked in lemon, and a marvelous red snapper stew. He eventually relented and shared his recipe for Red Snapper Stew with Mary:

Red Snapper Stew

One of the terribly unfortunate consequences of life aboard the Pilar *was that the fish was often too fresh. Mary recalled Gregorio's standards on this matter:*

> He never liked fish to be too fresh, he mentioned, because the skin shrinks in the cooking.
>
> "How fresh is too fresh, Gregorio?" We were slupping [sic] up beef-stew juice from our plates on the generator box aft, while Ernest ate, plate in hand, cross-legged on his bunk.
>
> "Oh, under an hour, depending on the size, depending on the fish. Two hours maybe."
>
> "Not a universal dilemma," murmured Ernest.[26]

1 large whole red snapper (or 2 small fish), cleaned and gutted

Salt

2 cloves garlic, coarsely chopped and 1 clove, halved

1 medium onion, coarsely chopped

3 tablespoons olive oil

1 red bell pepper, chopped

½ cup tomato sauce

1 bay leaf

1 teaspoon crushed dried oregano

¼ cup finely chopped pimiento

2 tablespoons capers

¼ cup raisins

¼ cup sliced green olives

½ cup manzanilla sherry

135

One hour before beginning to cook, score the fish diagonally on both sides and rub inside and out with salt. In a pan large enough to hold the entire fish, sauté the garlic and onion in the olive oil until the onion is translucent. Add the red pepper, tomato sauce, bay leaf, and oregano. Simmer over low heat, stirring occasionally, for 30 minutes. Add the pimiento, capers, raisins, olives, sherry, and salt to taste. Stir. Place the fish in the stew and simmer slowly for about 20 minutes, or until the flesh turns from opalescent to white.

Mary's Kitchen

Except for his writing, Ernest never finds any sort of work so important that it cannot be abandoned in an instant in favor of making or having fun. Of course, as he well knows, it is that kind of fun which impels me to try every day to make our food more interesting and better-tasting. A while ago he came into my room and, peering under my desk and into corners, busily put on a show of hunting for something. When I asked him what, he said, "An accolade. For you. Because lunch was the best meal I've ever eaten, ever."[27]

Mary Hemingway, Ernest's fourth wife, may have been honored to receive Gregorio's recipe for Red Snapper Stew, but she also created a masterpiece or two of her own during her years in Cuba. Mary met Ernest in London in 1944, after he followed Martha Gellhorn to war yet again. After the war, Ernest returned to Finca Vigía alone, his marriage to Martha finished. Mary later joined him there, and they were married in March 1946. Mary loved their Cuban lifestyle, replete with an endless stream of guests, a house filled with cats, and innumerable stunning sunsets. She became the kindly and generous matron of the Finca, a role that she enjoyed and Ernest needed: "It is a manner of living about as formal and regulated as the wag of a dog's tail, and Ernest seems to thrive in it and our friends to revel in it. I find it instructive, stimulating and busy."[28]

Originally, the Hemingways hired a cook at the Finca. But "after a certain amount of experimentation—and an otherwise tranquil luncheon during which our then butler rushed into the dining room brandishing a cocked pistol ready to kill the Chinese cook because he didn't like the food—[Mary] decided that it was not worth the bother to hunt a cook who could do or was willing to learn such an assortment of cooking."[29] So she took over the cooking, a responsibility she did not take lightly. With the international guest list and Ernest's taste for variety, she was constantly expanding her repertoire, including Chinese, Mexican, and Indian cuisine as well as local Cuban specialties.

Mary first began experimenting with Chinese cuisine in 1948, shortly before she and Ernest left Cuba for a long trip to Italy. Upon their return, she prepared a festive Chinese lunch for Ernest's 50th birthday that included slippery chicken with almonds in champagne sauce, melon soup, and a "miniature feast of stir-fry dishes."[30] In 1959, after Ernest and Mary had moved to Ketchum, Idaho, Mary shared her very thorough and comprehensive Chinese sweet-sour stir-fry recipe with friend and occasional cooking partner Forrest "Duke" MacMullen. Thanks to Duke for sharing Mary's letter which included the following recipe.

The Chinese use whole, small fish, lobster, crab, shrimp, chicken, spare-ribs of crisp-fried chunks (bite-size) of loin of port for their sweet-sour dishes. Rarely they do sweet-sour eggs, never beef. (Sweet-sour belongs to the large category of Chinese Stir-fry dishes which are all prepared in advance and then cooked quickly when ready to eat.)

Sweet-Sour Sauce for a Dish for Six People

2–3 tablespoons cornstarch

2–3 tablespoons white sugar (except brown when doing spareribs or pork loin)

2 tablespoons white vinegar

2 tablespoons white wine

2 tablespoons soy sauce

½ teaspoon salt

Juice, if any, from the vegetables or the principal ingredient, or a little chicken broth—to make about 1½ cups altogether

Stir all this together cold and have ready to dump on the Stir-Fry things 3 minutes before serving. There should be enough juice so that when the dish is served it is plenty wet but not sloppy or like soup.

The Chinese always use sliced fresh ginger, thin and square like postage stamps in some dishes (pork loin, eggs, lobster), long thin-like toothpicks for the others. In Classic Chinese cookery, the way a thing is sliced is very important—they think it affects the flavor.

For most sweet-sour you use about half as much ginger, measured sliced, as you do for the next constant ingredient—onion. For something for 6 people, about one-third cup of ginger to two-thirds cup sliced onion.

Besides ginger and onion, you add two more, seldom more than four more, things, besides the principal ingredient. With fish, add the delicate flavored things—celery, bean sprouts, and/or water-chestnuts. If possible, always put in something crunchy—and never cook the vegetables until they are soft.

With lobster or crab or shrimp, add mushrooms, green pepper, maybe—for fancy meals—blanched almonds.

The classic Chinese sweet-sour chicken has ginger, onion, celery, sliced pineapple and almonds—and you go easy—1 tablespoon only—on the soy sauce since this is White-meat (breast only) Stir-Fry dish. (This is a party dish, the chicken breast being sliced, square and ⅛ inch thick while raw and stir-fried at the last moment.)

137

With pork loin chunks, you use ginger, onion, celery, red and green pepper (cut square, ginger cut square too) and blanched almonds.

It is permissible to use garlic in the pork sweet-sour, but the Chinese don't use it in the other dishes.

Proportions of things vary according to the cook's personality, but the standard rule is that the total vegetables add up to half—about half—as much as the main ingredient.

Fry the vegetables briefly in oil (add the bean-sprouts last), add the chief ingredient, to heat it, pour on the sauce, stir three minutes, or until thickened.

Two all-time favorites, the dishes which constituted the "best meal [he'd] ever eaten ever," were Mary's chop suey and lime ice.

Chop Suey

Mary's adventurous culinary style certainly resonated with the Chinese-American tradition of chop suey, the name of which translates from Cantonese as "miscellaneous odds and ends." Her recipe includes chicken, shrimp, various vegetables, canned fried noodles, and even something that the Chinese in Cuba called orejas *or "ears," which Mary thought were either membranes of pig or monkey ears or some sort of vegetable. Most likely she was using a type of Chinese mushroom called "tree ears," which are available in most*

Asian markets. She may even have added slices of mango to this dish on occasion.

4 SERVINGS

For the Marinade

    ½ teaspoon salt

    ½ teaspoon sugar

    1 teaspoon soy sauce

    ½ teaspoon sesame oil

    2 tablespoons white wine

For the Chop Suey

    ½ pound chicken, cut into strips

    4 tablespoons olive or sesame oil

    ½ pound shrimp, shelled and deveined

    1 onion, chopped

    ¼ cup bamboo shoots

    1 red bell pepper, sliced thin

    1 scallion, chopped

    ½ cup sliced tree ears, or Chinese mushrooms

    1 2-ounce can fried Chinese noodles

    2 cloves garlic, finely chopped

    1-inch piece ginger, minced

    ½ cup bean sprouts

    1 mango, cubed (optional)

For the Gravy

½ teaspoon salt

½ teaspoon sugar

1 teaspoon cornstarch

2 teaspoons soy sauce

¼ cup water

Whisk together all the marinade ingredients in a large bowl. Add the chicken, cover, and let stand for at least 10 minutes.

Heat half the olive or sesame oil in a large skillet over high heat. When hot, add the chicken and stir-fry for 1–2 minutes. Add the shrimp and stir-fry until the shrimp turns bright pink. Remove the chicken and shrimp from the skillet and set aside. Return the skillet to high heat and add the remaining 2 tablespoons oil. Add the vegetables, mushrooms, fried noodles, garlic, and ginger and stir-fry for 2–3 minutes. Whisk together the gravy ingredients in a small bowl. Return the chicken and shrimp to the skillet. Toss together along with the sprouts and the mango. Pour in the gravy and cook for another 2–3 minutes. Serve immediately. Mary recommends that this dish be eaten with chopsticks, which she found helped the flavor.

Lime Ice

This dessert, clean and tart with just enough kick, is the perfect refreshment on a hot July afternoon in the hills just outside of Havana.

4 TO 6 SERVINGS

1½ cups sugar syrup (see below)

Juice of 6 limes

½ tablespoon lemon juice

1 cup water

1 egg white

3½ tablespoons gin

2 tablespoons crème de menthe

Rind of ½ lime, very finely chopped (optional)

To make the sugar syrup, dissolve 1¼ cups sugar in 1 cup water. This may be done by stirring the sugar into the water either at room temperature or over low heat. If done over heat, allow the syrup to cool completely before proceeding.

Remove the rind of half of 1 lime and cover with plastic wrap. Combine the juice of the 6 limes, lemon juice, sugar syrup, water, and egg white in a large-bottomed, sturdy plastic container, so that the liquid is no more than 2 inches deep. Stir the mixture completely. Cover and place in the freezer for 1½–2 hours. When ice has formed around the edge of the mixture and the center is slushy, blend for a few seconds with a hand mixer or whisk. Cover and return to the freezer for another 1½ hours or so. Repeat process, adding the gin, crème de menthe, and minced lime rind after the third freezing.

Return the mixture to the freezer for another 30–60 minutes, or until firmly frozen. The ice may be served directly from the freezer, as it will stay somewhat soft and scoopable with the alcohol included.

———————

Mary had access to a dozen different varieties of mangoes in Cuba, and she and Ernest enjoyed every type. Mary added mango slices to virtually every dish, whether it was Chinese, Mexican, or Italian. She froze mangoes in batches separated by flavor, which ranged from strawberry to honeydew, and served them with game or as dessert. She also made preserves and chutney to ensure there would be mango every day of the year. Mango chutney is a fresh alternative to regular salsas or chutneys and is easily prepared any time ripe mangoes are available.

Mango Chutney

8 TO 10 SERVINGS

> 2 large underripe mangoes, diced (see below)
>
> ¾ cup white vinegar
>
> ½ cup brown sugar
>
> 1 medium onion, chopped fine
>
> 1 clove garlic, finely minced
>
> ½ cup raisins
>
> ½ cup chopped crystallized ginger
>
> ½ teaspoon ground cloves
>
> 1 teaspoon salt
>
> 1 teaspoon cumin
>
> ½ cup hot water
>
> ½ teaspoon curry powder
>
> 1 tablespoon olive oil
>
> Dash of black pepper

Mangoes have a large, flat pit. The easiest way to dice the flesh of a mango is to cut the fruit in half, working the knife flush against the flat side of the pit. Then repeat on the other side to cut away the other half. With a bread knife, cut a grid into the flesh, not cutting through the skin of the mango. Then push from the skin side and invert each half from concave to convex. You can then simply cut away the already cubed flesh.

Place the cubed mango in a medium saucepan. Add the remaining ingredients and mix together. Place the saucepan over medium heat and bring to a boil.

Lower the heat and simmer for 30–45 minutes, or until thickened. You may need to add more hot water if the chutney is too thick at this point. Allow to cool to room temperature before serving.

———————

While Mary enjoyed cooking a vast variety of international dishes, she also embraced the cuisine of Cuba. One of her favorite hot-weather dishes was *picadillo* a classic Cuban dish. This recipe is based on Mary's and includes the ubiquitous mango, which adds an extra splash of sweetness. The directions for this dish are Mary's own and come from an article that she wrote for *Flair* magazine in 1951 entitled "Life with Papa."

Picadillo

4 SERVINGS

> 2 medium onions, finely sliced
> 3 cloves garlic, finely chopped
> 3 tablespoons butter
> 1 pound ground beef
> Salt
> Pepper
> Big dash of marjoram
> Big dash of oregano
> ½ cup dry white wine
> ½ cup raisins

> 1 cup mango or peach, fairly finely chopped
> ½ cup sliced celery
> ¼ cup sliced stuffed olives
> ¼ cup chopped almonds, (optional)

Slice fine and fry in plenty of butter a medium-sized onion, or more if your family is big and you are using more than a pound of beef, also shredded garlic according to your taste. Stir in the meat with salt, pepper, a big dash of marjoram and a big dash of oregano, and before the meat starts burning or sticking to the pan, add about one-half cup of dry white wine. (Here the Cubans use, instead, tomato paste and water, but I prefer this dish without tomatoes.) Let this simmer gently for a while during which you make a platter of fluffy white rice. About five minutes before serving, add to the frying-pan mixture a half cup of previously soaked raisins, a cup of fairly finely chopped mango or fresh peach, half a cup of sliced celery, a handful of sliced stuffed olives and, if you wish to be fancy, a handful of blanched, chopped almonds [blanching briefly in boiling water is only necessary if the almonds still have their skin]. Pour the frying-pan mixture on top of the rice. Very small rivulets of the juice of the meat mixture should appear around the edges of the platter, or you haven't used enough butter, wine or fruit. Garnish it with something dark green and very crisp.

Another dessert that was an all-time favorite of Mary and Ernest's was coconut ice cream, which she prepared and served within the half-shells of real coconuts.

Coconut Ice Cream

1¼ QUARTS ICE CREAM

2½ cups heavy cream
1½ cups coconut milk
1 vanilla bean
8 egg yolks
¾ cup sugar

In a heavy saucepan, combine the cream and coconut milk. Cut the vanilla bean in half lengthwise. Scrape the seeds into the cream mixture and add the bean. Bring the cream mixture to a boil over medium heat and set aside.

In a mixing bowl, whisk together the egg yolks and sugar. When the cream mixture has cooled slightly, whisk about 1 cup into the egg yolks and sugar. Add this mixture to the remaining cream mixture in the saucepan. Return the saucepan to medium heat, stirring constantly with a wooden spoon. Heat for 3–5 minutes, or until the custard reaches 175° F and coats the back of the spoon. Remove from the heat. Pour the custard into a bowl and set over a larger bowl half-filled with ice water. Cool the custard for 10 minutes, stirring often.

Cover the custard with plastic wrap, allowing the plastic to settle on the surface. Refrigerate for 2 hours. Remove the vanilla bean, transfer the custard to an ice cream maker, and freeze according to manufacturer's instructions. When finished, scoop the ice cream into halfshells of coconut, split open with a chisel and hammer.

EAST AFRICA AND IDAHO

A Hunter's Culinary Sketches

In my nocturnal dreams, I am always between 25 and 30 years old, I am irresistible to women, dogs and, on one recent occasion, to a very beautiful lioness. . . . One of the aspects of this dream that I remember was that the lioness was killing game for me exactly as she would for a male of her own species; but instead of our having to devour the meat raw, she cooked it in a most appetizing manner. She used only butter for basting the impala chops. She braised the tenderloin and served it, on the grass, in a manner worthy of the Ritz in Paris. She asked me if I wanted any vegetables, and knowing that she herself was completely nonherbivorious, I refused in order to be polite. In any case, there were no vegetables.

—From "The Christmas Gift"

(Left to right) Ben Fourie, Charles Thompson, Philip Percival, and Hemingway displaying the bounty of a hunt.

Hemingway's father, with his deep-set eyes and sharp, clear vision, was an excellent shot and avid hunter. As young Ernest grew older in a house increasingly dominated by women, Dr. Hemingway was eager to teach his young son the ways of the wild. Ernest's older sister Marcelline was also included in Ed Hemingway's regimented training but as Ernest himself would do later in life, Ed used these shared experiences to express his love for his son in particular.

By age five, Ernest had already begun to develop a love of fishing and hunting that would last his entire life. It was not until his teens, though, that his father would graduate him from his air rifle to target practice with a .22. Ed imparted discipline and respect for the weapons to his children and shared his contempt for hunters who killed for folly. The latter point, you may recall, resulted in the unfortunate porcupine incident of 1913 with Ernest and Harold Sampson.

These early experiences brought Ernest close to his father, even if they would later grow apart in many other ways. Years later he would thank his father, in a not wholly complimentary way through the semifictional voice of Nick Adams in the short story "Fathers and Sons":

> . . . the quail country made him remember him as he was when Nick was a boy and he was very grateful to him for two things: fishing and shooting. His father was as sound on those two things as he was unsound on sex, for instance, and Nick was glad that it had been that way; for some one has to give you your first gun or the opportunity to get it and use it, and you have to live where there is game or fish if you are to learn about them, and now, at thirty-eight, he loved to fish and to shoot exactly as much as when he first had gone with his father.[1]

As with all of his great passions—the bullfights, fishing for trout or marlin, or writing well—the heightened reality of the hunt awakened in Ernest that voracious appetite for food and drink. It has been noted that his appetite was only truly piqued while hunting or fishing for marlin. We find, particularly in writing about his safaris in East Africa, detailed and enthusiastic accounts of the exotic meals and potent drinks that provided sustenance for the hunters. His hunting adventures formed in large part the legend of Hemingway that remains today. From the Kapiti Plains of East Africa to the mountains of Wyoming and Idaho, as we partake of the foods and drinks of the hunt, replete with images of great successes and mortal failures, we may yet again participate that much more fully in the Hemingway legend. Our first stop is Kenya, where Ernest and Pauline arrived in 1933 for Hemingway's first major safari.

African Safari

Hemingway went on two major safaris to East Africa. The first, in 1933–34, resulted in *The Green Hills of Africa*, an ambitious effort at re-creating reality from the young and newly famous writer, as well as two of his most memorable short stories, "The Short Happy Life of Francis Macomber" and "The Snows of Kilimanjaro." The second safari, in 1953–54, ended with serious internal injuries and a fractured skull, the result of not one, but two, plane crashes.

In November 1933, Ernest and Pauline sailed from Marseilles for Mombasa, Kenya. Financed with $25,000 from Pauline's Uncle Gus, the Hemingways hunted for seven weeks in the Great Rift Valley and the Serengeti Plain of Tanganyika. They were joined by Key West friend Charles Thompson and the English hunter Philip Percival, who once hunted with Churchill and Theodore Roosevelt. They were also joined briefly by Baron Bror von Blixen, the director of Tanganyika Guides, Ltd., who, along with Percival, served as models for Wilson in "The Short Happy Life of Francis Macomber."

The drama and danger of the safari brought Hemingway in touch with his own struggles with cowardice and courage. He discovered that by having confronted the former he could eventually live and hunt and work firmly rooted in the latter.[2] The safari also brought out his volatile, competitive spirit, as the less experienced Thompson continually bettered Hemingway with larger kills.

The details of their safari would eventually make it into Hemingway's fiction. The finest piece to come of the early safari and one of his most intriguing short stories was "The Short Happy Life of Francis Macomber." Based very loosely on a tale told by Percival around their campfire, Hemingway embroidered a deliciously dark and taut story. Francis and Margot Macomber, a deeply embittered couple, are on safari with their white hunter, Wilson. Francis Macomber wallows in his cowardice, confronting it when there is nothing left to lose after Margot has betrayed him. He finds his courage in the path of a wounded and charging buffalo, but Margot ends the story with "a sudden white-hot, blinding flash."[3]

FRANCIS MACOMBER'S LAST MEAL

Having bolted from a charging lion the day before, Francis must contend with the ceaseless barbs of his wife and the contemptuous silence of Wilson. Over lunch, Margot takes ample opportunity to register her distaste at her husband's retreat:

"That's eland he's offering you," Wilson said.

"They're the big cowy things that jump like hares, aren't they?"

"I suppose that describes them," Wilson said.

"It's very good meat," Macomber said.

"Did you shoot it, Francis?" she asked.

"Yes."

"They're not dangerous, are they?"

"Only if they fall on you," Wilson told her.

"I'm so glad."

"Why not let up on the bitchery just a little, Margot," Macomber said, cutting the eland steak and putting some mashed potato, gravy and carrot on the down-turned fork that tined through the piece of meat.[4]

Hunter's Safari Steak

This recipe, adapted from The African Cookbook, *utilizes a method used by Kenyan hunters for preparing game such as eland, antelope, or zebra. If eland is not available, you may substitute veal, beef, or even buffalo.*

4 SERVINGS

2 pounds eland steaks
2 tablespoons olive oil
2 tablespoons butter
Salt
Pepper
½ cup dry red wine
½ cup sweet wine
2 cloves garlic, minced
½ cup tomato sauce
1½ cups mashed potatoes
1 cup mashed sweet potatoes
Chopped parsley, for garnish

Cut the meat into 4 steaks, each about ½ inch thick. Dry the steaks with a paper towel. Heat the olive oil and butter in a large skillet just to the smoking point. Add the steaks and cook for about 3 minutes on each side, adding more oil as necessary. Season the steaks with salt and pepper to taste and set aside on a warm plate.

Keep the skillet over low heat and add the wines. Deglaze the pan by stirring the wine and scraping up any browned bits that may have stuck. Add the garlic and simmer for 2 minutes. Stir in the tomato sauce and continue to simmer until the sauce has thickened.

In a large bowl, mix together the mashed potatoes and the mashed sweet potatoes. Add salt and pepper to taste. Spread the potatoes on a large serving plate. Place the steaks on top of the potatoes and pour the sauce over the steaks. Garnish with chopped parsley and serve immediately.

———————————

The second safari needed no such fictional veil to become the thing of legend. Ernest and Mary sailed from Marseilles in 1953 to hunt again with Percival, who came out of retirement to hunt with Hemingway. Ernest once again became aggressively competitive, this time with Mario Menocal, a friend from Cuba, but the drama of their dueling was nothing when compared with the accidents that would soon befall Ernest and Mary.

At the close of the safari in January 1954, the Hemingways planned to depart from Nairobi for a vacation in the Belgian Congo. Ernest arranged a flight from Nairobi airport as a belated Christmas present for Mary. Their flight plan was circuitous, allowing them ample time to view the wonders of the African landscape from above. They flew south over the Ngorongoro Crater and the Serengeti Plain, over the sight of Ernest and Pauline's 1933 safari campsite. They turned north and flew over the White Nile, eventually flying east, following the Victoria Nile to the Murchison Falls. Roy Marsh, their pilot, circled the falls three times, giving Mary a spectacular view where the river plunged in a series of cataracts toward the Sudan and Egypt. On the third pass, Marsh dived to avoid a flight of ibis in their path, striking a telegraph wire and raking the plane's tail assembly. They crash-landed three miles south-southwest of the falls. Mary suffered two broken ribs and Ernest a shoulder sprain, but otherwise they escaped serious injury.

After a night of restless sleep by a campfire, they spotted a passing riverboat. They boarded the *Murchison*, which was rented to John Huston during the shooting of *The African Queen*, and sailed to Butiaba. Upon arrival the Hemingways discovered that local officials had searched the wreckage and found no survivors. The news had quickly got out, and the world believed that Hemingway was dead.

In the early evening of that same day, they boarded another plane at the Butiaba airstrip en route to Entebbe. Upon takeoff, after barrelling down the makeshift runway, the de Havilland Rapide 12-seater promptly stopped and burst into flames. Mary and the others escaped through a kicked-out window while Ernest used his head and injured shoulder to butt his way through the port door. He had survived yet again, but not unscathed this time. His injuries included ruptured liver, spleen, and kidney, a fractured skull resulting in loss of vision in one eye and hearing in one ear, a crushed vertebra, several sprains, and first-degree burns.

148

Ernest and Mary prepare game for the safari pot.

The following day the world discovered that Hemingway was alive after all. Groggy and seeing double, he met the press in relatively good humor. As if the truth were not amazing enough, the press prompted the myth that the great Hemingway had emerged from the jungle sporting a bottle of gin and a bunch of bananas. The myths and the legends spread, as did the effects of his injuries. He had out-Hemingway'd himself yet again, and the world's appetite for the legend grew accordingly.

DINNER AFTER THE HUNT

We've almost come to expect such drama and adventure while keeping company with Ernest. As we learned at the Finca Vigía in Cuba, we could also expect wonderful food when Mary was around. While their post-safari accidents were pure Ernest, the food they enjoyed while hunting was inspired by Mary's culinary enthusiasm. She recalled, in her memoirs *How It Was*, the marvelous food they ate in the bush:

> N'bebia, our cook, had once cooked at the Governor's house, and, squatting beside the battered pots around the edge of his fire, big as a Hollywood bed, he provided us with food good enough for governors or gourmets. Lunch was usually cold roast of game we had shot, with hot baked potatoes, salad, fruit and cheese. Dinner began with a rich strained soup enlivened by onion or barley and continued with such main dishes as oxtail stew, roast Tommy, roast eland, curries

of wild bird we'd shot, with such extras as grated fresh coconut, bananas, chutney, and Bombay duck, saffron rice with sautéed guinea hen, or deepdish eland pie, the pie crust, rolled out on a wine box with a wine bottle, light as feathers. With our appetites constantly whetted by excitement and by walking in the fresh air, we all ate too much and my pants accordingly shrank.[5]

A successful pheasant hunt.

149

Curry of Wild Bird

This recipe is based on a basic African curry dish with one important element added—bananas. Mary Hemingway would add small, sweet bananas to this dish to add a smooth, starchy consistency to the sauce. This habit may have grown out of her common practice of adding mangoes to many of her favorite recipes in Cuba.

4 SERVINGS

¼ cup olive oil

2 onions, chopped

4 cloves garlic, chopped

1 tablespoon cumin

1 teaspoon cardamom

1 cinnamon stick

4 cloves

½ teaspoon crushed red pepper flakes

1 teaspoon turmeric

1-inch piece of fresh ginger, sliced

½ cup tomato purée

½ cup chicken stock

4 pounds wild fowl such as pheasant, quail, or sandgrouse, cut up

3 potatoes, peeled and quartered

2 small, ripe bananas, chopped

½ cup chopped fresh cilantro

Heat the olive oil in a large skillet. Add the onions, garlic, cumin, cardamom, cinnamon, cloves, red pepper, turmeric, and ginger. Stir until well mixed. Add the tomato purée and stock and simmer over low heat for 10 minutes, stirring occasionally. Add the birds, cover, and cook for 10 minutes. Add the potatoes and bananas and cook, covered, for 15 minutes, or until the potatoes are just tender. Add the cilantro and cook, uncovered, for 5 minutes, or to desired consistency.

A good day in Sun Valley, Idaho.

150

Mike Reynolds, one of Hemingway's preeminent biographers, and his wife, Ann, visited Marty Peterson, Hemingway Society member and codirector of the 1996 International Hemingway Conference, in Boise. Marty set out to host a small dinner party with a Hemingway theme. His cousin, Bill Tate, had a small breeding herd of eland at his ranch in Grandview, Idaho. He provided the meat for a memorable meal. Eland is remarkably similar to veal and he prepared it picata style. Given N'bebia's training at the Governor's house, it is likely that this dish was in his vast repertoire. Many thanks to Marty Peterson for sharing this recipe.

Eland Piccata

4 SERVINGS

1 yellow onion, diced

4 green onions, chopped

2 cloves garlic, chopped

2 tablespoons olive oil

2 pounds eland, cut into thin slices

Salt

Freshly ground pepper

All-purpose flour, for dredging

¼ cup butter

3 tablespoons dry sherry

3 tablespoons lemon juice

2 tablespoons capers, chopped

¼ cup chicken stock (optional)

Thin-cut lemon slices

¼ cup chopped Italian parsley

Sauté the yellow and green onions and garlic in olive oil until yellow onions begin to become transparent. Set aside. Pound the eland slices with a meat pounder until flat. Sprinkle them with salt and pepper to taste and dredge lightly in flour. Heat the butter in a large skillet over moderately high heat and lightly brown the eland, turning each piece once. Add the onions and garlic. Transfer the meat to a serving platter and keep in warm oven.

Place the skillet over high heat and add the sherry and lemon juice. Scrape up the brown particles in the pan. Add the capers. Allow the sauce to thicken. The chicken stock may be used to dilute the sauce or extend it if desired. Pour over the meat. Garnish with lemon slices and parsley and serve immediately.

Oxtail Stew

4 SERVINGS

2 pounds oxtails, cut into pieces

Salt

Freshly ground pepper

3 tablespoons peanut oil

4 cups water

2 onions, chopped

2 cloves garlic, minced

½ teaspoon crumbled dried oregano

1 green bell pepper, chopped

3 tomatoes, peeled and chopped

1 tablespoon capers

2 potatoes, peeled and cut into 1-inch pieces

Season the oxtails with salt and pepper to taste. Heat the peanut oil in a stockpot over medium heat. Add the tail pieces and brown thoroughly for 8–10 minutes. Add water, onions, garlic, oregano, and green peppers, and cook for about 1 hour, or until the tail meat is just tender. Add the tomatoes, capers, and potatoes and continue cooking until the potatoes are tender, about 15 minutes. Mash up some of the potatoes to thicken the stew. Cook for another 15–20 minutes and serve.

It was also over N'bebia's campfire that Ernest and Mary cultivated their taste for lion, which they first ate raw after Ernest's first kill in 1953:

> Ernest's lion was a young male in his prime, four or five years old, with immense fore- and hind-leg muscles and thick bones and muscles in his paws. Watching the skinning, Ernest bent down and with his pocketknife cut out a bit of the tenderloin beside the spine, chewed some and offered me a tidbit. We both thought the clean pink flesh delicious, steak tartare without the capers. Denis scoffed that it would make us sick and Philip (Percival) politely declined a taste. In Kenya neither the natives nor the whites ate lion, having against it some taboo which they would never define for me.[6]

They would eventually develop several recipes for lion meat, which they found "firmer than Italian veal, but not tough, and as bland in flavor without a hint of the wilderness. Later [they] dressed it up with garlic and onion and various tomato and cheese sauces, as [they] had done with *vitello* in Italy."[7] In December 1955, Ernest provided a recipe for a *Sports Illustrated* article entitled "A Christmas Choice of Fair and Fancy Game." Receiving top billing above President Eisenhower's Colorado Mountain Trout and Baron de Rothschild's Hare à la Royale was the following dish by the most famous sportsman of them all. Although its creator is falsely claimed to be a "first-rate cook," the recipe itself is pure Hemingway. To re-create this dish, simply follow Ernest's instructions, substituting veal for the lion fillet.

152

Ernest Hemingway's Fillet of Lion

First obtain your lion. Skin him out and remove the two strips of tenderloin from either side of the backbone. These should hang overnight in a tree out of reach of hyenas and should be wrapped in cheesecloth to prevent them being hit by blowflies.

The following day, either for breakfast, lunch or dinner, slice the tenderloin as though you were cutting small tenderloin steaks. You may cut them as thin or as thick as you like, and if you should be fortunate enough to have eggs, which will usually be brought in by natives for whom you have killed the lion, if these natives possess chickens, dip the small steaks in beaten and seasoned egg and then in either corn meal or cracker meal or bread crumbs. Then grill the steaks over the coals of an open fire.

If you have no eggs, simply grill the steaks, basting them preferably with the lard made from eland fat, after having salted and peppered them liberally, but not using too much salt to destroy the delicate flavor.

If you are fortunate enough to have lemon or sour orange in camp, serve a half of lemon or sour orange with each portion of lion steak.[8]

Sun Valley and Ketchum, Idaho

In September 1936, shortly before he left to cover the Spanish Civil War, Hemingway hunted grizzly bears near the Nordquist Ranch on the far edge of Yellowstone National Park near the Montana border. Ernest killed two bears and experienced that familiar yet fleeting elation when the hunting or the fishing or the writing went very well. When a third grizzly was killed a few days later, "he insisted on a lunch of bear steaks. . . . The meat was rank and stringy, cooked middling rare, and eaten in the form of sandwiches made from sourdough pancakes spread with orange marmalade. But Ernest consumed his portion with obvious gusto, chewing long and appreciatively, his black beard glossy with bear fat."[9]

This was Ernest Hemingway in his element. As much as he enjoyed living and fishing in Cuba, and as much as Spain drew him in the late 1930s, he felt most genuinely at home in the mountains and valleys of Wyoming and eventually in and around Sun Valley, Idaho, where Ernest lived the last few years of his life.

Ernest's arrival in Idaho in 1939 coincided with the outbreak of war across Europe and the de facto end of his second marriage to Pauline Pfeiffer. Returned from war in Spain, working hard on *For Whom the Bell Tolls*, and having recently moved to Cuba with soon-to-be third wife Martha Gellhorn, Hemingway returned for another fall season of hunting in Wyoming. When Pauline joined him there, recently back from Europe with a bad cold, Hemingway's fear

Hemingway and the lion that succumbed to his bullet on the Serengeti Plain, January 1934.

of illness and desire to escape his marriage drove him to summon Martha to meet him at the newly opened Sun Valley resort in central Idaho.

Averell Harriman and the Union Pacific Railroad developed the village of Sun Valley to be a world-class ski resort. Gene Van Guilder ran publicity for the resort, and Lloyd Arnold was its photographer. The chief publicity campaign for the resort involved attracting celebrities to show off the skiing and hunting that Sun Valley offered. Hemingway and Martha occupied suite 206 in the Sun Valley lodge, which he later renamed "Glamour House." Although Ernest was suspicious of Gene and Lloyd at first, they quickly became good friends and hunted together regularly. When Gene was tragically killed in a hunting accident, Ernest delivered a stirring eulogy, part of which now graces Hemingway's own memorial just outside Sun Valley, overlooking Trail Creek. Lloyd Arnold would eventually write a book about Hemingway's days in Idaho, *High on the Wild*, which contains many of his wonderful photographs of Papa with his friends and family and other celebrities such as Gary Cooper, Ingrid Bergman, and Clark Gable.

In the late 1950s, when Ernest and his last wife, Mary, decided it was time to finally leave Cuba, they returned to Idaho to settle in the land they truly loved. They bought the Topping estate, with dramatic views of Ketchum, Adam's Gulch, and the mountains. Hemingway lived out his final few years in Ketchum, until he ended it, on his own terms, on a sunny morning in July 1961. He is buried in the Ketchum Cemetery.

Hemingway was drawn to Idaho for the hunting. He did very little fishing and in fact hunted primarily birds, including duck, pheasant, sage hen, and partridge. Lloyd Arnold recounts one of his first hunting trips with Hemingway, who was characteristically enthusiastic about his forthcoming adventures:

My wife Tillie and I were barely out of bed the morning of September 22 [1939] when Ernest called about breakfast with us.

"Good morning, Chief. What a beauty Indian summer day. . . ."

Ernest said that the ducks on the lagoon by the sun deck at Glamour House were his alarm clock that morning. "I came to, reaching for a gun. . . ."

He'd gone to sleep on my Idaho Encyclopedia and had been absorbing it since first light. "A hell of a lot of state, this Idaho, that I don't know about."[10]

Ernest's standard western-ranch-style breakfast was a fried-egg sandwich, complete with the ubiquitous raw onion. He would later revive his taste for this breakfast while on safari in 1953, when the overabundance of exotic game dishes rekindled his appetite for the simple, hearty breakfast of his days in Wyoming and Idaho. To re-create Ernest's hunting breakfast, fry up an egg in plenty of butter and make the sandwich of the egg, ham, some thickly sliced onion, ketchup, Worcestershire sauce, and a mustard pickle on slices of hearty bread.[11]

In the later years, the Hemingways rarely ate out in Ketchum. Occasionally they would have a steak at the Alpine, dine on leg of lamb prepared by Gloria, the Basque owner of the Rio Club, host a party at the Trail Creek Cabin, or have a special meal at the Christiania Restaurant on Sun Valley Road, where Ernest had his last meal on the evening of July 1, 1961. But Ernest and Mary usually ate at home in the later years, or shared a meal with close friends like Duke MacMullen or Lloyd and Tillie Arnold.

Tillie Arnold recalls once preparing an excellent roast on a rotisserie, which Ernest loved. When Papa asked if he could take some home, Mary gently chided him that it was rude to ask such a thing. "Well," Tillie fondly recalls, "Mary didn't know it then, but Papa always had some to take home."

Ernest and Mary were very fond of a delicious fruit compote for dessert, reminiscent of the fruit cup that Ernest and Hadley enjoyed in Milan in the early 1920s. This version is a little more elaborate and a lot stronger! Keep in mind that if any of the ingredients are out of season, you can substitute any favorite fruit that is available.

Fruit Compote

8 TO 10 SERVINGS

- 2 cups each honeydew melon, crenshaw melon, cantaloupe, and watermelon, cut into ¾ inch chunks
- 1 cup halved grapes
- 2 apples, peeled, cored, and cut into ¾-inch chunks
- 2 pears, peeled, cored, and cut into ¾-inch chunks
- 2 peaches, peeled, pitted, and cut into ¾-inch chunks
- 1 orange, peeled, sections cut in half
- ½ cup pitted and halved cherries
- 2 bananas, sliced
- 1½ cups kirsch

Cut all of the fruit over a large salad bowl or punch bowl, so as not to lose any of the juice. Stir the fruit to mix thoroughly. Pour the kirsch over the fruit and place in the refrigerator for several hours. Stir the fruit frequently. MacMullen recommends that you resist the temptation to throw away the fruit and just drink the sauce.

MOUNTAINSIDE PICNIC

During his frequent hunting trips, or any time hunger called in the mountains, Hemingway loved to picnic. In fact, his granddaughter, Joan Hemingway, wrote a wonderful book entitled *The Picnic Gourmet* (New York: Random House, 1977), that re-creates "a boating picnic" that she enjoyed as a young girl with Ernest and Mary in Cuba.

For Ernest, eating outdoors beside an open fire with a small group of friends was the only way to satisfy the hunger that the hunt and the mountain air inspired. As he had learned from his father never to shoot over the limit or waste what he killed, Hemingway's hunting meals invariably included leftovers. After a dinner of venison, Ernest would look at a half-full platter and think aloud that it would make a "good sandwich in a duck blind."[12] More often than not, it eventually did just that. The picnics, too, were nothing fancy and included mostly leftovers brought along by Mary or Tillie Arnold. Mary would bring her chili and Tillie a leftover roast, and they would cook them together and tailgate beside the road.

Forest MacMullen recalls taking along Cornish pasties, or deep-dish meat pies, when he and Ernest went down country hunting. This dish, perfectly suited for leftovers, is delicious either hot or cold.

Cornish Pasties

4 SERVINGS

For the Piecrust, see Campfire Apple Pie, page 11, with below exceptions

For the Filling

¾- to 1-pound round steak, cut into ¾-inch cubes

2 medium potatoes, cut into ¾-inch cubes

2 medium onions, chopped

¼ cup fresh, flat parsley leaves

2 tablespoons butter, softened

1 package Lipton's French Onion Soup mix

To make the piecrust, follow the instructions for Hemingway's Campfire Apple Pie (see page 11) with the following alterations. First, before rolling the dough, form it gently into a ball, wrap it in plastic wrap, and refrigerate for at least 1 hour up to several days. Second, you need not spread the extra shortening on the crust. Third, you may want to use a rolling pin rather than an old bottle (although the bottle works perfectly well).

Preheat the oven to 350° F.

For the filling, mix all of the ingredients, except the butter and the soup mix, together in a large bowl. Pour the mixture into the pie shell, press the mixture firmly into the shell, and smooth level. Rub the butter over the filling and sprinkle on the soup mix. Roll the top piecrust onto a floured rolling pin and unroll over the pie. Seal the edges of the crust with your thumb and cut two slashes in the top crust to let steam escape. Place the pie on the center rack and bake for about 1 hour. To test for doneness, stick a toothpick in the center. It should pull out easily. Remove from the oven and let stand 5 minutes before serving. Serve with plenty of ketchup to taste.

With this hearty meat pie as a starter, you may indulge in true Hemingway fashion whenever the opportunity to picnic presents itself. Take along some dishes from Ernest's past. The recipes may be decades old, but a few minutes over the fire may render them, and the memories they evoke, more delicious than when they were first enjoyed. Take along some of the venison prepared by Frau Nels at the Hotel Taube in Schruns, Cipriani's duck from Harry's in Venice, Gregorio's beef stew from Cuba, and some fruit cup from Biffi's in the Galleria in Milan. It is a Hemingway buffet of sorts, leaping effortlessly across space and time, from real life to the reality of great fiction, igniting the senses to degrees only possible through indulgence in honest art and great food.

158

FORREST "DUKE" MACMULLEN

Hemingway, Forrest "Duke" MacMullen, and Mr. Owl, who was shot accidentally and then nursed back to health by Hemingway.

THE HEMINGWAY WINE CELLAR

"Wine is one of the most civilized things in the world and one of the natural things of the world that has been brought to the greatest perfection, and it offers a greater range for enjoyment and appreciation than, possibly, any other purely sensory thing which may be purchased."

—*Death in the Afternoon*

Hotel de la Mère Poularde, Mont-Saint-Michel, August 1944

(Left to right) *Time* magazine correspondent Bill Walton, Mademoiselle Chevalier, Hemingway, an Army Signal Corp photographer, Monsieur Chevalier, and *Life* photographer Bob Capa.

In his treatise on bullfighting, *Death in the Afternoon*, Hemingway included in his glossary of terms an entry for Vino. With the air of authority of a world-class sommelier, he provided for the reader a complete introduction to Spanish wine:

> For any one who comes to Spain thinking only in terms of Sherry and Malaga the splendid, light, dry, red wines will be a revelation. The vin ordinaire in Spain is consistently superior to that of France since it is never tricked or adulterated, and is only about a third as expensive. I believe it to be the best in Europe by far.[1]

That Hemingway could speak with such authority in his early 30s is not surprising. He had been living in Paris through most of the 1920s and had traveled throughout Europe during that time. In addition, he had already developed a knack for speaking as an authority on subjects of which he knew far less than he knew of wine. Wine was a lifelong indulgence for Hemingway, from the days of his "boyhood when all red wines were bitter except port and drinking was the process of getting down enough of anything to make you feel restless," to the time when he developed "a palate that will give me the pleasure of enjoying completely a Chateaux Margaux or a Haut Brion."[2]

The Hemingway Wine Cellar contains only a fraction of the wines associated with Ernest Hemingway and those mentioned in his work. I have chosen to include here only those wines that are given prominent mention in his writing, wines of which he was especially fond, wines that accompany recipes in this book particularly well, and wines around which intriguing anecdotes arose. Without further ado, let us adjourn to the cellar.

Algerian Wine

> We ate very cheaply in an Algerian restaurant and I liked the food and the Algerian wine. The fire-eater was a nice man and it was interesting to see him eat, as he could chew with his gums as well as most people can with their teeth.[3]

As Hemingway waited to meet Fitzgerald in Lyon in *A Moveable Feast*, he met a man who ate fire and bent coins with his gums for a living. It is fitting that they should choose Algerian wine to wash away the aftertaste of the gentleman's vocation. Algeria's dark, heavy red wines are highly alcoholic, as much as 15 percent, due to the high sugar content produced by extremely hot Algerian summers. These wines were often blended with French wines to produce deeper color, fuller body, and higher alcohol content.

Asti

On Saturday night, August 31, 1918, Ernest and Agnes von Kurowsky dined together at the Du Nord restaurant in Milan. It was probably their first real date, at least in Ernest's eyes. Agnes had just ended a relationship with an Italian captain and was being careful not to do "anything foolish."[4] But Ernest's charms and boyish enthusiasm eventually wore her down. Their love affair formed the romantic centerpiece of *A Farewell to Arms*.

At the Du Nord, Agnes and Ernest shared a bottle of Asti Spumante, the sparkling white wine that had become her favorite. If Ernest was able to stomach this often "sickly sweet"[5] low-alcohol wine in 1918, he certainly could not do so after living in Paris, marrying and remarrying, and sitting down to write his second novel. After Agnes betrayed his love, Ernest reserved a special place for Agnes's favorite beverage in that novel of the war:

> Later, below in the town, I watched the snow falling, looking out of the window of the bawdy house, the house for officers, where I sat with a friend and two glasses drinking a bottle of Asti, and, looking out at the snow falling slowly and heavily, we knew it was all over for that year.[6]

Barbera

It is false to say that Ernest Hemingway wrote exclusively from his firsthand experience. What is true is that he created characters who appeared to have had such experiences even if their creator in fact had not. Hemingway was a great student of those things about which he wrote, be it war or revolution or bullfighting. In *A Farewell to Arms*, he re-created the retreat from Caporetto "so accurately that his Italian readers will later say he was present at that nation's embarrassment."[7] He was not. And yet, he was able to capture not only the events and the landscapes of the retreat, but also the essence of a national character. In one instance, Hemingway included a reference to Barbera wine—a heavy, deep red wine from the Piedmont region in the extreme northwest corner of Italy—to convey that character:

> We ate in the kitchen before we started. Aymo had a basin of spaghetti with onions and tinned meat chopped up in it [pasta asciutta]. We sat around the table and drank two bottles of the wine that had been left in the cellar of the villa. It was dark outside and still raining. Piani sat at the table very sleepy.

> "I like a retreat better than an advance," Bonello said. "On a retreat we drink barbera."[8]

Beaune

Hemingway recalls in *A Moveable Feast* that this is the wine he and Hadley enjoy with dinner at home after they pay Sylvia Beach her book deposit and cannot afford to eat out:

> We'll come home and eat here and have a lovely meal and drink Beaune from the cooperative you can see right out the window there with the price of the Beaune on the window. And afterwards we'll read and then go to bed and make love.[9]

As the story goes, an English wine merchant introduced his apprentices to Burgundies by telling them "there are two kinds of Burgundy: Beaune and the rest. We sell the rest." Beaune, the major city of the Côte de Beaune in central France, is considered the "Capital of Burgundian Wines." The region produces red and white wines, which are light and quick to mature. Most will hold for less than five years. We can assume that they purchased a red beaune, as Ernest later recommends this wine, along with Corton, Pommard, and Chambertin, as accompaniment to the Woodcock Flambé in Armagnac (see page 20).[10]

Cahors

An extremely dark, heavy, and ignoble red wine from southwest France, Cahors was often used, as was Algerian wine, to add color and flavor to lighter wines. Cahors was described as "black" and, like several other wines in the Hemingway cellar, was once very high in alcohol. Ernest and Hadley drank this wine, diluted by one-third, at the Nègre de Toulouse in Paris. By contrast, they brought home a bottle of Corsican wine, another cheap and rough wine, and could dilute that by one-half "and still receive its message."[11] Ernest always had a talent for finding pleasure in cheap wines, particularly in the early days when he had no choice. Much later, when money was hardly an issue, he wrote to the art critic Bernard Berenson, "I do not know why the wines you love should be so expensive. If I had all the money in the world I would drink Cahors and water."[12] Cahors is rather slow to mature, and should be aerated longer than most red wines for drinking.

Capri

> Because we would not wear any clothes because it was so hot and the window open and the swallows flying over the roofs of the houses and when it was dark afterward and you went to the window very small bats hunting over the houses and close down over the trees and we would drink the capri and the door locked and it hot and only a sheet and the whole night and we would both love each other all night in the hot night in Milan.[13]

This is how Frederic Henry imagined it would be with the women he had fallen for. Ernest, too, must have imagined such scenes with himself and Agnes during the war. He was able to give Frederic his evening of romance later in the

163

novel. At first, when Frederic was on his crutches, they went into Milan and, after trying several sweet white wines (including Freisa: "...imagine a country that makes a wine because it tastes like strawberries"[14]). They drank Capri and made it "their" wine. When they finally had their night of love in Milan, a bottle of Capri (as well as a bottle of St. Estephe) accompanied the woodcock, soufflé potatoes, purée de marron, salad, and zabaglione.

Capri was a dry, white wine from southwest Italy. It was made in very small quantities and was hardly ever found outside Capri itself. Often similar wines were imported and bottled under Capri labels. This was likely the case with Frederic and Catherine in Milan, adding an air of deceit and betrayal to their love, a vestige from Ernest's relationship with Agnes.

In the early 1920s, when Ernest returned with Hadley to his old front, they visited Biffi's in the Galleria in Milan and enjoyed a fruit cup with Capri. In *A Moveable Feast*, Hemingway remembered Biffi's and the fruit cup with wild strawberries and peaches, served in a glass pitcher.[15]

Biffi's Fruit Cup

4 SERVINGS

3 peaches, pitted and cut into bite-size slices
2 cups wild strawberries, hulled, or very small regular strawberries, halved
1 tablespoon sugar (optional)
2 cups Capri, or other dry white wine

Combine the peaches and strawberries in a bowl. Sprinkle with sugar, then pour the wine over the fruit. Mix the ingredients together gently. Chill in the refrigerator for 1 hour. Pour the fruit and wine into a tall glass pitcher and serve in a large bowl surrounded with crushed ice.

Chablis

Chablis is the well-known green-tinted yellow-gold wine from central France. It is known for its dryness and austere flavor.

In *The Sun Also Rises*, Jake Barnes and Bill Gorton order Chablis and sandwiches as an alternative to lunch as they find themselves stuck behind an endless procession of Catholic pilgrims aboard a train from Paris to Spain:

> We ate the sandwiches and drank the Chablis and watched the country out of the window. The grain was just beginning to ripen and the fields were full of poppies. The pastureland was green, and there were fine trees, and sometimes big rivers and chateaux off in the trees.[16]

The wine seems a lovely complement to the scene vista passing by the train window. Before the madness of Pamplona and San Fermín, replete with twirling dancers, drums pounding, and shirts stained with deep, rich Spanish red wine, a glass of Chablis and a rolling pastoral landscape may deceive our travelers as to what exactly awaits them.

Chateau Mouton-Rothschild

In 1937, Hemingway covered the Spanish Civil War for the North American News Alliance. As he watched his beloved Spain torn apart, he cultivated an affair with fellow journalist Martha Gellhorn, who he had met at Sloppy Joe's in Key West late the previous year. In Madrid, a city devastated by war, Ernest and Martha stayed in adjoining rooms at the Hotel Florida, venturing into the war torn streets to eat and drink at Chicote's on the Gran Via. Food and supplies were running very short. Hemingway remembered those times in the short story "Night Before Battle":

> "Comrade," I called the waiter. . . . "Bring another bottle of wine, please."

> "What kind?"

> "Any that is not too old so that the red is faded."

> "It's all the same."

> I said the equivalent of like hell it is in Spanish, and the waiter brought over a bottle of Château Mouton-Rothschild 1906 that was just as good as the last claret we had was rotten.

> "Boy that's wine," Al said. "What did you tell him to get that?"

> "Nothing. He just made a lucky draw out of the bin."[17]

Château Mouton-Rothschild is afforded eminent status among the Bordeaux due to its excellent quality and prestige, imparted by Philippe de Rothschild, who took over administration of the vineyard in 1926. Mouton-Rothschild was once known for its unique, faintly metallic flavor. That special quality is gone, but what remains is a wonderfully heavy, full-bodied wine. Coming from the Hotel Florida, whose top two floors had been destroyed by shelling, a 30-year-old bottle of this very fashionable wine must have been quite a pleasant surprise.

Châteauneuf du Pape

Ernest had great difficulty getting his early fiction published in the United States. Literary magazine editors were simply not prepared to accept his style, subjects, or choice of words. Many editors agreed with Gertrude Stein that his work was "inaccroachable," like a painting whose creator cannot hang it for view because it will no doubt offend. One magazine toward which Hemingway remained bitter for those early rejections was the *Dial*. Ernest Walsh, an editor at the *Dial*, once asked Ernest to lunch shortly after rumors spread that the magazine was going to award a sizeable sum to their most outstanding contributor. Walsh took Hemingway to a very expensive restaurant in the Boulevard St. Michel, and they dined on all the things that Ernest could not afford.

"What about red wine?" he asked. The sommelier came and I ordered a Châteauneuf du Pape. I would walk it off afterwards along the quais. He could sleep it off, or do what he wanted to do.[18]

Ernest knew that Châteauneuf du Pape was "not a luncheon wine." In fact, it has the highest minimum alcohol content of any French wine (between 12% and 14%). Perhaps he was out to prove, as he had often done and would continue to do, that he could drink anyone under the table, especially some con-man editor from the *Dial*.

After they were almost through with the wine, Walsh told Ernest that he was to receive the award, not Ezra Pound or James Joyce. Years later, Hemingway found out that Joyce, too, was told he would win the award.

Fleurie

Hemingway finishes a carafe of this Beaujolais wine he and Fitzgerald shared on their layover en route from Lyon to Paris. They order the wine as an accompaniment to *Escargots à la Bourguignonne* (see page 64). Fleurie is known as the queen of Beaujolais wines (Moulin-à-Vent is the king), exhibiting the quintessential characteristics of the region: heavy, yet exceedingly fruity. This wine should be drunk, not sipped, which Ernest no doubt does as he awaits Scott's return.

Mâcon

Mâcon is a dry white wine of southern Burgundy, "moderately full-bodied but with a low alcoholic content."[19] On their epic journey from Lyon to Paris, Hemingway sees to it that he and Scott have plenty of Mâcon with their picnic lunch of Truffle-Roasted Chicken (see page 63). He is surprised that "a few bottles of fairly light, dry white Mâcon could cause chemical changes in Scott that would turn him into a fool."[20] No doubt the drinks before breakfast, the whiskey and Perrier after, and the double whiskies before lunch contributed to Scott's eventual episode of hypochondria.

Marsala

Marsala, a dark wine sometimes served as an aperitif, is the principal dessert wine of Sicily. Made from a blend of aromatic white wine, a mash of dried grapes fortified with brandy, and grape-juice syrup, marsala has a mild taste of burnt sugar. While Ernest was recovering at the Red Cross Hospital in Milan, a man "with beautiful manners and a great name,"[21] came bearing marsala and Campari and made homosexual advances toward him.

Montagny

According to Lichine, "pleasant is the word most frequently used to describe"[22] this white wine of the Côte Chalonnais. In fact, as Hemingway and Fitzgerald sat down for a meal of Poularde de Bresse, it was accompanied by this wine which Ernest called "a light, pleasant white wine of the neighborhood."[23] After one sip, with no theatrics and apparently being careful not to spill anything, Scott proceeded to pass out at the table.

Muscadet

This pale, slightly musky white wine from vineyards on the River Loire south of Nantes, goes perfectly with fresh fish. In *A Moveable Feast*, Ernest recalled walking along the Seine to clear his head, watching the fisherman catch goujon with long cane poles. When he had money he would dine at La Pêche Miraculeuse and eat goujon fried whole, accompanied perfectly with Muscadet. Other times, he would dine al fresco:

> I knew several of the men who fished the fruitful parts of the Seine between the Île St.-Louis and the Place du Verte Galente and sometimes, if the day was bright, I would buy a liter of wine and a piece of bread and some sausage and sit in the sun and read one of the books I had bought and watch the fishing.[24]

Pouilly-Fuisse

Hemingway and Ernest Walsh drank this very fine dry white wine from southern Burgundy as an accompaniment to their oysters. The wine goes superbly with oysters.

Rioja

> We lunched up-stairs at Botín's. It is one of the best restaurants in the world. We had roast suckling pig and drank rioja alta. Brett did not eat much. She never ate much. I ate a very big meal and drank three bottles of rioja alta.[25]

Hemingway's recognition as early as 1925 of the superior quality of Rioja Alta is less impressive today, now that Rioja is widely considered one of the world's finest wine-producing regions. Rioja, in north-central Spain, produces wines that rival a fine Bordeaux or Burgundy. Interestingly, Rioja Alta, the northernmost and highest part of Rioja, is tantalizingly close to the Basque coast and San Sebastián, from where Jake was summoned to Madrid and Brett Ashley and Casa Botín. As when he was served Izzarra, a Basque liqueur, while in France, it seems that Jake has a hard time chasing the Basque presence from his memory.

Sancerre

After a good day at the track, Ernest and Hadley stop at Pruniers and spend their winnings on the "clearly priced"[26] oysters, *Crabe Mexicaine* (see page 55) and glasses of this crisp, very dry white wine from the Loire Valley.

Sherry

Sherry, a wine fortified with grape brandy from the Jerez region, is the most famous wine of Spain. The Spaniards' passion for sherry eclipses that of the Portuguese for port. When Jake Barnes, Bill Gorton, and Robert Cohn sit beside the Plaza del Castillo as the Fiesta de San Fermín begins its week-long burn, it is no wonder that Hemingway bestows upon them this most Spanish of aperitifs:

> The café was like a battleship stripped for action. To-day the waiters did not leave you alone all morning to read without asking if you wanted to order something. A waiter came up as soon as I sat down.
>
> "What are you drinking?" I asked Bill and Robert.
>
> "Sherry," Cohn said.
>
> "Jerez," I said to the waiter.[27]

In *A Moveable Feast*, Hemingway recalled drinking dry sherry with James Joyce despite Joyce's reputation for drinking exclusively Swiss white wine.[28]

MANZANILLA

Manzanilla is the palest of the Fino sherries, an extremely light, tart wine. It is the most popular accompaniment to tapas, the exquisite appetizers served in bars throughout Spain. When David and Catherine visit Madrid and the Prado in *The Garden of Eden*, they drink this "light and nutty tasting"[29] wine with their tapas: thin slices of jamón serrano, bright red and spicy sausages, anchovies, and garlic olives.

Sion

Sion is a Swiss white wine from the province of Valais. This is the suggested accompaniment, along with Aigle, to *Trout au Bleu*, page 58. Both wines come from vineyards at the foot of the Bernese Alps.

> Do you remember how Mrs. Gangeswisch cooked the trout au bleu when we got back to the chalet? They were such wonderful trout, Tatie, and we drank the Sion wine and ate out on the porch with the mountainside dropping off below and we could look across the lake and see the Dent du Midi with the snow half down it and the trees at the mouth of the Rhône where it flowed into the lake.[30]

St. Estephe

Along with Capri, Frederic and Catherine drink this fruity, full Bordeaux red with their exquisite "last supper" together at the hotel in Milan.

HEMINGWAY COLLECTION, JOHN F. KENNEDY LIBRARY

Hemingway opens a bottle of wine to enjoy in the majesty of the Swiss Alps.

169

Tavel

Norberto Fuentes, in his book *Hemingway in Cuba*, wrote that Tavel was Ernest's favorite French rosé.[31] Tavel is sturdy and full bodied for a rosé and should be drunk in "its first blush of youth."[32] In *The Garden of Eden*, a novel of the peril of new and adventurous love, Tavel seems to be the wine of choice, along with Perrier-Jouët Champagne. After Catherine returns with her hair cropped short, like a boy's, she orders Tavel with lunch. "It is a great wine for people that [sic] are in love,"[33] she says. Later, David and Marita have Tavel with the artichoke hearts dipped in mustard sauce.[34]

Valdepeñas

Before the recent ascension of wines from Rioja to the ranks of great celebrity, Valdepeñas was the best-known nonfortified Spanish wine. Throughout Hemingway's days in Madrid, this was the favorite wine in the cafés. Smooth, ruby red, and well balanced, this valiantly alcoholic wine was no doubt enjoyed by Hemingway at Casa Botín in Madrid, along with Rioja Alta, over roast suckling pig. In *The Garden of Eden*, David and Catherine drink pitchers of Valdepeñas with their gazpacho:

> They drank Valdepeñas now from a big pitcher and it started to build with the foundation of the marismeño only held back temporarily by the dilution of the gazpacho which it moved in on confidently. It built solidly.

"What is this wine?" Catherine asked.

"It's an African wine," David said.

"They always say that Africa begins at the Pyrenees," Catherine said. "I remember how impressed I was when I first heard it."[35]

Valpolicella

Colonel Richard Cantwell enjoys this red wine, from the Veneto region in northeast Italy, at the Gritti Palace Hotel in Venice. He knows what he wants: "the light, dry, red wine which was as friendly as the house of your brother, if you and your brother are good friends."[36] Cantwell also knows that Valpolicella is best if consumed within two years: "I believe that the Valpolicella is better when it is newer. It is not a grand vin and bottling it and putting years on it only adds sediment."[37] Ostensibly because of this sediment, but more likely to save money, Cantwell persists in demanding that the wine be decanted from two-litre fiascos rather than from the bottle:

> "He has your Valpolicella in the big wicker fiascos of two litres and I have brought this decanter with it."
>
> "That one," the Colonel said. "I wish to Christ I could give him a regiment."[38]

8

THE HEMINGWAY BAR

"I have drunk since I was fifteen and few things have given me more pleasure. When you work hard all day with your head and know you must work again the next day what else can change your ideas and make them run on a different plane like whiskey? When you are cold and wet what else can warm you? Before an attack who can say anything that gives you the momentary well being that rum does?"

—Letter to Russian critic Ivan Kashkin

Hemingway and Mary by his table-bar at the Finca Vigía, the house on their fifteen-acre estate in Cuba.

Hemingway drank. A lot. For most of his life. The statement to Ivan Kashkin can be read in different ways, depending on the role (or roles) the reader believes alcohol played in Hemingway's life. That he was an alcoholic is indisputable. The source of that alcoholism, while ultimately unimportant, remains a source of debate. Hemingway never openly admitted that he had a problem, yet he was quick to publicly point it out in others such as Scott Fitzgerald and William Faulkner.

Alcohol served him well in his early years. He spoke enthusiastically of its idea-changing properties and actively embraced the culture of alcohol while living in Paris. In an August 1922 dispatch to the *Toronto Star* weekly, young Hemingway captured the hedonistic lure of early-evening Paris in a discourse on apéritifs:

> Apéritifs, or appetizers, are those tall, bright red or yellow drinks that are poured from two or three bottles by hurried waiters during the hour before lunch and the hour before dinner, when all Paris gathers at the cafés to poison themselves into a cheerful pre-eating glow.[1]

Later in his life, alcohol became the "giant killer," helping him fight off his anxieties and bouts with severe depression. He needed it to get to sleep and to wake up. Eventually, as with Fitzgerald and Faulkner, it eroded his talent and certainly contributed to his death.

Why, then, has Hemingway remained the consummate "drinking writer," inspiring a carefree indulgence for countless fans and readers?

Because, for much of his life, he truly enjoyed drinking, and it did help him to maintain his craft. The eventual devastation notwithstanding, the image of the smiling, boisterous Hemingway, drink in hand and surrounded by friends, is one of the lasting images he left behind. If we live in the moment, get caught up in his generosity, and succumb to the charge he bestowed on a room upon entering, we may with honor and respect raise a glass to Ernest Hemingway and toast the good times.

To do so, we must familiarize ourselves with the Hemingway bar. Ernest was fastidious in his habit, indulging in his drinks of choice with the same dedication to detail that he had for his writing. While that may help us to understand why he wrote so much about drinking and drinkers, it in no way detracts from the magic he created when doing so. This may hint at another reason why the deleterious effects of drinking are often overlooked in Hemingway's case: he made it sound like so damned much fun.

Absinthe

It took the place of the evening papers, of all
the old evenings in cafés, of all chestnut trees
that would be in bloom now in this month, of
the great slow horses of the outer boulevards,
of book shops, of kiosques, and of galleries, of
the Parc Montsouris, of the Stade Buffalo, and
of the Butte Chaumont, of the Guaranty Trust
Company and the Ile de la Cité, of Foyot's old
hotel, and of being able to read and relax in
the evening; of all the things he had enjoyed
and forgotten and that came back to him
when he tasted that opaque, bitter, tongue-
numbing, brain-warming, stomach-warming,
idea-changing liquid alchemy.[2]

174

It's a very strange thing," he said. "This drink
tastes exactly like remorse. It has the true
taste of it and yet it takes it away."[3]

Absinthe is an emerald-green, very bitter liquor
infused with herbs, primarily anise and wormwood.
First distilled in the mountains of Switzerland,
absinthe was later brought to fabulous popularity
by the Frenchman Henri-Louis Pernod. Originally
considered a stimulant to creativity, it was later
believed that prolonged use of wormwood was
harmful to the nervous system, producing a syn-
drome know as absinthism. Absinthe was banned
throughout most Western countries between 1912
and 1915, although Spain continued to allow its
use for some time thereafter.

Hemingway first discovered absinthe on his initial trips to Spain and the bullfights in the early
1920s. Absinthe was banned in France before he
arrived, or else he would certainly have discovered
it much earlier. Despite the ban, Hemingway continued to drink absinthe (and Pernod, the brand
name of the imitation absinthe, produced without
wormwood) well into the 1930s. In *Death in the
Afternoon*, he explained, with tongue firmly in
cheek, why he has decided to give up bullfighting
(an endeavor that, in fact, he had never begun):
". . . it became increasingly harder as I grew older
to enter the ring happily except after drinking
three or four absinthes which, while they inflamed
my courage, slightly distorted my reflexes."[4]

Hemingway's taste for absinthe no doubt stems
from the purported mind-altering effects it
bestowed upon the drinker. After emerging from
his fiction, in which he would often become
deeply immersed, Hemingway would look to alcohol to attain some distraction from his work, some
transformation of the mind. As Robert Jordon says
after introducing a gypsy to absinthe in *For Whom
the Bell Tolls*: "It's supposed to rot your brain out
but I don't believe it. It only changes the ideas."[5] Of
course, it can also have other, less philosophically
intriguing effects: "It had the slow, culminating
wallop that made the boulevardier want to get up
and jump on his new straw hat in ecstasy."

Today, you may indulge in other anise-flavored
drinks without wormwood, such as Pernod or
Ricard, but you will probably end up waiting in
vain for "the feeling that makes [you] want to
shimmy rapidly up the side of the Eiffel Tower."[6]

Pernod

Pernod is a greenish imitation absinthe. When you add water it turns milky. It tastes like licorice and it has a good uplift, but it drops you just as far. We sat and drank it, and the girl looked sullen.[7]

1 SERVING

> 1½ ounces Pernod
> 1 sugar cube
> Drip glass
> Drip spoon

Pour Pernod into the drip glass or an old-fashioned glass. Place the drip spoon over the glass and the sugar cube on the spoon. Slowly pour cold water over the spoon to fill. If you do not have a drip spoon, place the sugar in a teaspoon and slowly pour the water over the sugar and allow it to run into the glass. Be careful to pour the water into the Pernod very slowly, otherwise it will be "flat and worthless."[8]

Armagnac and Perrier

Armagnac is a full-bodied and potent brandy produced in southwest France bordering on France's Basque country.The Armagnac's brandy is a reflection of its swarthy, hot-blooded people. For Hemingway, Armagnac has great diversity of use, from quelling arguments among guerrillas advancing toward occupied Paris to igniting woodcock in flambé. For David and Catherine Bourne, honeymooning in Mediterranean France in *The Garden of Eden*, Armagnac and Perrier satisfies their taste for something real:

> The waiter brought the Armagnac and the young man told him to bring a cold bottle of Perrier water instead of the syphon. The waiter poured two large Armagnacs and the young man put ice in the big glasses and poured in the Perrier.
>
> "This will fix us," he said. "It's a hell of a thing to drink before lunch though."
>
> The girl took a long sip. "It's good," she said. "It has a fresh clean healthy ugly taste." She took another long sip. "I can really feel it. Can you?"
>
> "Yes," he said and took a deep breath. "I can feel it."
>
> She drank from the glass again and smiled and the laugh wrinkles came at the corner of her eyes. The cold Perrier had made the heavy brandy alive.[9]

1 SERVING

> 2–4 ounces Armagnac
> Perrier to fill

Pour the brandy into a highball glass over ice cubes and fill with Perrier. Stir.

Hemingway's Bloody Marys

Hemingway's taste for Bloody Marys was probably cultivated in the 1920s at Harry's New York Bar in Paris, allegedly the birthplace of the drink. Twenty years later he claimed to have introduced the drink to Hong Kong, which "did more than any other single factor except perhaps the Japanese Army to precipitate the Fall of that Crown Colony."[10] In 1947, Ernest shared his own Bloody Mary recipe with friend Bernard Peyton.

Hemingway's recipe makes a full pitcher, as he insisted that "any smaller amount is worthless."[11] You will note that when the recipe calls for stirring, Hemingway deliberately spelled *stir* with two r's. As you create the drink, catching its sweet and spicy aroma and eagerly awaiting its taste, you'll want to "stirr" it also.

2 SERVINGS

2 cups Russian vodka
2 cups chilled tomato juice
1 tablespoon Worcestershire sauce
1 jigger fresh lime juice
Pinch of celery salt
Pinch of cayenne pepper, or to taste
Pinch of black pepper, or to taste

Place as large a lump of ice as will fit in a large pitcher. The single piece of ice is important, as it keeps the drink very cold while not watering it down. If you are using ice cubes, be sure that the vodka and tomato juice are very cold, and only add the ice to individual glasses when serving.

Combine the vodka, tomato juice, and Worcestershire sauce and stirr. Add the lime juice and stirr again. Add the seasonings, keep stirring, and taste. If it is too strong, add more tomato juice, if it "lacks authority," add vodka. Hemingway recommends adding more Worcestershire sauce to avoid a bad hangover, as well as adding a few drops of Mexican hot sauce to taste.

Campari and Gordon's Gin

He heard her coming up the stairs and noticed the difference in her tread when she was carrying two glasses and when she had walked down bare-handed. He heard the rain on the windowpane and he smelled the beech logs burning in the fireplace. As she came into the room he put his hand out for the drink and closed his hand on it and felt her touch the glass with her own.

"It's our drink for out here," she said. "Campari and Gordon's with ice."

"I'm certainly glad you're not a girl who would say 'on the rocks.'"[12]

Ernest was likely first introduced to Campari in Milan by the Italian gentleman with the great name and the fine manners (see Marsala, page 169). Campari, made in Milan by Fratelli Campari, is a deep red, bitter liqueur infused with herbs and orange peel.

Gordon's was Hemingway's gin of choice. He specifically requested it for his martinis and twice has his characters in his fiction mention this brand of gin in their Campari and gin. In the story quoted above, a blind American writer and his wife drink their "drinks for out here" in Venice. In *Across the River and into the Trees*, when Colonel Cantwell arrives at a Venice bar, the bartender sends down, via dumbwaiter, for a Gordon's gin and Campari before the Colonel even orders it. Could it be that this drink tastes of Venetian homecomings? It's worth a shot.

1 SERVING

> 2 ounces Gordon's gin
>
> 1 ounce Campari

Pour the gin and Campari over ice in an old-fashioned cocktail glass. Stir. Garnish with a twist of orange peel, if desired.

Chambéry Cassis

> On this evening I was sitting at a table outside of the Lilas watching the light change on the trees and the buildings and the passage of the great slow horses of the outer boulevards. The door of the café opened behind me and to my right, and a man came out and walked to my table.[13]

The man was Ford Madox Ford, a British writer who was editor of the *transatlantic review* in Paris, for which Ernest was an associate editor for some time. Ford had earlier published Hemingway's "Indian Camp" at a time when popular magazines would never accept such a graphic story. He considered Ernest the best writer of his time. Of course, good deeds did not always exempt people from Hemingway's biting, often vicious sense of satire. Hemingway laid into Ford in *The Sun Also Rises* as Braddocks, and later in *A Moveable Feast*.

When Ford joins Ernest at the Closerie des Lilas, he orders a Chambéry Cassis, known commonly in France as *rince cochon*, or "pig rinse." This is fitting for a man who Ernest described as "an ambulatory, well clothed, up-ended hogshead."[14] In *Death in the Afternoon*, Hemingway warns his lady friend against befriending writers (himself in particular?). Unfortunately, it was a warning that Ford, and many others along the way, never heard or heeded.

Chambéry Cassis is made with Chambéry vermouth, a very dry vermouth, and cassis, a sweet red liqueur made from black currants. Put ¾ ounce cassis in a glass with crushed ice and then fill with Chambéry vermouth.

Citron Pressé with Whiskey (The Hemingway Whiskey Sour)

Stopped by heavy rains en route from Lyon to Paris, Hemingway and Scott Fitzgerald took refuge at a hotel in Châlon-sur-Saône. Once there, Hemingway attempted to stave off Scott's hypochondria with his version of a whiskey sour.

Citron pressé is a classic French aperitif, its components presented to the drinker to assemble to his or her own taste. Ernest and Scott's drinks are served with the glasses of pressed lemon juice and ice accompanied by two double whiskeys and a bottle of Perrier. You may add sugar to taste, but Hemingway likely took his *citron pressé* sugar-free.

2 SERVINGS, BUT KEEP THEM COMING

> 2 lemons
> 2 double whiskies
> 1 bottle Perrier
> Sugar to taste (optional)
> Ice

Cut the lemons in half. Squeeze the juice from each lemon and strain into two tall cocktail glasses. Add 1 double whiskey to each glass. Top with Perrier. Add sugar to taste if desired. Drop a few ice cubes into each glass. Stir and serve.

Cuba Libre (Chasing a Straight Whiskey)

The disparity between rich and poor in Depression-era Key West appears throughout *To Have and Have Not*. In the closing pages, as Harry Morgan's blood-soaked boat is towed in from the Gulf, Hemingway turns his astute, satirical eye toward the yachts that are tied up at the pier. It is a moment of supreme tragedy. Earlier, the "haves" and "have-nots" met up at Freddy's Bar, modeled on the original Sloppy Joe's in Key West (see p. 117). A rich young woman, with "the face and build of a lady wrestler,"[15] sized up Harry as he entered the bar, coyly asked her husband to buy him for her, and interrupted Harry's conversation with Freddy.

"Shut up, you whore," Harry replied curtly and walked to the back room. When Harry returned to the bar the woman looked away from him to register disgust.

"What will you have?" asked Freddy.

"What's the lady drinking," Harry asked.

"A Cuba Libre."

"Then give me a straight whiskey."[16]

Straight Whiskey

When Hemingway drank at Sloppy Joe's he drank scotch on the rocks. He'd order Chivas or Cutty Sark or J&B, but mostly Chivas. In reality it didn't matter because Joe Russell, the owner, would fill up empty Chivas, Cutty, and J&B bottles with "skunk piss" Scotch. One can only assume that he poured a similar quality of whiskey straight as well. Obviously, the sensitive palate that Hemingway developed for wine in Paris had not yet caught up with his taste for whiskey in Key West.

Cuba Libre

1 SERVING

> 2 ounces Havana Club or Bacardi White rum
> Juice of ½ lime, plus the rind
> Cola
> Ice

Pour the rum and lime juice into a highball glass. Add the lime rind. Fill the glass with cola and ice cubes.

The Hemingway Daiquirí

He was drinking another of the frozen daiquirís with no sugar in it and as he lifted it, heavy and the glass frost-rimmed, he looked at the clear part below the frappéd top and it reminded him of the sea. The frappéd part of the drink was like the wake of a ship and the clear part was the way the water looked when the bow cut it when you were in shallow water over marl bottom. That was almost the exact color.

"I wish they had a drink the color of sea water when you have a depth of eight hundred fathoms and there is a dead calm with the sun straight up and down and the sea full of plankton," he said.

"What?"

"Nothing. Let's drink this shallow water drink."[17]

If there is one drink that is synonymous with Ernest Hemingway, it is the Daiquirí. If there is one bar that is synonymous with both Hemingway and the Daiquirí, it is El Floridita in Old Havana. Hemingway found El Floridita in the 1930s and, as with so many other bars, cities, and even countries, he left it, years later, a very different place.

In Hemingway's time, Constantino Ribailagua owned El Floridita. Constante, as his customers called him, also served as bartender. If Constante did not invent the Daiquirí, he certainly nurtured it to a position of great notoriety. Constante would blend rum, lemon, sugar, crushed ice, and maraschino with the precision and finesse of an artist at work on his masterpiece. His artistry was not lost on the famous American writer sitting in his regular stool in the first corner to the left at the end of the bar. It was here where Hemingway invented his own version of the Daiquirí, known as the Papa Doble, the Hemingway Daiquirí, the Daiquirí Special, or the Wild Daiquirí.[18]

He made two simple changes. First, due to his distaste for sugar in his drinks, he had the Daiquirí made without it. Second, to save time and effort while drinking, he began to order doubles. He would often drink a dozen of these frothy elixirs in one sitting. Legend has it (and what respectable drinker could deny such a legend), that Hemingway once drank 16 Papa Dobles in one run at El Floridita. With 3¾ ounces of rum in each drink, that comes to 60 ounces! Needless to say, El Floridita, and Hemingway, would never be the same.

Today, El Floridita is more refined than in Hemingway's day. When Mary Hemingway visited Cuba in 1977, she was not interested in visiting the Floridita, which had lost its charm when all the prostitutes and *maricones* left. Nonetheless, El Floridita thrives on the memory of its most famous patron.

The Myth of the Mojito

Curiously, El Floridita was not the only bar to capitalize on Hemingway's star status. La Bodeguita del Medio, a "claustrophobic little hole-in-the-wall,"[19] has carved out its own piece of the Hemingway legend. Above the bar, a sign reads:

MY MOJITO IN LA BODEGUITA
MY DAIQUIRÍ IN EL FLORIDITA

The quote is signed "Ernest Hemingway" in his unmistakable script. Thanks to the insatiable appetites of tourists and journalists for Hemingway lore, the *mojito* has made its way into The Hemingway Bar. In fact, that sign was not created until well after the Castro revolution in 1959. The owners needed a way to increase business and attract tourists, and Hemingway seemed like the perfect spokesman. It did not matter that Hemingway probably never set foot in the place, which was nothing more than a *bodeguita*, or grocery store, in Hemingway's drinking days. They did not even have a bar until the mid-1950s. All that aside, there was no place on the narrow street outside El Bodeguita for Ernest's chauffeur to park, and the fact that there is no such thing as a sugarless *mojito* confirms that the Hemingway connection with the drink is completely fictional. Nonetheless, it is a marvelously refreshing drink, and truly Cuban. As close as Hemingway came to the *mojito* was a drink invented by Gregorio Fuentes—at once mate, cook, and bartender aboard the *Pilar*—to prevent or cure colds. It is very similar to a *mojito*, sweetened with honey instead of sugar:

    2 tablespoons honey
    Juice of 2 lemons
    Sprig of mint
    2 ice cubes
    Bacardi White rum

Place the honey, lemon juice, and mint sprig in a tall glass. Stir, pressing the mint against the side of the glass to release the oils. Add the ice and rum. Stir and serve.

Hemingway Daiquirí, Papa Doble, Wild Daiquirí, Daiquirí Special

The following recipe is based upon the Daiquirí recipe from El Floridita that Hemingway drinks with A. E. Hotchner in his book *Papa Hemingway*.

1 SERVING

    2½ jiggers Bacardi or Havana Club rum
      (1 jigger = 1½ ounces)
    Juice of 2 limes
    Juice of ½ grapefruit
    6 drops of maraschino (cherry brandy)

Fill a blender one-quarter full of ice, preferably shaved or cracked. Add the rum, lime juice, grapefruit juice, and maraschino.

Blend on high until the mixture turns cloudy and light-colored, "like the sea where the wave falls away from the bow of a ship when she is doing thirty knots."[20]

Serve immediately in large, conical goblets.

Deusico (Turkish Coffee)

In the late summer of 1922, Asia Minor was smoldering, ready to ignite yet again in the final, tragic chapter of the Greco-Turkish War. Hemingway to went Constantinople as a correspondent for the *Toronto Star*, to cover the Greek expulsion from Thrace. He witnessed their forced exodus from the city, an experience he would draw upon when he described the Italian retreat from Caporetto in *A Farewell to Arms*. He took in the entire spectacle, resting his imagination on certain things he found most intriguing. As he wrote about Constantinople, he described the food, eventually focusing on a drink that he must have deeply respected, if for nothing other than its brute, unrelenting potency:

> Turks sit in front of the little coffee houses in the narrow blind-alley streets at all hours, puffing on their bubble-bubble pipes and drinking deusico, the tremendously poisonous, stomach rotting drink that has a greater kick than absinthe.[21]

Duesico, or Turkish coffee, refers to a method of grinding and preparation rather than a type of bean. You may either grind the coffee yourself, which involves pulverizing dark beans (such as arabica or viennese) to a very fine powder and adding a pinch of cardamom. Or, you may purchase the coffee already ground. Be certain to note that there is cardamom in the mix. The coffee is prepared in a small, long-handled pot called a *jezve*, which you may find in finer cookware stores or Turkish markets. It may also be made in a small saucepan.

1 SERVING

1 tablespoon Turkish coffee

2 teaspoons sugar

4 tablespoons water

Mix the coffee, sugar, and water together in a *jezve*. Place the *jezve* over low heat and bring it to a boil three times, removing it from the heat each time before the foam runs over. After the third boil, rap the *jezve* sharply on the side to settle the grounds (you may also add a small splash of water to obtain the same effect). Pour the coffee slowly into a demitasse.

Hemingway with Perico Chicote, Mary, and friends at Chicote's in Madrid, Spain.

Gimlet

The overt tension between Francis Macomber and his wife throughout the story about his "Short Happy Life" on safari in Africa begins at the very start of the story, over lunchtime cocktails with their white hunter, Robert Wilson:

> It was now lunch time and they were all sitting under the double green fly of the dining tent pretending that nothing had happened.
>
> "Will you have lime juice or lemon squash?" Macomber asked.
>
> "I'll have a gimlet," Robert Wilson told him.
>
> "I'll have a gimlet too. I need something," Macomber's wife said.
>
> "I suppose it's the thing to do," Macomber agreed. "Tell him to make three gimlets."
>
> The mess boy had started them already, lifting the bottles out of the canvas cooling bags that sweated wet in the wind that blew through the trees that shaded the tents.[22]

While Raymond Chandler's legendary detective Philip Marlowe insisted that the only way to make a gimlet was with equal parts vodka and Rose's (lime juice), the gimlet of the Macombers' day was still a gin drink.

1 SERVING

> 1 ounce gin
>
> 1 ounce Rose's lime juice

Fill an old-fashioned glass halfway with ice. Add the gin and lime juice and stir.

Gin and Tonic

Chicote's on the Gran Via in Madrid "was a very cheerful place, and because really cheerful people are usually the bravest, and the bravest get killed quickest, a big part of Chicote's old customers are now dead."[23] Perico Chicote opened his bar in 1931. It was a favorite hangout of Hemingway's during the Spanish Civil War in the late 1930s. When he began writing "The Denunciation," a story of old friends and new betrayals, in Paris in the spring of 1938, he brought the narrator Henry Emmunds to Chicote's to escape the shelling on the Gran Via. Once inside, a waiter tells him of the presence of Luis Delgado, a fascist spy. Before he denounced Delgado to the counterespionage bureau, he recalled gambling with him in San Sebastián over gin and tonics, the same drink he is drinking at Chicote's:

> "What about a gin and tonic? That's a marvelous drink you know."
>
> So we had a gin and tonic and I felt very badly to have broken him and I felt awfully good to have won the money, and a gin and

tonic never tasted better to me in all my life. There is no use to lie about these things or pretend you do not enjoy winning; but this boy Luis Delgado was a very pretty gambler.[24]

The true Hemingway gin and tonic uses Schweppes Indian tonic water, which they served at Chicote's, and Gordon's gin, Hemingway's favorite. (He once wrote that Gordon's gin could "fortify, mollify and cauterize practically all internal and external injuries."[25]) The measure of gin and the lemon are included in honor of Gregorio Fuentes, who served gin and tonics of these proportions aboard the *Pilar*.

The Ernest Hemingway Gin and Tonic

1 SERVING

> 2 fingers Gordon's gin
> Schweppes Indian tonic water
> Lemon wedge

Pour the gin into a tall glass over ice. Fill the glass with tonic water. Add the lemon wedge and stir.

Glühwein

The German word glühwein translates literally as "glowing wine." It is a hot, spiced wine drink that served Frederic and Catherine well during the cold nights in Switzerland in the middle of January:

> There was an inn in the trees at the Bains de l'Alliaz where the woodcutters stopped to drink, and we sat inside and warmed by the stove and drank hot red wine with spices and lemon in it. They called it glühwein and it was a good thing to warm you and to celebrate with. . . . It was a fine country and every time that we went out it was fun.[26]

> ¼ cup black tea (made by steeping 1 tea bag per ½ cup boiling water)
> 2–3 slices of lemon with peel (use orange for a less bitter version)
> 3 teaspoons sugar
> 1–2 dried juniper berries
> 2 cloves
> 1 cinnamon stick (optional)
> 1¾ cups red wine

Heat all ingredients in a saucepan over low heat until very warm. Strain through a sieve into warmed tumblers or drink with teeth clenched.

Grappa

In *A Farewell to Arms*, Frederic Henry has a peculiar relationship with grappa, a harsh Italian brandy distilled from grape husks, the residue that remains when the grapes have been pressed and relieved of their juice. He never seems to want it, and yet he drinks it throughout the novel, with often dramatic consequences. During a layover, en route from the field hospital to the Red Cross Hospital in Milan, Frederic pays a young boy to get him some cognac. All the boy can find is grappa. Henry shares the bottle with the man invalided next to him, and they both suffer from what Hemingway called "gastric remorse."

Grappa could never be accused of being smooth. It hits like a roundhouse right and sears life phosphorus. In *Across the River and into the Trees*, Colonel Cantwell reminisces about his war days with a friend and former comrade:

> "I drank grappa and could not even feel the taste."
>
> "We must have been tough then," the Colonel said.[27]

Highball (*Highbalito con Agua Mineral*)

In his book *Straight Up or on the Rocks*, William Grimes calls the highball "about the laziest cocktail in existence."[28] Although originally a whiskey or gin drink, the highball now refers to any liquor on the rocks with soda. Compared with the high art of the Daiquirí, the highball is simple pedestrian fare:

> The Floridita was open now and he bought the two papers that were out, Crisol and Alerta, and took them to the bar with him. He took his seat on a tall bar stool at the extreme left of the bar. His back was against the wall toward the street and his left was covered by the wall behind the bar. He ordered a double frozen daiquiri with no sugar from Pedrico, who smiled his smile which was almost like the rictus on a dead man who has died from a suddenly broken back, and yet was a true and legitimate smile. . . .
>
> Pedrico set out a bottle of Victoria Vat, a glass with large chunks of ice in it, and a bottle of Canada Dry soda in front of Ignacio Natera Revello and he made a highball hurriedly and then turned toward Thomas Hudson, looking at him through his green-tinted, hornrimmed glasses and feigning to have just seen him.[29]

Highball

1 SERVING

>2 ounces Victoria Vat, or whiskey
>
>Canada Dry soda water (Honest Lil, the old prostitute from El Floridita, orders her *highbalito* with mineral water)

Pour the whiskey over ice in a highball glass. Fill the glass with soda and stir.

Izzarra

In Bayonne, France, after the madness of the Fiesta, Jake Barnes enjoys the pleasure of eating and drinking alone. Afterward, "the waiter recommended a Basque liqueur called Izzarra. He brought in the bottle and poured a liqueur-glass full. He said Izzarra was made of the flowers of the Pyrenees . . . It looked like hair-oil and smelled like Italian strega. I told him to take the flowers of the Pyrenees away."[30]

It is interesting that the French waiter should offer Jake Izzarra, the Basque version of Chartreuse, which is made right there in Bayonne. Perhaps it is an indication of how persistent the specter of Spain will be for Jake. He shakes it off, though, rejecting the Izzarra in favor of the veritable French marc (see page 189). There are two types of Izzarra, green and yellow. We could presume that Jake (and Ernest) sampled the green, as it is the more highly alcoholic of the two.

Jack Rose

At five o' clock I was in the Hotel Crillon, waiting for Brett. She was not there, so I sat down and wrote some letters. They were not very good letters but I hoped their being on Crillon stationary would help them. Brett did not turn up, so about quarter to six I went down to the bar and had a Jack Rose with George the barman.[31]

The Hotel Crillon in Paris is one of the great and grand hotels. In the early days, Hemingway could scarcely afford to drink there. He would, no doubt, employ the free stationary to keep up appearances.

1 SERVING

>1½ ounces applejack brandy
>
>Juice of ½ lime
>
>½ ounce grenadine

Combine the brandy, lime juice, and grenadine in a shaker filled with ice. Shake, and strain into a cocktail glass.

Kirsch

Kirsch is a brandy distilled from cherries, including the stones, which impart an almond flavor. This was a favorite of Hemingway's, which he drank frequently during the Paris years. He kept a bottle in his rented writing room in Paris, drinking it to keep warm during damp Parisian winters. When the Hemingways escaped from Paris to Austria in the wintertime, Ernest's taste for kirsch followed. As he immersed himself in the rugged mountain environs and let his black beard thicken, he delighted in hearing the residents refer to him as the "black, kirsch-drinking Christ."[32]

Kümmel

Kümmel was on the roll call of Hemingway's "army of dead men," the empty liquor bottles that littered his bedside armoire at the hospital in Milan. In *A Farewell to Arms*, the little bear-shaped bottle stands out amongst its fallen brethren:

> One day while I was in bed with jaundice Miss Van Campen came in the room, opened the door into the armoire and saw the empty bottles there. . . . The bear-shaped bottle enraged her particularly. She held it up, the bear was sitting up on his haunches with his paws up, there was a cork in his glass head and a few sticky crystals at the bottom. I laughed.

"It is kümmel," I said. "The best kümmel comes in those bear shaped bottles. It comes from Russia.[33]

Kümmel is a sweet, clear liqueur distilled from grain alcohol. Its flavor comes from caraway seeds. As in Frederic Henry's case, sugar is some-

HEMINGWAY COLLECTION, JOHN F. KENNEDY LIBRARY

In Austria, the "black kirsch-drinking Christ" gives his son John Hadley Nicanor Hemingway, affectionately called Bumby, a skiing lesson.

times allowed to crystallize in the bottle. This type of kümmel is known as Kümmel Crystallize. Although invented in either Germany or Holland, the best kümmel does, in fact, come from Russia. (See Zabaglione, page 22.)

Marc

Marc is a powerful brandy distilled from grape pomace, essentially the French counterpart of grappa. With the help of Krebs Friend, with whom Ernest worked in Chicago and who eventually married an heiress and became benefactor to Ford Madox Ford's *transatlantic review* in Paris, we may understand the dubious allure of marc. In 1923, Hemingway wrote of Friend's boar-hunting trip in a little town in the Côte d'Or:

> Krebs was wakened before daylight. The boar hunters were assembled at the café. They were waiting for him. He arrived half asleep. Inside the café were about twenty men. Bicycles were stacked outside. Hunting the boar was nothing to be undertaken on an empty stomach. They must have a small drink of some sort. Something to warm the stomach.
>
> Krebs suggested coffee. What a joke. What a supreme and delightful joker the American. Coffee. Imagine it. Coffee before going off to hunt the sanglier. What a thing. Drôle enough, eh?

Marc. Marc was the stuff. No one ever started after the wild boar without first a little marc. Patron, the marc. The marc was produced. Now marc, pronounced mar as in marvelous, is one of the three most powerful drinks known. As an early morning potion it can give vodka, douzico, absinthe, grappa, and other famous stomach destroyers two furlongs and beat them as far as Zev beat Papyrus. It is the great specialty of Burgundy and the Côte d'Or and three drops of it on the tongue of a canary will send him out in a grim, deadly, silent search for eagles.[34]

The Montgomery (Hemingway's Martini)

HARRY'S BAR, VENICE

"Waiter," the Colonel called; then asked, "Do you want a dry Martini, too?"

"Yes," she said, "I'd love one."

"Two very dry Martinis," the Colonel said. "Montgomerys. Fifteen to one."[35]

Like James Bond with his Vesper, Hemingway, too, had his special martini called the Montgomery. Named after the World War II British General, Sir Bernard Law Montgomery, General of the British Eighth Army, who would not attack unless he outnumbered the enemy 15 to 1, Hemingway's martini contains that same proportion

189

of gin to vermouth. The Montgomery is a house special at Harry's Bar in Venice, where they make their Montgomerys 10 to 1. For this recipe, we'll use Hemingway's favorite ingredients: Gordon's gin and Noilly Prat vermouth.[36]

1 SERVING

> 3 ounces Gordon's gin
>
> 1 teaspoon plus a few drops Noilly Prat vermouth
>
> 1 olive

Pour the gin and vermouth into an ice-filled shaker. Shake, then strain into a martini glass. Place the filled glass in the freezer until ready to serve. Garnish with the olive.

Option #1: To make a Super Montgomery, garnish with a garlic olive (see page 95).

Option #2: Multiply the recipe by 73, as Hemingway did after liberating the Ritz Hotel in Paris from the Nazis with a thirsty band of FFI (*Forces Françaises l'Intérieur*) on August 25, 1944.

Rum Punch

In *The Sun Also Rises*, Jake and Bill spend a cold, blustery night in the Hostal Burguete in the Spanish Pyrenees before trout fishing. While Jake negotiates with the woman who owns the inn, Bill plays the piano to keep warm:

"How about a hot rum punch?" he said. "This isn't going to keep me warm permanently."

I went and told the woman what a rum punch was and how to make it. In a few minutes a girl brought a stone pitcher, steaming, into the room. Bill came over from the piano and we drank the hot punch and listened to the wind.

"There isn't too much rum in that."

I went over to the cupboard and brought the rum bottle and poured a half-tumblerful into the pitcher.

"Direct action," said Bill. "It beats legislation."[37]

1¾ cups dark rum

¾ cup sugar

1½ teaspoons ground cloves

6 teaspoons lemon juice

2 tablespoons butter

3 cups boiling water

Combine all ingredients except ½ cup rum in a medium saucepan and heat over medium-high heat until hot. Transfer the punch to a ceramic pitcher. Taste to verify insufficient volume of rum. Add remaining rum. Serve immediately.

Tomini or Green Isaak's Special

Hemingway's passion for romantic descriptions of the Daiquirí in *Islands in the Stream* overflowed Constante's blender to include other favorites as well. Several times throughout the novel, Thomas Hudson truly enjoys a sort of embellished Tom Collins, made with coconut water and bitters:

> Thomas Hudson took a sip of the ice-cold drink that tasted of the fresh green lime juice mixed with the tasteless coconut water that was still so much more full-bodied than any charged water, strong with the real Gordon's gin that made it alive to his tongue and rewarding to swallow, and all of it tautened by the bitters that gave it color. It tastes as good as a drawing sail feels, he thought. It is a hell of a good drink.[38]

2 ounces Gordon's gin

Dash of Angostura bitters ("just enough Angostura bitters to give it a rusty, rose color.")[39]

Juice of 1 lime

Coconut water

In a tall cocktail glass filled with ice, combine the gin, bitters, and lime juice. Add coconut water to fill. Stir and serve.

Note: Coconut water is not the same as coconut milk. The water is simply the juice found in fresh coconut, while the milk is produced by pouring boiling water over the coconut flesh.

Vermouth and Bitters

Drinks made with vermouth, the fortified wine blended with a secret combination of herbs and spices, appear throughout Hemingway's life and fiction. He was usually quite specific with his choice of vermouths, employing Noilly Prat for his best martini, providing Frederic Henry with a bottle of Cinzano for his bedside stash and keeping one for himself in the living room bar at home in Cuba, creating fictional Negronis in Mestre outside Venice made with two sweet vermouths, and twice specifying that the drink be made with 2 parts French to 1 part Italian vermouth. These last specifications refer more to the dryness of the vermouths than to their countries of origin. Italian vermouth was originally red and sweet, while French was white and dry. Today, the distinctions are no longer set.

In the fall of 1935, while drifting for marlin four miles east of Havana and an onshore gunnery range, the crew aboard the *Pilar* were suddenly startled away from their drinks when a loud blast was heard well to the east of the boat. Only such a blast, in actuality the breaching of a whale, could take their attention from their manly talk and freshly mixed drinks:

> We had the tall glasses with of Italian vermouth (two parts of French to one of Italian, with a dash of bitters and a lemon peel, fill glass with ice, stir and serve) in our hands and I was just raising mine when Carlos shouted "Que canonazo!" Oh, what a cannon shot!
>
> "Where?"
>
> "Way out there. To the eastward. Like the spout from a twelve inch shell."[40]

Before the frantic pursuit of the whale becomes all-consuming, let's not forget those drinks:

1 SERVING

2 ounces dry vermouth
1 ounce sweet vermouth
Dash of bitters
Lemon peel for garnish
Ice

Pour the vermouths over ice into a tall glass. Add the bitters and lemon peel. Stir and serve.

Whiskey

I went back to the papers and the war in the papers and poured the soda slowly over the ice into the whiskey. I would have to tell them not to put the ice in the whiskey. Let them bring the ice separately. That way you could tell how much whiskey there was and it would not suddenly be too thin from the soda. I would get a bottle of whiskey and have them bring ice and soda. That was the sensible way. Good whiskey was very pleasant. It was one of the pleasant parts of life.

"What are you thinking, darling?"

"About whiskey."

"What about whiskey?"

"About how nice it is."

Catherine made a face. "All right," she said.[41]

Hemingway employs whiskey in innumerable and novel ways, from fending off F. Scott Fitzgerald's hypochondria[42] to curing athlete's foot.[43] He was also known to drink it on occasion. In fact, whiskey appears in his writing more than any other liquor, being consumed, alluded to, or admired over 100 times. It is consumed straight, on the rocks, or mixed with ginger ale, lemonade,

192

mineral water, or Perrier, and even mixed with beer or wine.

In the short story "The Strange Country" the characters imagine the pleasure of a uniquely concocted Giant Killer Scotch:

> You can make a wonderful one with wild strawberries. If you have a lemon you cut half of it and squeeze it into the cup and leave the rind in the cup. Then you crush the wild strawberries into the cup and wash the sawdust off a piece of ice from the icehouse and put it in and then fill the cup with Scotch and then stir it till it's all mixed and cold.[44]

Hemingway himself enjoyed some interesting variations of Scotch drinks. Susan Buckley, wife of Hemingway's friend and biographer Peter Buckley, recalls Hemingway's fondness for a drink of equal parts Scotch and lime juice.

Above all these, though, there is one whiskey drink that is perfectly Hemingway, absolutely Ernestly earnest. It is his own invention, evoking images of trout fishing, spring thaws, and infinite wilderness. It is the Mountain Stream Scotch.

With great pride, Hemingway shared this creation with A. E. Hotchner. He poured the Scotch into glasses, added water and placed them in the freezer. A few hours later, Hemingway retrieved the glasses (replacing them with two more) and presented Hotchner with the drink. You see, as you bring the glass to your lips, the water trickles through the ice like a cold mountain stream made of Scotch.[45]

1 SERVING

3 ounces Scotch
Water

Pour the Scotch into a tumbler. Add water to fill. Place in the freezer for approximately two to three hours, or until ice has formed on top.

193

AN AFTER-DINNER TREAT

The Fable of the Good Lion

The following short story is one of my all-time favorites. It shows Hemingway's mastery of storytelling as well as his warmth, sense of humor, and insatiable love of food. He wrote "The Fable of the Good Lion" in January 1950 in Venice, for a young nephew of Adriana Ivancich. It eventually appeared in the March 1951 issue of *Holiday* magazine.

While the style of the story itself is hardly typical of Hemingway, the details are uniquely his. In it we return to Africa and Venice where we enjoy familiar food and drink and old friends like Cipriani at Harry's Bar. Once again we recognize a protagonist and the development of his character through the food and drink he chooses.

The Fable of the Good Lion

Once upon a time there was a lion that lived in Africa with all the other lions. The other lions were all bad lions and every day they ate zebras and wildebeests and every kind of antelope. Sometimes the bad lions ate people too. They ate Swahilis, Umbulus and Wandorobos and they especially liked to eat Hindu traders. All Hindu traders are very fat and delicious to a lion.

But this lion, that we love because he was so good, had wings on his back. Because he had wings on his back the other lions all made fun of him.

"Look at him with the wings on his back," they would say and then they would all roar with laughter.

"Look at what he eats," they would say because the good lion only ate pasta and scampi because he was so good.

The bad lions would roar with laughter and eat another Hindu trader and their wives would drink his blood, going lap, lap, lap with their tongues like big cats. They only stopped to growl with laughter or to roar with laughter at the good lion and to snarl at his wings. They were very bad and wicked lions indeed.

But the good lion would sit and fold his wings back and ask politely if he might have a Negroni or an Americano and he always drank that instead of the blood of the Hindu traders. One day he refused to eat eight Masai cattle and only ate some tagliatelli and drank a glass of pomodoro.

This made the wicked lions very angry and one of the lionesses, who was the wickedest of them all and could never get the blood of Hindu traders off her whiskers even when she rubbed her face in the grass, said, "Who are you that you think you are so much better than we are? Where do you come from, you pasta-eating lion? What are you doing here anyway?" She growled at him and they all roared without laughter.

"My father lives in a city where he stands under the clock tower and looks down on a thousand pigeons, all of whom are his subjects. When they fly they make a noise like a rushing river. There are more palaces in my father's city than in all of Africa and there are four great bronze horses that face him and they all have one foot in the air because they fear him."

"In my father's city men go on foot or in boats and no real horse would enter the city for fear of my father."

"Your father was a griffon," the wicked lioness said, licking her whiskers.

"You are a liar," one of the wicked lions said. "There is no such city."

"Pass me a piece of Hindu trader," another very wicked lion said. "This Masai cattle is too newly killed."

"You are a worthless liar and the son of a griffon," the wickedest of all the lionesses said. "And now I think I shall kill you and eat you, wings and all."

This frightened the good lion very much because he could see her yellow eyes and her tail going up and down and the blood caked on her whiskers and he smelled her breath which was very bad because she never brushed her teeth ever. Also she had old pieces of Hindu trader under her claws.

"Don't kill me," the good lion said. "My father is a noble lion and always has been respected and everything is true as I said."

Just then the wicked lioness sprang at him. But he rose into the air on his wings and circled the group of wicked lions once, with them all roaring and looking at him. He looked down and thought, "What savages these lions are."

He circled them once more to make them roar more loudly. Then he swooped low so he could look at the eyes of the wicked lioness who rose on her hind legs to try and catch him. But she missed him with her claws.

"Adios," he said, for he spoke beautiful Spanish, being a lion of culture.

"Au revoir," he called to them in his exemplary French.

They all roared and growled in African lion dialect.

Then the good lion circled higher and higher and set his course for Venice. He alighted in the Piazza and everyone was delighted to see him. He flew up for a moment and kissed his father on both cheeks and saw the horses still had their feet up and the Basilica looked more beautiful than a soap bubble. The Campanile was in place and the pigeons were going to their nests for the evening.

"How was Africa?" his father said.

"Very savage, father," the good lion replied.

"We have night lighting here now," his father said.

"So I see," the good lion answered like a dutiful son.

"It bothers my eyes a little," his father confided to him. "Where are you going now, my son?"

"To Harry's Bar," the good lion said.

"Remember me to Cipriani and tell him I will be in some day soon to see about my bill," said his father.

"Yes, father," said the good lion and he flew down lightly and walked to Harry's bar on his own four paws.

In Cipriani's nothing was changed. All of his friends were there. But he was a little changed himself from being in Africa.

"A Negroni, Signor Barone?" asked Mr. Cipriani.

But the good lion had flown all the way from Africa and Africa had changed him.

"Do you have any Hindu trader sandwiches?" he asked Cipriani.

"No, but I can get some."

"While you are sending for them, make me a very dry martini." He added, "With Gordon's gin."

"Very good," said Cipriani. "Very good indeed."

Now the lion looked about him at the faces of all the nice people and he knew that he was at home but that he had also traveled. He was very happy."[1]

Notes

CHAPTER 1

1. Sanford, Marcelline Hemingway, *At the Hemingways*, pp. 34–35.

2. Sanford, p. 90.

3. Sanford, p. 89.

4. Sanford, p. 81.

5. Sanford, pp. 23–26.

6. Hemingway, Ernest, *Dateline: Toronto*, p. 34.

7. *Dateline: Toronto*, p. 46.

8. *Dateline: Toronto*, p. 46.

9. *Dateline: Toronto*, p. 46.

10. *Dateline: Toronto*, p. 46.

11. *Dateline: Toronto*, pp. 46–47.

12. Hotchner, A. E., *Papa Hemingway*, p. 91.

13. Doctorow, E. L., *Jack London, Hemingway and the Constitution*, p. 41.

14. Hemingway, Ernest, *The Complete Short Stories of Ernest Hemingway*, pp. 167–68.

15. *Complete Short Stories*, p. 169.

16. *Complete Short Stories*, p. 168.

CHAPTER 2

1. Baker, Carlos, *Ernest Hemingway: A Life Story*, p. 34.

2. MacLeish, Archibald, "The Human Season," *A Continuing Journey*, p. 307.

3. Villard, Henry S. and James Nagel, *Hemingway in Love and War*, p. 2.

4. Hemingway, Ernest, *A Farewell to Arms*, p. 43.

5. *A Farewell to Arms*, pp. 151–53.

6. Hemingway, Ernest, *By-Line: Ernest Hemingway*, "Remembering Shooting-Flying: A Key West Letter," pp. 189–90.

7. Savarin, *Real French Cooking*, p. 247.

8. *A Farewell to Arms*, p. 5.

9. *A Farewell to Arms*, p. 318.

10. *A Farewell to Arms*, p. 329.

11. Underhill, Linda, "Food for Fiction: Lessons from Ernest Hemingway's Writing," p. 90.

12. *Toronto Daily Star*, June 22, 1922.

13. Baker, *Ernest Hemingway: A Life Story*, p. 468.

14. Baker, *Ernest Hemingway: A Life Story*, p. 467.

15. Reynolds, Michael, *The Young Hemingway*, p. 212.

16. Hotchner, A. E., *Hemingway & His World*, p. 178.

17. Hemingway, Ernest, *Across the River and into the Trees*, p. 82.

18. Cipriani, Arrigo, *Harry's Bar: The Life and Times of the Legendary Venice Landmark*, p. 20.

19. *By-Line: Ernest Hemingway*, pp. 189–91.

20. *Across the River and into the Trees*, p. 5.

21. *Across the River and into the Trees*, p. 69.

22. *Across the River and into the Trees*, p. 57.

23. *Across the River and into the Trees*, p. 107.

24. *Across the River and into the Trees*, p. 116.

25. Baker, Carlos, (Ed.), *Ernest Hemingway: Selected Letters*, p. 728.

26. *Across the River and into the Trees*, p. 128.

27. *Across the River and into the Trees*, pp. 190–93.

28. *Across the River and into the Trees*, p. 200.

29. *Across the River and into the Trees*, p. 200.

30. *Across the River and into the Trees*, p. 203.

31. *Across the River and into the Trees*, p. 203.

CHAPTER 3

1. Baker, Carlos, (Ed.), *Ernest Hemingway: Selected Letters*, p. 25.

2. Desnoyers, Megan Floyd, "Ernest Hemingway: A Storyteller's Legacy," p. 339.

3. Hemingway, Ernest, *The Complete Short Stories of Ernest Hemingway*, p. xvi.

4. Reynolds, Michael, *Hemingway: The Paris Years*, p. 11.

5. Hemingway, Ernest, *A Moveable Feast*, p. 37.

6. *A Moveable Feast*, pp. 13–14.

7. *A Moveable Feast*, p. 5.

8. *A Moveable Feast*, pp. 100–101.

9. *A Moveable Feast*, p. 69.

10. *A Moveable Feast*, p. 69.

11. *A Moveable Feast*, p. 72.

12. *A Moveable Feast*, p. 72.

13. *A Moveable Feast*, pp. 43–44.

14. *A Moveable Feast*, p. 43.

15. *A Moveable Feast*, p. 45.

16. *A Moveable Feast*, p. 45.

17. Dos Passos, John, *The Best Times: An Informal Memoir*, p. 143.

18. Hemingway, Ernest, *The Torrents of Spring*, pp. 121–22.

19. Street, Julian, *Where Paris Dines*, p. 193.

20. Hemingway, Ernest, *By-Line: Ernest Hemingway*: "Trout Fishing in Europe," pp. 113–14.

21. *A Moveable Feast*, p. 55.

22. *By-Line: Ernest Hemingway*, pp. 113–14.

23. *By-Line: Ernest Hemingway*, pp. 113–14.

24. *A Moveable Feast*, pp. 125–26.

25. *A Moveable Feast*, p. 127.

26. *A Moveable Feast*, p. 149.

27. *A Moveable Feast*, p. 167.

28. *A Moveable Feast*, p. 162.

29. *A Moveable Feast*, p. 173.

30. *A Moveable Feast*, p. 174.

31. *A Moveable Feast*, p. 174.

32. *A Moveable Feast*, p. 198.

33. *A Moveable Feast*, p. 201.

34. Baker, Carlos, *Ernest Hemingway: A Life Story*, p. 154.

35. Charters, James, *This Must Be the Place: Memoirs of Montparnasse*, p. 38.

36. Rodriguez-Hunter, Suzanne, *Found Meals of the Lost Generation*, p. 180.

37. Hemingway, Ernest, *The Sun Also Rises*, p. 76.

38. Street, p. 203.

39. *The Sun Also Rises*, p. 76–77.

40. Rodriguez-Hunter, p. 185.

41. Solomon, Barbara, "Where's Papa?" *The New Republic*, March 9, 1987, p. 33.

42. Solomon, p. 33.

43. Griffin, Peter, *Less than a Treason*, p. 142.

44. Hemingway, Ernest, *The Garden of Eden*, p. 4.

45. Stoneback, H. R., "Memorable Eggs 'in Danger of Getting Cold' and Mackerel 'Perilous with Edge-Level Juice': Eating in Hemingway's Garden," p. 27.

46. *The Garden of Eden*, pp. 10–11.

47. *The Garden of Eden*, p. 10.

CHAPTER 4

1. Hemingway, Ernest, *Death in the Afternoon*, p. 264.

2. Hemingway, Ernest, *The Sun Also Rises*, p. 183.

3. Hemingway, Ernest, *By-Line: Ernest Hemingway*, p. 16.

4. *The Sun Also Rises*, p. 157.

5. *The Sun Also Rises*, pp. 104–105.

6. Castillo-Puche, Jose Luis, *Hemingway in Spain*, p. 181.

7. Fuentes, Norberto, *Hemingway in Cuba*, p. 103.

8. *Death in the Afternoon*, p. 48.

9. Hemingway, Ernest, *The Garden of Eden*, p. 52.

10. *The Sun Also Rises*, pp. 245–46.

11. Hemingway, Ernest, *For Whom the Bell Tolls*, p. 26.

12. *For Whom the Bell Tolls*, p. 22–23.

13. *For Whom the Bell Tolls*, pp. 84–85.

14. Hemingway, Ernest, *The Dangerous Summer*, p. 139.

15. *The Dangerous Summer*, p. 125.

16. Casas, Penelope, *The Foods and Wines of Spain*, p. 174.

CHAPTER 5

1. Reynolds, Michael, *Hemingway: The American Homecoming*, pp. 168–76, 194.

2. Hemingway, Ernest, *The Green Hills of Africa*, p. 149.

3. Hemingway, Mary Welsh, *"Life with Papa,"* p. 117.

4. Hemingway, Ernest, *To Have and Have Not*, p. 30.

5. Hemingway, Mary Welsh, *How It Was*, p. 318, pp. 419–20.

6. *To Have and Have Not*, p. 135.

7. Hemingway, Ernest, *Islands in the Stream*, p. 208.

8. *Islands in the Stream*, p. 208.

9. Hotchner, A. E., *Papa Hemingway*, p. 37.

10. Hotchner, *Papa Hemingway*, p. 7.

11. Hemingway, Mary, *How It Was*, p. 311.

12. Hemingway, Mary, *How It Was*, p. 311.

13. *Islands in the Stream*, p. 214.

14. *Islands in the Stream*, p. 65.

15. *Islands in the Stream*, p. 222.

16. *Islands in the Stream*, p. 223.

17. *Islands in the Stream*, p. 230.

18. Lang, Jennifer Harvey, (Ed.), *Larousse Gastronomique*, pp. 124–25.

19. *Islands in the Stream*, pp. 288–89.

20. Hemingway, Ernest, *By-Line: Ernest Hemingway*, pp. 239–49.

21. Hemingway, Ernest, *The Enduring Hemingway*, p. xxi.

22. Hemingway, Ernest, *The Old Man and the Sea*, p. 17.

23. *Islands in the Stream*, pp. 390–91.

24. Hotchner, *Papa Hemingway*, p. 194.

25. Hemingway, Mary, *How It Was*, p. 103.

26. Hemingway, Mary, *How It Was*, p. 420.

27. Hemingway, Mary, "Life with Papa," p. 116.

28. Hemingway, Mary, "Life with Papa," p. 29.

29. Hemingway, Mary, "Life with Papa," p. 116.

30. Hemingway, Mary, *How It Was*, p. 242.

CHAPTER 6

1. Hemingway, Ernest, *The Complete Short Stories of Ernest Hemingway*, p. 370.

2. Baker, Carlos, *Ernest Hemingway: A Life Story*, p. 609.

3. *Complete Short Stories*, p. 27.

4. *Complete Short Stories*, pp. 9–10.

5. Hemingway, Mary, *How It Was*, pp. 355–56.

6. Hemingway, Mary, *How It Was*, pp. 347–48.

7. Hemingway, Mary, *How It Was*, pp. 347–48.

8. Wells, Reginald, "A Christmas Choice of Fair and Fancy Game," *Sports Illustrated*, pp. 40–41.

9. Baker, *Ernest Hemingway: A Life Story*, p. 294.

10. Arnold, Lloyd, *High on the Wild*, p. 7.

11. Baker, *Ernest Hemingway: A Life Story*, p. 517.

12. MacMullen, Forrest, conversation with author, September 4, 1997.

CHAPTER 7

1. Hemingway, Ernest, *Death in the Afternoon*, p. 462.

2. *Death in the Afternoon*, p. 11.

3. Hemingway, Ernest, *A Moveable Feast*, p. 158.

4. Villard, Henry S. and James Nagel, *Hemingway in Love and War: The Lost Diary of Agnes von Kurowsky*, p. 73.

5. Lichine, Alexis, *New Encyclopedia of Wine & Spirits*, p. 384.

6. Hemingway, Ernest, *A Farewell to Arms*, p. 6.

7. Reynolds, Michael, *Hemingway: The 1930's*, p. 2.

8. *A Farewell to Arms*, p. 191.

9. *A Moveable Feast*, p. 37.

10. Hemingway, Ernest, *By-Line: Ernest Hemingway*, p. 190.

11. *A Moveable Feast*, p. 101.

12. Baker, Carlos, (Ed.), *Selected Letters*, p. 808.

13. *A Farewell to Arms*, p. 38.

14. *A Farewell to Arms*, p. 113.

15. *A Moveable Feast*, pp. 53–54.

16. Hemingway, Ernest, *The Sun Also Rises*, p. 87.

17. Hemingway, Ernest, *The Complete Short Stories of Ernest Hemingway*, p. 450.

18. *A Moveable Feast*, p. 127.

19. *A Moveable Feast*, p. 162.

20. *A Moveable Feast*, p. 167.

21. *A Moveable Feast*, p. 19.

22. Lichine, p. 159.

23. *A Moveable Feast*, p. 174.

24. *A Moveable Feast*, pp. 43–44.

25. *The Sun Also Rises*, p. 246.

26. *A Moveable Feast*, p. 52.

27. *The Sun Also Rises*, p. 153.

28. *A Moveable Feast*, p. 128.

29. Hemingway, Ernest, *The Garden of Eden*, pp. 51–52.

30. *A Moveable Feast*, p. 55.

31. Fuentes, Norberto, *Hemingway in Cuba*, p. 64.

32. Lichine, p. 495.

33. *The Garden of Eden*, p. 16.

34. *The Garden of Eden*, p. 243.

35. *The Garden of Eden*, p. 52.

36. Hemingway, Ernest, *Across the River and into the Trees*, p. 232.

37. *Across the River and into the Trees*, p. 130.

38. *Across the River and into the Trees*, p. 177.

CHAPTER 8

1. Hemingway, Ernest, *Dateline: Toronto*, p. 182.

2. Hemingway, Ernest, *For Whom the Bell Tolls*, p. 51.

3. Hemingway, Ernest, *The Garden of Eden*, p. 69.

4. Hemingway, Ernest, *Death in the Afternoon*, p. 172.

5. *For Whom the Bell Tolls*, p. 50.

6. *Dateline: Toronto*, p. 182.

7. Hemingway, Ernest, *The Sun Also Rises*, p. 15.

8. *The Garden of Eden*, p. 39.

9. *The Garden of Eden*, p. 26.

10. Baker, Carlos (Ed.), *Selected Letters*, p. 619.

11. Baker, *Selected Letters*, p. 618.

12. Hemingway, Ernest, *The Complete Short Stories of Ernest Hemingway*, p. 488.

13. Hemingway, Ernest, *A Moveable Feast*, p. 83.

14. *A Moveable Feast*, p. 83.

15. Hemingway, Ernest, *To Have and Have Not*, p. 129.

16. *To Have and Have Not*, p. 134.

17. Hemingway, Ernest, *Islands in the Stream*, p. 276.

18. Fuentes, Norberto, *Hemingway in Cuba*, pp. 228–29.

19. Houk, Walter, E-mail, July 22, 1997.

20. *Islands in the Stream*, p. 281.

21. Hemingway, Ernest, *By-Line: Ernest Hemingway*, p. 55.

22. *Complete Short Stories*, p. 5.

23. *Complete Short Stories*, p. 421.

24. *Complete Short Stories*, p. 425.

25. *By-Line: Ernest Hemingway*, p. 449.

26. Hemingway, Ernest, *A Farewell to Arms*, pp. 302–303.

27. Hemingway, Ernest, *Across the River and into the Trees*, p. 121.

28. Grimes, William, *Straight Up Or on the Rocks*, p. 109.

29. *Islands in the Stream*, p. 258.

30. *The Sun Also Rises*, p. 233.

31. *The Sun Also Rises*, p. 41.

32. *A Moveable Feast*, p. 206.

33. *A Farewell to Arms*, p. 143.

34. *Dateline: Toronto*, pp. 356–57.

35. *Across the River and into the Trees*, p. 82.

36. Griffin, *Less than a Treason*, p. 142.

37. *The Sun Also Rises*, p. 110.

38. *Islands in the Stream*, p. 244.

39. *Islands in the Stream*, p. 84.

40. *By-Line: Ernest Hemingway*, p. 247

41. *A Farewell to Arms*, p. 310.

42. *A Moveable Feast*, p. 170.

43. *By-Line: Ernest Hemingway*, p. 275.

44. *Complete Short Stories*, pp. 612–13.

45. Hotchner, *Papa Hemingway*, pp. 158, 161.

EPILOGUE

1. Hemingway, Ernest, *The Complete Short Stories of Ernest Hemingway*, pp. 482–84.

Bibliography

BOOKS

Arnold, Lloyd. *High on the Wild*. Caldwell, ID: Caxton Printers, 1968.

Baker, Carlos, ed. *Ernest Hemingway: Selected Letters*. New York: Charles Scribner's Sons, 1981.

——————. *Ernest Hemingway: A Life Story*. New York: Scribners, 1969.

Beard, James, et. al. *The Great Cooks Cookbook*. New York: Ferguson/Doubleday, 1974.

Bertholle, Louisette. *Secrets of the Great French Restaurants*. New York: Macmillan, 1974.

Brennan, Georgeanne. *Aperitif*. San Francisco: Chronicle Books, 1997.

Cappel, Constance. *Hemingway in Michigan*. New York: Fleet Publishing, 1966.

Casas, Penelope. *Discovering Spain*. New York: Alfred A. Knopf, 1992.

——————. *Tapas: The Little Dishes of Spain*. New York: Knopf, 1989.

——————. *The Foods and Wines of Spain*. New York: Knopf, 1982.

Castillo-Puche, Jose Luis. *Hemingway in Spain*. New York: Doubleday, 1961.

Charters, James. *This Must Be the Place: Memoirs of Montparnasse*. New York: Collier Books, 1989.

Child, Julia. *Baking with Julia*. New York: William Morrow & Company, 1996.

Cipriani, Arrigo. *Harry's Bar: The Life and Times of the Legendary Venice Landmark*. New York: Arcade Publishing, 1996.

Cipriani, Arrigo. *The Harry's Bar Cookbook*. New York: Bantam Books, 1991.

Collins, Larry, and Dominique Lapierre. *Is Paris Burning?* New York: Pocket Books, 1977.

Conrad, Barnaby III. *Absinthe: History in a Bottle*. San Francisco: Chronicle Books, 1988.

——————. *Martini*. San Francisco: Chronicle Books, 1994.

Curnonsky and Rouff, Marcel. *The Yellow Guides for Epicures: Paris*. New York: Harper and Brothers, 1926.

Dannenberg, Linda. *Paris Boulangerie-Pâtisserie*. New York: Clarkson Potter, 1994.

Dardis, Tom. *The Thirsty Muse: Alcohol and the American Writer*. New York: Ticknor and Fields, 1989.

Doctorow, E. L. *Jack London, Hemingway and the Constitution*. New York: Random House, 1993.

Dos Passos, John. *The Best Times: An Informal Memoir*. London: Andre Deutsch, 1968.

Fuentes, Norberto. *Hemingway in Cuba*. Secaucus, NJ: Lyle Stuart, 1984.

Giusti-Lanham, Hedy and Andrez Dodi. *The Cuisine of Venice and Surrounding Northern Regions*. Woodbury, New York: Barron's, 1987.

Griffin, Peter. *Less than a Treason*. New York: Oxford University Press, 1990.

Grimes, William. *Straight Up Or on the Rocks: A Cultural History of American Drink*. New York: Simon & Schuster, 1993.

Heath, Ambrose, ed. *Madame Prunier's Fish Cookery Book*. New York: Julian Messner, 1939.

Hemingway, Ernest. *Across the River and into the Trees*. New York: Charles Scribner's Sons, 1950.

——————. *By-Line: Ernest Hemingway*. New York: Charles Scribner's Sons, 1967.

——————. *The Complete Short Stories of Ernest Hemingway*. New York: Charles Scribner's Sons, 1987.

——————. *Conversations with Ernest Hemingway*. Edited by Matthew J. Bruccoli. Jackson, MS: University Press of Mississippi, 1986.

——————. *The Dangerous Summer*. New York: Charles Scribner's Sons, 1985.

——————. *Dateline: Toronto*. New York: Charles Scribner's Sons, 1985.

——————. *Death in the Afternoon*. New York: Charles Scribner's Sons, 1932.

——————. *The Enduring Hemingway*. Edited by Charles Scribner. New York: Charles Scribner's Sons, 1974.

——————. *A Farewell to Arms*. New York: Charles Scribner's Sons, 1929.

——————. *For Whom the Bell Tolls*. New York: Charles Scribner's Sons, 1940.

——————. *The Garden of Eden*. New York: Charles Scribner's Sons, 1986.

——————. *Green Hills of Africa*. New York: Charles Scribner's Sons, 1935.

——————. *Islands in the Stream*. New York: Charles Scribner's Sons, 1970.

——————. *A Moveable Feast*. New York: Charles Scribner's Sons, 1964.

——————. *The Old Man and the Sea*. New York: Charles Scribner's Sons, 1952.

——————. *The Sun Also Rises*. New York: Charles Scribner's Sons, 1926.

——————. *To Have and Have Not*. New York: P. F. Collier & Son, 1937.

——————. *The Torrents of Spring*. New York: Charles Scribner's Sons, 1972.

Hemingway, Mary Welsh. *How It Was*. New York: Alfred A. Knopf, 1951.

Hotchner, A. E. *Hemingway & His World*. New York: Vendome, 1989.

——————. *Papa Hemingway*. New York: Random House, 1966.

Iribarren, Jose Maria. *Hemingway y los Sanfermines*. Pamplona: Editorial Gomez, 1970.

Jacques, Marie. *Colette's Best Recipes*. Boston: Little, Brown & Co., 1923.

Lang, Jennifer Harvey, ed. *Larousse Gastronomique*. Paris: Larousse, 1938.

Lawrence, H. Lea. *Prowling Papa's Waters*. Marietta, GA: Longstreet Press, 1992.

Lichine, Alexis. *New Encyclopedia of Wine & Spirits*. New York: Alfred A. Knopf, 1987.

MacLeish, Archibald. *A Continuing Journey*. Boston: Houghton Mifflin, 1967.

McIver, Stuart. *Hemingway's Key West*. Sarasota, FL: Pineapple Press, 1993.

Miller, Tom. *Trading with the Enemy: A Yankee Travels through Castro's Cuba*. New York: Atheneum, 1992.

Reynolds, Michael. *Hemingway: The American Homecoming*. Cambridge, MA: Basil Blackwell Ltd., 1992.

——————. *Hemingway: The Paris Years*. New York: Blackwell, 1989.

——————. *Hemingway: The 1930's*. New York: W. W. Norton & Company, 1997.

——————. *The Young Hemingway*. New York: Blackwell, 1986.

Rodriguez-Hunter, Suzanne. *Found Meals of the Lost Generation*. Boston: Faber & Faber, 1994.

Rogal, Samuel J. *For Whom the Dinner Bell Tolls.* Bethesda, MD: International Scholars Publications, 1997.

Samuelson, Arnold. *With Hemingway: A Year in Key West & Cuba.* New York: Random House, 1984.

Sandler, Bea. *The African Cookbook.* New York: Citadel Press, 1993.

Sanford, Marcelline Hemingway. *At the Hemingways.* Boston: Little, Brown & Co., 1962.

Savarin, *Real French Cooking.* Garden City, New York: Doubleday & Co., 1956.

Sheraton, Mimi. *The German Cookbook.* New York: Random House, 1965.

Street, Julian. *Where Paris Dines.* Garden City, New York: Doubleday Doran & Co., 1929.

Toklas, Alice B. *The Alice B. Toklas Cookbook.* New York: Harper & Brothers, 1954.

Villard, Henry S. and James Nagel. *Hemingway in Love and War: The Lost Diary of Agnes von Kurowsky.* New York: Hyperion, 1995.

Villas, James. *The French Country Kitchen.* New York: Bantam Books, 1992.

Waldo, Myra. *The Flavor of Spain.* New York: Macmillan, 1965.

SELECTED ARTICLES

Beegel, Susan. "Hemingway Gatronomique: A Guide to Food and Drink in *A Moveable Feast.*" *The Hemingway Review.* v4, n1, Fall 1984, pp. 14–26.

Belzer, S. A. "Savoring the Soup of Hemingway Country." *The New York Times.* December 17, 1997, p. F13.

Benoit, Raymond. "The Complete Walker: Food and Lodging in Hemingway's 'Big Two-Hearted River.'" *Notes on Contemporary Literature.* v20, n3, May 1990, pp. 10–12.

Desnoyers, Megan Floyd. "Ernest Hemingway: A Story-teller's Legacy." *Prologue*, v24, n4, Winter, 1992, pp. 335–49.

Hemingway, Mary. "Life with Papa." *Flair*, January 1951, p. 29, 116–7.

Lanier, Doris. "The Bittersweet Taste of Absinthe in Hemingway's 'Hills Like White Elephants.'" *Studies in Short Fiction*, v26, Summer 1989, pp. 279–88.

Lyons, Nick. "Hemingway's Many Hearted Fox River." *National Geographic*, June 1997, pp. 106–23.

Slough, Andrew. "An Immoveable Feast." *SKI*, v59, n3, Nov. 1994, pp. 180–7.

Solomon, Barbara, "Where's Papa?" *The New Republic*, March 9, 1987, pp. 30–34.

Stoneback, H. R. "Memorable Eggs 'in Danger of Getting Cold' and Mackerel 'Perilous with Edge-Level Juice': Eating in Hemingway's Garden." *The Hemingway Review*, v8, n2, Spring 1989, pp. 22–29.

Underhill, Linda and Jeanne Nakjavani. "Food for Fiction: Lessons from Ernest Hemingway's Writing." *Journal of American Culture*, v15, n2, Summer 1992, pp. 87–90.

Vivant, Don. "Literary Drinks." *Forbes* (FYI Supplement), v156, n10, October 23, 1995, p. 162.

Wells, Reginald. "A Christmas Choice of Fair and Fancy Game." *Sports Illustrated*, December 1955, pp. 40–3.

Acknowledgments

More often than not, I have felt like the editor of this book rather than the writer. It has been a collaborative effort in many ways, and there are several people without whose assistance this book would not have been possible.

First, my eternal gratitude goes out to all those who were genuinely enthusiastic about this book from the outset, who found some fun in helping me, and whose support helped me overcome whatever lingering doubts remained along the way: Thomas Bahr, whose trip to Schruns triggered this wild ride and whose friendship, research assistance, and interest has been invaluable; Peter Johnson, who saw through the free booze and seemed to embody the essence of this project (maybe it was just the free booze); Jack Murphy, a Hemingway fan who helped me remember why I wrote this thing in the first place; Tillie Arnold, Don Anderson, and Forrest MacMullen, all friends of Ernest from his Idaho days, whose fond memories of Papa brought the subject to life for me; and finally, Jennifer Wheeler, executive director of The Hemingway Foundation of Oak Park, who helped out so much along the way and who seems to truly love her work.

I would also like to thank the community of scholars who have dedicated much of their careers to the study of Hemingway's life and work. I was warned at the outset of this project that "the Hemingway folks" were a tough lot. I have found them, without exception, to be scholarly, generous, forthcoming, and downright friendly. They are genuinely interested in advancing the body of work on Ernest Hemingway. In particular, I would like to thank the following: Susan Beegel, editor of the *Hemingway Review,* and Miriam Mandel, both walking Papa encyclopedias; Allen Josephs, president of The Hemingway Society and inspirer of restauranteurs; Marty Peterson; John Bittner; Charlotte Ponder; Ruth Hawkins; Walter Houk for exposing the mojito; Megan Desnoyers and Stephen Plotkin of the Hemingway Collection at the John F. Kennedy Library in Boston; Allan Goodrich at the John F. Kennedy Library; Marla Metzner; the Hemingway Foundation; Susan Buckley; Lydia Zelaya; Sam Rogal for his comprehensive research on Hemingway and food; Robert Trogden and everyone on the Hemingway E-mail-list service whose comments and debate provides an ongoing education for everyone who tunes in; Michael Reynolds and Carlos Baker, without whose brilliant biographies none of this would be possible.

Along the way, I have had the honor of meeting many wonderful and talented people who

208

donated their time and wisdom to this book: Juanita Bellaguer, Juan, José, and everyone at La Pepica in Valencia; Penelope Casas, grand dame of Spanish cuisine in America; Mario Leon Iriarte, owner of Dalí in Cambridge; everyone at the Schlesinger Library at Radcliffe College; Sandy Block, Master of Wine; Teresa Merenges, Cuban cuisine expert and super-nice lady; Walter Nels at the Hotel Taube in Schruns; Antonio Gonzalez and the wonderful people who make Casa Botín in Madrid a magical place; Joe Faber at Capt. Tony's in Key West; Maria Luisa Nieto Moneo in Pamplona who, had she been around in 1925, would have found a starring role in *The Sun Also Rises*; the folks at the Hostals Burguete and Loizu in Burguete; Paul Christie and Neil Palmer at Gargoyle's on the Square; and a special thank you to Cynthia Sherry and Lisa Rosenthal-Hogarth at Chicago Review Press.

Finally, a toast to all of my friends and family who helped out along the way: Katie Sharkey; Eric S. A. Reed; Jason Soslow; Mike and Tori Palmer; Bart Laurijssens and his mom; Joan and Sandy; Gary and Sandrijn; Korina; Chris Richards; Jill and Ryan; Sean and Elana; Penny and Arnie; Harry and Phyllis; Janice and Stu; Karen Bender; Marty Jones; Martin and Margaret Bendersky; Abby Gitlitz; Ayshe Yildiz; Missy Maxfield; Steve Halloran; Jeffrey Isaacs; Joe "See ya in Church" Murphy; Eileen Boreth; M. Brad Boreth; everyone at Ben-Eve's Beauty Salon and Fat Oscar's Bar & Grill; and of course, my mom and dad, Bessie and Ziegfried Borethkovitz, of the Flying Borethkovitzes.

General Index

A

Across the River and into the Trees, 18, 26–28, 30–36
Adams, Nick, 12–14
Anderson, Sherwood, 39, 51
Anita (boat), 112, 132
Anoz, Matías, 89
Arnold, Lloyd, 155–56
Arnold, Tillie, 155–57
At the Hemingways, 7

B

Barkley, Catherine, 18–25
Barnes, Jake, 72, 82–83, 85, 90–91
Beach, Sylvia, 39–40
Berenson, Bernard, 129
"Big Two–Hearted River," 12–13
Boise (cat), 120–22
Bourne, Catherine, 75
Bourne, David, 75
Brasserie Lipp (restaurant), 47–48
Burguete, Hostal, 82–83

C

Cannell, Kitty, 71
Cantwell, Richard, 26–28, 30–36
Capt. Tony's Saloon, 119
Casa Botín, 97

Casa Marceliano, 89
Cipriani, Arrigo, 27–28
Cipriani, Giuseppe, 27–28
Civil War, Spanish, 99
Clyne, Frances, 71

D

Dangerous Summer, The, 81, 104
Death in the Afternoon, 81, 104, 111
Dingo Bar, 62
Dominguín, Luis Miguel, 104
Dos Passos, John, 50–51

F

Farewell to Arms, A, 18–25, 26–27
"Fathers and Sons," 145
Fiesta de San Fermín, 81, 85–86
Finca Vigía, 112, 136
Fitzgerald, F. Scott, 62–63, 65–66
"Food for Fiction," 25
Ford, Ford Madox, 45, 177
For Whom the Bell Tolls, 81, 99–101
Found Meals of the Lost Generation, 71–72
Fuentes, Gregorio, 112, 132

G

Garden of Eden, The, 75

Gorton, Bill, 72, 82–83, 85, 88, 90
Green Hills of Africa, The, 111, 146
Gritti Palace Hotel, 26, 30

H

Harry's Bar, 27–28
Hatuey beer, 116
Hemingway, Clarence Edmonds (Ed), 3, 5–7, 14, 145
Hemingway, Ernest
    as an ambulance driver in Italy, 17–18
    birth, 3
    in China, 129
    in Cuba, 111–13, 116, 120–24, 131, 136
    death of, 155
    drinking habits, 173
    on duck hunting, 27–28
    father's influence on, 5–7
    at the French Riviera, 75
    on hunger, 47
    and the hunt, 145
    in Key West, 111–13, 117, 119
    love affair with Agnes von Kurowsky, 17–18, 162
    marriage to Hadley Richardson, 39
    marriage to Mary Hemingway, 136
    in Paris, 39–40, 44–45, 47–51, 54, 57, 60, 65–66
    return to Italy, 26
    on safari in Africa, 146–49, 151–52
    in Schruns (Austria), 66–68, 71
    in Spain, 81–83
    and the Spanish Civil War, 99
    in Sun Valley and Ketchum, Idaho, 153, 155–56
    traveling with F. Scott Fitzgerald, 62–63, 65–66
Hemingway, Grace Hall, 3, 14

Hemingway, Hadley Richardson, 39–40, 44–45, 47–51, 54, 57, 71
Hemingway, Joan, 156
Hemingway, John ("Bumby"), 66
Hemingway, Marcelline, 3, 6–7, 145
Hemingway, Martha Gellhorn, 99, 112, 119, 129, 153, 155
Hemingway, Mary, 30, 54, 112, 136–42, 147–49, 155–57
Hemingway, Patrick, 111
Hemingway, Pauline Pfeiffer, 71, 111–12, 146, 153, 155
Hemingway, Tyler, 17
Henry, Fredric, 18–25
High on the Wild, 155
Hotchner, A. E., 121
How It Was, 149
Hudson, Thomas, 120–24, 129

I

Islands in the Stream, 112, 120–24, 129
Ivancich, Adriana, 26

J

Jordan, Robert, 99–101

L

Loeb, Harold, 71, 81

M

MacMullen, Forrest, 64, 136, 156–57
Macomber, Francis, 146–47
Macomber, Margot, 146–47
Madrid (Spain), 95, 99
Morgan, Harry, 113

N

Nakjavani, Jeanne, 25
Nobel Prize, 116, 130

O

Oak Park (IL), 1, 3, 14
Old Man and the Sea, The, 104, 112, 129–30
Ordoñez, Antonio, 104
Ordoñez, Cayetano, 71

P

Pamplona (Spain), 81, 85–86
Pepica, La, 105–7
Percival, Philip, 146
Pickering, Harry, 27
Pilar (boat), 112, 120, 131–32
Pound, Ezra, 39–40, 47, 81
Pruniers, 54
Pulitzer Prize, 130

R

Red Cross hospital, American, 17–18
Renata, 26–28, 30–36
Rendezvous-des-Mariniers, 71–72
Rodriguez-Hunter, Suzanne, 71–72
Royal Order of Shrimp Eaters, 120–21
Russell, Joe, 117

S

Sampson, Harold, 6, 145
San Sebastián (Spain), 91–92
Schruns (Austria), 66–68, 71
Scribner, Charles, Jr., 40

Shakespeare and Company, 39–40, 45
"Short, Happy Life of Francis Macomber, The," 111, 146–47
Silver Slipper, 117
Sloppy Joe's, 111, 117, 119
Smith, Bill, 39, 71, 81
"Snows of Kilimanjaro, The," 111, 146
Stein, Gertrude, 39–40, 44–45, 47, 81
Street, Julian, 72
Sun Also Rises, The, 71–72, 81–83, 85, 90–91

T

Taube, Hotel, 66–68
To Have and Have Not, 113, 119–20
Toklas, Alice B., 44–45
Torrents of Spring, The, 51

U

Underhill, Linda, 25

V

Valencia (Spain), 100–101
Van Guilder, Gene, 155
von Blixen, Baron Bror, 146
von Kurowsky, Agnes, 17–18, 162

W

Walloon Lake (MI), 4, 5
Walsh, Ernest, 60
Where Paris Dines, 72

Recipe Index

A

Absinthe, 174
Algerian wine, 161
Alioli (Garlic Mayonnaise), 94
appetizers
  Fried Octopus, 106
apples
  Apple Tart, 43–44
  Campfire Apple Pie, 11–12
  Marmelade de Pommes (Apple Conserve), 53
Apple Tart, 43–44
Apricots, Stewed, 11
Armagnac and Perrier, 175
Artichoke Vinaigrette, 33–34
Asti wine, 162
Avocado, Boise's, 122

B

Bacalao de Pamplona (Salt Cod), 89–90
Bacon, Canadian, 36
Bananas, Fried, 130–31
Barbera wine, 162
beans
  Black Bean Soup, 114
  New Green Beans, 74
  Pork and Beans and Spaghetti, 13
Beaune wine, 163

beef
  Beef Stew with Boiled Potatoes, 114, 116
  Châteaubriand, 127
  Cornish Pasties, 157
  Foie de Veau à l'Anglaise, 42
  Oxtail Stew, 152
  Picadillo, 141
  Tournedos with Sauce Béarnaise, 61
Beef Stew with Boiled Potatoes, 114, 116
beverages, alcoholic
  Absinthe, 174
  Algerian wine, 161
  Armagnac and Perrier, 175
  Asti wine, 162
  Barbera wine, 162
  Beaune wine, 163
  Cahors wine, 163
  Campari and Gordon's Gin, 176–77
  Capri wine, 163–64
  Chablis wine, 165
  Chambéry Cassis, 177
  Chateau Mouton-Rothschild wine, 165–66
  Châteauneuf du Pape wine, 166
  Citron Pressé with Whiskey (The Hemingway Whiskey Sour), 178
  Cuba Libre (Chasing a Straight Whiskey), 178–79
  Daiquirí Special, 181
  Ernest Hemingway Gin and Tonic, The, 185

Fleurie wine, 166
Gimlet, 184
Gin and Tonic, 184–85
Glühwein, 185
Grappa, 186
Green Isaak's Special, 191
Hemingway Daiquirí, 179–80, 181
Hemingway's Bloody Marys, 176
Highball (*Highbalito con Agua Mineral*), 186–87
Izzarra, 187
Jack Rose, 187
Kirsch, 188
Kümmel, 188–89
Mâcon wine, 167
Marc, 189
Marsala wine, 167
Mojito, 180–81
Montagny wine, 167
Montgomery, The, 189–90
Muscadet wine, 167
Papa Doble, 181
Pernod, 175
Pouilly-Fuisse wine, 168
Rioja wine, 108
Rum Punch, 190–91
Sancerre wine, 168
Sangría, 105
Sherry, 168–69
Sion wine, 169
St. Estephe wine, 169
Tavel wine, 170
Tomini, 191
Valdepeñas wine, 170
Valpolicella wine, 170

Vermouth and Bitters, 191–92
Whiskey, 192–93
Wild Daiquirí, 181
Biffi's Fruit Cup, 164
Black Bean Soup, 114
Black Currant Liqueur, 46
Bloody Marys, Hemingway's, 176
Bocadilla de Tortilla de Patata (Potato Omelet Sandwich), 86, 88
Boise's Avocado, 122
Bouillabaisse de Marseilles, 126–27
breads
    Brioche, 23–24, 76
Brioche, 23–24, 76
Burgundy Snails (*Escargots à la Bourguignonne*), 64

C
Cabbage, Red (*Rotweinkraut*), 70
Café au Lait, 76
Cahors wine, 163
cakes
    Grace Hall Hemingway's English Tea Cakes, 4
    Visitandines, 46
Campari and Gordon's Gin, 176–77
Campfire Apple Pie, 11–12
Canadian Bacon, 36
Canapé of Fried Fish, 94
Capri wine, 163–64
Cauliflower Braised with Butter, 33
Celery Rémoulade, 78
Cervelas with Mustard Sauce, 49
Chablis wine, 165
Chambéry Cassis, 177
Châteaubriand, 127

Chateau Mouton-Rothschild wine, 165–66

Châteauneuf du Pape wine, 166

chestnuts

    Purée de Marron (Chestnut Purée), 21–22

chicken

    Poularde de Bresse, 65–66

    Roast Chicken, 73–74

    Truffle-Roasted Chicken (*Poularde Truffée*), 63

Chop Suey, 138–39

Choucroute Garni (Garnished Sauerkraut), 25

Citron Pressé with Whiskey (The Hemingway Whiskey Sour), 178

Civet de Lièvre à la Cocotte (Jugged Hare), 53

Clams on the Half-Shell, 34–35

Cochinillo Asado (Roast Suckling Pig), 98–99

Coconut Ice Cream, 142

coffee

    Café au Lait, 76

    Coffee According to Hopkins, 14

    Deusico (Turkish Coffee), 182

Coffee According to Hopkins, 14

Cold Cucumber Soup, Ernest Hemingway's, 5

condiments

    Alioli (Garlic Mayonnaise), 94

    Mango Chutney, 140–41

Cornish Pasties, 157

crab

    Crabe Mexicaine, 55–57

Crabe Mexicaine, 55–57

Cuba Libre (Chasing a Straight Whiskey), 178–79

cucumbers

    Ernest Hemingway's Cold Cucumber Soup, 5

currants

    Black Currant Liqueur, 46

Curry of Wild Bird, 150

D

Daiquirí, Hemingway, 179–80, 181

Daiquirí Special, 181

desserts

    Apple Tart, 43–44

    Biffi's Fruit Cup, 164

    Campfire Apple Pie, 11–12

    Coconut Ice Cream, 142

    Fruit Compote, 156

    Lime Ice, 139

    Zabaglione, 22

Deusico (Turkish Coffee), 182

dolphin

    Dorado Fillet in Damn Good Sauce, 134

Dorado Fillet in Damn Good Sauce, 134

duck

    Roast Duckling (*Anitra Arrosto*), 28–29

E

eggs

    Bocadilla de Tortilla de Patata (Potato Omelet Sandwich), 86, 88

    Omelet with Truffles, 36

    Zabaglione, 22

eland

    Eland Piccata, 151

    Hunter's Safari Steak, 147

Eland Piccata, 151

Endive Salad, 42

English Tea Cakes, Grace Hall Hemingway's, 4

Ernest Hemingway Gin and Tonic, The, 185

Ernest Hemingway's Cold Cucumber Soup, 5

Ernest Hemingway's Fillet of Lion, 153

Escabeche de Atún (Marinated Tuna with Onions), 88–89

F

Fillet of Lion, Ernest Hemingway's, 153

fish

    Bacalao de Pamplona (Salt Cod), 89–90

    Bouillabaisse de Marseilles, 126–27

    Canapé of Fried Fish, 94

    Dorado Fillet in Damn Good Sauce, 134

    Escabeche de Atún (Marinated Tuna with Onions), 88–89

    Fried Trout, 9–10

    Friture de Goujon (Fried Gudgeon), 50

    Pastry of Fish, Peppers, and Pine Nuts (*Empanadilla de Pescado*), 102

    Red Snapper Stew, 135

    Rollmops, 52

    Sea Bass Grilled with Butter and Herbs, 77–78

    Sole Meunière (Fillet of Sole Miller's Wife Style), 52

    Swordfish á la *Pilar*, 134

    Trout au bleu, 58

    Trucha a la Navarra (Trout Cooked with Cured Ham), 84–85

Fleurie wine, 166

Foie de Veau à l'Anglaise, 42

French-fried Potatoes (*Pommes de Terre Frites*), 61

Fried Baby Eels, 104

Fried Bananas, 130–31

Fried Octopus, 106

Fried Trout, 9–10

Friture de Goujon (Fried Gudgeon), 50

Fruit Compote, 156

fruits. *See under* specific fruit name

G

game

    Curry of Wild Bird, 150

    Eland Piccata, 151

    Ernest Hemingway's Fillet of Lion, 153

    Hunter's Safari Steak, 147

    Roast Duckling (*Anitra Arrosto*), 28–29

    Venison in Juniper Cream Sauce (*Hirschfilet in Wacholderrahmsauce*), 69

    Woodcock Flambé in Armagnac, 20–21

Garlic Olives, 95

Gazpacho, 96

Gimlet, 184

Gin and Tonic, 184–85

Gin and Tonic, Ernest Hemingway, The, 185

Glühwein, 185

Grace Hall Hemingway's English Tea Cakes, 4

Grappa, 186

Green Isaak's Special, 191

gudgeon

    Friture de Goujon (Fried Gudgeon), 50

H

hare

    Civet de Lièvre à la Cocotte (Jugged Hare), 53

Hemingway Daiquirí, 179–80, 181

Hemingway's Bloody Marys, 176

herring

    Rollmops, 52

Highball (*Highbalito con Agua Mineral*), 186–87

Home-Pickled Mushrooms, 78

Hunter's Safari Steak, 147

217

I

Izzarra, 187

J

Jack Rose, 187

K

kidneys
  Rognons Grilled with Champignons, 35–36
Kirsch, 188
Kümmel, 188–89

L

Leeks, Young Tom Hudson's, 123
Lime Ice, 139
lion
  Ernest Hemingway's Fillet of Lion, 153
liver
  Foie de Veau à l'Anglaise, 42
lobster
  Lobster Salad, 31–32
  Paella de Langosta, 106–8
Lobster Salad, 31–32

M

Mâcon wine, 167
Mango Chutney, 140–41
Marc, 189
Marmelade de Pommes (Apple Conserve), 53
Marsala wine, 167
Mashed Potatoes, 42
mayonnaise
  Alioli (Garlic Mayonnaise), 94

Mojito, 180–81
Montagny wine, 167
Montgomery, The, 189–90
Moules (Mussels) in Peppery Milk Broth, 125–26
Mount Everest Special, 131
Muscadet wine, 167
mushrooms
  Home-Pickled Mushrooms, 78
  Rognons Grilled with Champignons, 35–36
mussels
  Moules (Mussels) in Peppery Milk Broth, 125–26
Mustard Sauce, 49

N

New Green Beans, 74

O

octopus
  Fried Octopus, 106
  Pulpo a la Vinagreta (Octopus Vinaigrette), 92–93
Olives, Garlic, 95
omelets
  Bocadilla de Tortilla de Patata (Potato Omelet Sandwich), 86, 88
  Omelet with Truffles, 36
Omelet with Truffles, 36
Oxtail Stew, 152
Oysters, 54–55

P

Paella de Langosta, 106–8
Pancakes, 10–11
Papa Doble, 181

pasta
  Pork and Beans and Spaghetti, 13
  Spaghetti, 133
pastries
  Brioche, 23–24, 76
  Pastry of Fish, Peppers, and Pine Nuts (*Empanadilla de Pescado*), 102
Pastry of Fish, Peppers, and Pine Nuts (*Empanadilla de Pescado*), 102
Patatas Alioli (Potatoes in Garlic Mayonnaise), 93
peanut butter
  Mount Everest Special, 131
peppers
  Pastry of Fish, Peppers, and Pine Nuts (*Empanadilla de Pescado*), 102
  Pimientos, 94
Pernod, 175
Picadillo, 141
Pie, Campfire Apple, 11–12
Pilar's Rabbit Stew, 100
Pimientos, 94
pine nuts
  Pastry of Fish, Peppers, and Pine Nuts (*Empanadilla de Pescado*), 102
Pommes de Terre à l'Huile (Potatoes in Oil), 48
pork
  Canadian Bacon, 36
  Cervelas with Mustard Sauce, 49
  Cochinillo Asado (Roast Suckling Pig), 98–99
Pork and Beans and Spaghetti, 13
Potato Croquettes (*Kartoffelkroketten*), 70
potatoes
  Beef Stew with Boiled Potatoes, 114, 116
  Bocadilla de Tortilla de Patata (Potato Omelet Sandwich), 86, 88

French-fried Potatoes (*Pommes de Terre Frites*), 61
Mashed Potatoes, 42
Patatas Alioli (Potatoes in Garlic Mayonnaise), 93
Pommes de Terre à l'Huile (Potatoes in Oil), 48
Potato Croquettes (*Kartoffelkroketten*), 70
Soufflé Potatoes, 21
Pouilly-Fuisse wine, 168
Poularde de Bresse, 65–66
Prawns in Sea Water, 121
Pulpo a la Vinagreta (Octopus Vinaigrette), 92–93
Purée de Marron (Chestnut Purée), 21–22

R

Rabbit Stew, Pilar's, 100
Radishes, 41
raspberries
  Black Currant Liqueur, 46
Red Cabbage (*Rotweinkraut*), 70
Red Snapper Stew, 135
rice
  Paella de Langosta, 106–8
Rioja wine, 168
Roast Chicken, 73–74
Roast Duckling (*Anitra Arrosto*), 28–29
Rognons Grilled with Champignons, 35–36
Rollmops, 52
Rum Punch, 190–91

S

salads
  Endive Salad, 42
  Lobster Salad, 31–32
salt cod
  Bacalao de Pamplona (Salt Cod), 89–90

Sancerre wine, 168

sandwiches

Bocadilla de Tortilla de Patata (Potato Omelet Sandwich), 86, 88

Mount Everest Special, 131

Sangría, 105

sauces and syrups

Black Currant Liqueur, 46

Celery Rémoulade, 78

Marmelade de Pommes (Apple Conserve), 53

Mustard Sauce, 49

Purée de Marron (Chestnut Purée), 21–22

Sweet–Sour Sauce for a Dish for Six People, 137–38

Tournedos with Sauce Béarnaise, 61

sauerkraut

Choucroute Garni (Garnished Sauerkraut), 25

Scaloppine with Marsala, 32–33

Sea Bass Grilled with Butter and Herbs, 77–78

seafood

Bacalao de Pamplona (Salt Cod), 89–90

Clams on the Half-Shell, 34–35

Crabe Mexicaine, 55–57

Dorado Fillet in Damn Good Sauce, 134

Escabeche de Atún (Marinated Tuna with Onions), 88–89

Fried Baby Eels, 104

Fried Octopus, 106

Moules (Mussels) in Peppery Milk Broth, 125–26

Oysters, 54–55

Paella de Langosta, 106–8

Prawns in Sea Water, 121

Pulpo a la Vinagreta (Octopus Vinaigrette), 92–93

Red Snapper Stew, 135

Rollmops, 52

Sea Bass Grilled with Butter and Herbs, 77–78

Sole Meunière (Fillet of Sole Miller's Wife Style), 52

Swordfish á la *Pilar*, 134

Sherry, 168–69

Sion wine, 169

smelt

Friture de Goujon (Fried Gudgeon), 50

snails

Burgundy Snails (*Escargots à la Bourguignonne*), 64

Sole Meunière (Fillet of Sole Miller's Wife Style), 52

Sopa de Navarra a la Burguete (Hot Vegetable Soup), 84

Soufflé Potatoes, 21

soups and stews

Beef Stew with Boiled Potatoes, 114, 116

Black Bean Soup, 114

Bouillabaisse de Marseilles, 126–27

Ernest Hemingway's Cold Cucumber Soup, 5

Gazpacho, 96

Oxtail Stew, 152

Pilar's Rabbit Stew, 100

Red Snapper Stew, 135

Sopa de Navarra a la Burguete (Hot Vegetable Soup), 84

Spaghetti, 133

spaghetti

Pork and Beans and Spaghetti, 13

Spaghetti, 133

St. Estephe wine, 169

Stewed Apricots, 11

stews. *See* soups and stews

Sweet-Sour Sauce for a Dish for Six People, 137–38

Swordfish á la *Pilar*, 134

syrups. *See* sauces and syrups

T

Tavel wine, 170

Tomini, 191

Tournedos with Sauce Béarnaise, 61

trout

    Fried Trout, 9–10

    Trout au bleu, 58

    Trucha a la Navarra (Trout Cooked with Cured Ham), 84–85

Trout au bleu, 58

Trucha a la Navarra (Trout Cooked with Cured Ham), 84–85

Truffle-Roasted Chicken (*Poularde Truffée*), 63

truffles

    Omelet with Truffles, 36

    Truffle-Roasted Chicken (*Poularde Truffée*), 63

tuna

    Escabeche de Atún (Marinated Tuna with Onions), 88–89

V

Valdepeñas wine, 170

Valpolicella wine, 170

veal

    Rognons Grilled with Champignons, 35–36

    Scaloppine with Marsala, 32–33

vegetables. *See under* specific vegetable name

Venison in Juniper Cream Sauce (*Hirschfilet in Wacholderrahmsauce*), 69

Vermouth and Bitters, 191–92

Visitandines, 46

W

Whiskey, 192–93

Wild Daiquirí, 181

Woodcock Flambé in Armagnac, 20–21

Y

Young Tom Hudson's Leeks, 123

Z

Zabaglione, 22

Permissions

222